GOLF'S
CRITICAL DETAILS

The Secrets of Great Swings and Perfect Impact

George Hibbard

FIRST EDITION

Hibbard, George, 1932-
Golf's Critical Details, the Secrets of Great Swings and Perfect Impact
by George Hibbard.

Includes Index.

All photography including cover photo by Mike Ficocello
Printed by:
Athletic Guide Publishing, Inc.
P.O. Box 1050
Flagler Beach, FL 32136-1050

ISBN: 0-9673951-4-3

Library of Congress Registration Pending

Acknowledgments

My heartfelt gratitude to all those who have helped me with the editing and proofing of this work, particularly Karen "1-Putt" Roberts and Marcia Munsterman, whose generous input and good judgment enabled me to simplify and clarify some pretty convoluted first drafts. Their suggestions and advice had an enormous impact on my ability to make this complex and difficult material readable by a general audience. Thanks also to a few of my pupils for their suggestions and help, all of which improved on my own versions, specifically Clint Blundon, Bill Day, and Cathy Minnick.

I thank "Big Mike" Ficocello for his most professional and high quality photography. My thanks involve much more than how pleased I am with the pictures and the accuracy of detail he took pains to capture: it is not possible to measure the value of his patience and the earnest care he brought to this work. Mike, I am indebted to you big time!

My thanks to Tom Keegan and the rest of the professionals at Athletic Guide Publishing, for quality printing, for their help with the graphics, and especially for their extraordinary courtesies, friendship, and help to me for almost five years now. Again, what does not appear on the invoice is often of much more value than what does!

I need to express my gratitude to Corris Caro, Boss Advertising & Design, Palm Coast, FL, for her imaginative and professional cover design and, again, for kindnesses and courtesies over several years time. Her generosity to me, as with the others who have been helping me since my first effort in 1999, is not compensable in financial terms.

Finally, my thanks to the owners and management of the Ocean Palm Golf Club in Flagler Beach, Florida for their courtesies to us and for generously offering us their facility for our photography.

Dedication

This work is dedicated to my unutterably generous Creator, the source of my love for the game of golf and for the considerable passion and persistence with which he blessed me to struggle, experiment, and study the golf swing for nearly 60 years now. And thereby to discover its secrets.

He also gave me the ability to translate many of the dynamic principles of the swing into everyday images in a way that makes them understandable even by people without technical training or inclination.

And by extension, this is dedicated to you the reader, in the earnest hope that my discoveries will free you from the imprisonment of the 'not quite enough information' and 'not quite right' situation that was my own experience for so many years. When you truly know and have control over your golf game by understanding and putting into practice everything I have uncovered and explained here, you will discover a new level of unlimited joy in this remarkable game. He would have it no other way!

In a church bulletin article about things kids say in their prayers, one read, "God, when you made a giraffe, was that an accident, or did you do it on purpose?" The adult asks God, "Did you invent golf on purpose, or did we accidentally discover it?" I believe the answer to both questions is the same.

Table of Contents

Foreword

Why on earth would somebody take it upon himself to write a golf swing book at this time, or for a publisher to believe it to be a worthwhile undertaking? Hasn't it all been covered? Don't all the instruction materials produced in the last 50 years already handle golf instruction very well, including the work of Hogan, Nicklaus, Woods, Harmon, Leadbetter, and many other giants in the field?

And consider the hundreds of other books and videos, monthly magazines, and scores of television instruction programs so readily available. Besides this flood of available help, doesn't the PGA of America make instruction available to just about anyone in any area of the country, often at little or no expense? Well, yes it does.

So why do we find so many serious golfers frustrated and disillusioned? They take the lessons, they study authoritative sources and practice conscientiously. Is there some elusive talent necessary for golf that some 'get it' and some don't?

On top of this, wouldn't any new golf instruction book at this time, especially from a relatively unknown like this author, be an enormous presumption? And isn't it a given that no one should take upon himself to write a book of *any* kind unless he has something to say that hasn't been said before? Something pretty darned important, actually. So what hasn't been said that calls for *another 'golf book?'*

Well, preposterous though it may seem, I can unhesitatingly tell you that it is because so much golf instruction continues to fall short. It continues to fail the public. Year after year, book after book, video after video, and lesson after lesson, the public continues to be shortchanged! *This is why so many golfers continue to be frustrated and disillusioned!*

I am 71 years old. I have been playing golf for 57 years now. I have studied, watched, analyzed, tried, experimented, and passionately digested just about everything available, and I find the same problems perpetuated again and again and again. It is the norm in just about everything available in books, videos, and personal instruction. The failures exist in three forms:

- **Lack of clarity:** Despite great good faith given *to* thoroughness and clarification, the culture, delivery, and language of most instruction is not specific enough. Words chosen leave too many openings for misunderstanding.

- **Misleading information:** Some of it is just plain wrong, and what is most harmful is that what *is* written *is believed and obeyed without question* when it just plain doesn't fit the golfer reading it. So he struggles to *embed things that guarantee his failure*, clueless for a lifetime that he is on a wrong path unless his good sense stops him somehow. But whether he follows the advice or not, his poor performance remains to inform him that 'there is something wrong with this picture.'

- **The omission of important things:** Insufficiency of information leaves the golfer with having to figure out too much by himself. In fact, it is in *extremely* elusive subtlety and micro adjustments of detail, as will be seen, where the most important secrets are located that free a golfer for success and joy, and rare are those people who are able to discover all of them, whether by trial and error or from natural talent and instinct.

Some people object that, "There are no secrets. Just do the basics, practice hard and you will succeed." But a metaphor applies here. I will give you nine of the ten letters for a website address containing information you need. Or all ten, but one of them is wrong. Or ten correct letters, but two are out of sequence. Not only can't you access the website in any of these situations: *you will not be able to figure out where to look for the answer to your problem.* It is the same with the golf swing: an omission or error may mean that for most of your lifetime you will not be able to discover what is wrong or missing in your setup or procedure.

The situation is similar to computers where some glitch keeps us confused or unable to do something. We spend hours looking for the solution— it could be a setting or a wrong command (in the early days it was common to confuse the letter 'o' with the number 'zero', and this caused a lot of problems.) Perhaps we cannot find it by ourselves no matter how much time we spend looking. Then after several days or a tip from someone else, we find that *all it took was a click or two. The problem was not difficulty in clicking: the problem was about knowing where to click.* And that is what happens in golf: the correct help for our particular problem is often impossible to find.

Guess what! If you don't know something, to you it is a secret, and you find it impossible to proceed without knowing it! And searching *for* the secret turns out to be a full time job for too many earnest golfers.

So this book most definitely *is* a contribution, and to repeat what has already been reported by hundreds about my first book *Perfect Impact,* upon which this book expands and improves, "This is the most thorough book on the golf swing ever written!"

Golf's Critical Details replaces that first effort with much greater detail, simpler delivery, more specificity, and many more illustrations. In fact, I believe that everything that anyone needs to know about golf swing technique, ball striking and the teaching of them is contained in these pages and is stated as clearly as is possible in words and still pictures.

It is my intention to furnish you here with just that, i.e., the most thorough book ever written on the subject. I have tried to give you a complete understanding of the swing rather than direct you to 'do it my way because I said to.' I believe if you have *this* book in your golf library, that you will never need anything more than a knowledgeable observer to give you feedback, for you to reach whatever heights of proficiency your passion desires and the limits of your natural gifts permit.

When you have read it once and wish to advance, read it again. And again and again and again. Then, when you have incorporated the correct information and wish to achieve advanced level of accuracy and proficiency, don't go somewhere else in search of 'Golf 501." No, excellence is not to be found somewhere else. It will be found *in installing these critical details— the **real basics*** ('basics' as they are taught but including the details that make them work for you!) *with greater precision. Do them better and better, with more fidelity to detail, and with more care.*

So read, reread, study, and trust the accuracy and respect the importance of all the details. As the title says accurately, the secrets <u>*are*</u> *in the critical details, in the extremely subtle but real differences between NQR (not quite right) and EXACTLY RIGHT.*

Good luck, and I wish you true joy in your golf experience.

I wish to thank a pupil of mine, who also assisted me in the editing of this work, Marcia Munsterman, for the following tip. A local printer or copy center will be able to remove the book's present binding and place its sheets into a loose leaf finger binding that allows the pages to lay flat. This will make it easier for you to use it on the practice tee while you are working on your swing. What a neat idea!

NOTES

Introduction

A Look at the Nature of the Golf Swing and of the Game

Significant skill in the game of golf is probably the most subtle and elusive of all popular athletic achievements. While we recognize that the golf ball is small and fairly far away from us down there on the ground, most of us are not intimidated by that, especially since it sits there patiently waiting to be struck ("Take your time"). And we watch men and women golfers on TV every weekend who are not particularly strong or tall, or really very different in appearance from us in any remarkable way, play the game with ease and accuracy. But the difficulties in the game involve a lot more than meets the eye. Skill in this game is different from other sports that require great strength, height, speed or exceptional natural reflexes.

On the face of it, there is no apparent reason why we can't do what they do! But that is just the point. We try to do the same, and many of us fail miserably. "Why can't I do that?" The reasons are not apparent. Is there some kind of conspiracy of fate to seduce us to try it, but unknown to us we lack a particular mysterious talent that they have and we don't?

Emphatically NO! As you'll see shortly. My title actually addresses a profound reality about how to learn to play golf well with relish and significant skill. Specifically, there *are* secrets, and they are located in what I call the "critical details" that exist in almost every element involved in learning, practicing, and playing the game of golf. They are secrets because of their subtlety— someone suggested to me the term "micro adjustments."

I have recently returned from an out-of-town trip where I was working with two pupils over a period of four days. There were about forty practice tee boxes at the facility, and just about all of them were in use by earnest golfers for the entire period of time I was there. I witnessed probably two hundred serious, dedicated and athletic, mostly young people struggling, and it left me very sad.

I was sad for one simple reason: with no exception among all those golfers, I saw problems in swings and in impact that could have been overcome in a few moments by just about every golfer there with nothing more than a small adjustment in something, and a few minutes of explanation of how and why it was critical. (I remember reading a comment made by George Peper, then editor of *Golf Magazine,* in which he stated that he improved his single digit handicap index by some 4 strokes on the basis of a single tip— an event so significant to him that he immediately hired the teacher who gave him the tip for the magazine instruction staff!) These were competent people, serious and self-aware, and most of them were obviously doing everything they possibly could do to produce good swings and good impact.

But not one of them seemed to be able to improve the procedure or the results of his work, regardless of the effort, analysis, and care they were giving to their practice. Most swings were 'pretty good,' a few were *very* good, yet every one of these earnest people was struggling and at an impasse as to how to improve either his ball-striking accuracy or his direction control, or how to attain what would seem to be appropriate distance for his size and strength. I did not see a single golfer among them who I felt knew what to do to benefit from his practice or to improve significantly. I am sure that each one of them *felt* he was on a course of improvement. I have seen this phenomenon for half a century and it never changes— only the names and faces change— but the outcome is always the same. They are, in effect, trying to accomplish something without knowing what to do to accomplish it. It is not inability that prevents them. It is a simple failure of knowing exactly what to do.

The bottom line: an effective and efficient golf swing, and perfect impact *with* a good swing, are each dependent on dealing correctly with a relatively few extremely subtle and sensitive details. Not just a little subtle or sensitive, where "close is good enough!" But much more **critical, minute, precise, and unforgiving** than is recognized.

Once uncovered and explained, the reason for any of them will be seen to be simple common sense, and the procedure for achieving the precision required is nearly as easy to handle as putting your finger on a dime on the table in front of you. It is not a matter of extraordinary ability at all (playing at the level of professional tournament golf is, however, big time!). The issue is *what* the detail *is* and whether you are incorporating it into your swing, not whether you have special native talent for it.

A baseball player aspiring to play major league ball is obviously dependent on acute eyesight, quick reactions, speed, and strength to be able to hit a ball coming toward him at some 90 miles per hour. A basketball player is limited if he isn't tall or quick enough to evade a jungle of hands and bodies in his face with the intention of thwarting his best efforts. But the normal person who wishes to play golf well needs no more native talent than the ability to "stand like *this*," "put your hand *here*" as opposed to "there," and hold it like "*this*" instead of "that."

So the problem with the struggling and uninformed golfer is not his ability. It is the failure of his instruction to show him, and of his practice to install, the essential critical details. It is the same as trying to open a combination lock: the issue is not opening the lock; it is using the right combination!

In over fifty years of frustrating practice, study and obsessive self-analysis, I came to discover by myself many of these details that were never made known to me in any book, videocassette, lesson, or golf tip. Most of them I have never even seen addressed anywhere, to say nothing of seeing them given significant attention when they *are* hinted at or suggested. The failure of most golf instruction even to address them places a burden on the *pupil* to discover what he needs, instead of pointing them out to him at the outset of his golfing experience. He will not be *able*, in most cases, to discover them. So he typically struggles unnecessarily— a week, a month, a year, and probably all his life! The fact remains— and this is the *real* reason for lack of improvement in the average handicap over the years— very few people *ever* uncover all the subtleties of a truly efficient swing or of perfect impact; so because of the omission of those few simple facts in their training, most golfers remain dreadfully short-changed for life.

For those skeptics who insist "There are no secrets. The basics (posture, grip, stance, etc.) take care of good ball striking if practiced enough." I answer simply, but at the top of my lungs,

"Absolutely not! Life is not long enough." This is confirmed overwhelmingly by golfers of all ages, all levels of skill, and years in the game, in testimonial letters and emails sent to me daily— often with *very* emotional outbursts of joy and gratitude— upon *finally* learning of the things that I uncover here. Nearly all of the testimonials we receive come from people already in possession of many of the best-known instruction books and videos— some of my "converts" own literally hundreds of them, and most of them have had lessons from 'certified pros,' many at well-known golf academies, some from 'top teachers.' The approach of nearly all other instruction they have ever had *is* in fact *to* "start with the basics," but the testimonials cry out loudly in unison, *"It doesn't work!"* Problems remain, *and they lie in the incomplete or even harmful nature of what is often taught.*

What exactly *are* those "basics?" What's wrong with them? Let me answer with the following analogy.

I once heard the term "NQR" used by a friend who had spent time in another country to describe how on a daily basis so many things were "Not Quite Right." The lights often failed just when needed most, replacement parts were not available or those purchased didn't fit, the bus didn't show up, the taxi ran out of gas three miles from nowhere, etc. I like to use 'NQR' to describe the kind of golf instruction I refer to, and I have added the 'NQEI' factor— "Not Quite Enough Information!"

Two illustrations of this will make my point. The first is the nearly universal unqualified counsel to "put your feet shoulder width apart" when you address a golf ball. The problem for most people is that the stance advocated necessarily limits or inhibits lower body turn, effectively shutting down the 'main power source' of the golf swing, the turn of the hips. So the golfer must instead try to move his *upper* body, which is less powerful and has less range of motion by itself, requiring him to muscle or force his swing. The golfer obeys the instruction unaware of its built-in flaw.

The second is likewise about as central to good golf as can be imagined— it is the way in which people are shown how to place the left hand on the club in many books, magazines, and videos. By picturing the grip as they do— placed somewhat diagonally across the palm of the hand— the pupil is seriously compromised. He remains unaware how to fit his left hand to his club so that he can create power and accuracy efficiently, and following the counsel takes a grip that **prevents** it. He believes that the comfort of his hands at address is proof of the quality of the way he holds the club. But in fact, a comfortable hold on the club at address is secondary to the central issue, the function of that hand during delivery! *Both hands need to be placed in a way that will enable a full 90°degree angle of the clubshaft relative to the left forearm at the top of the backswing*— a position not possible for most golfers if they obey the instruction, due to the limit of range of motion of the left wrist. There happens to be virtually zero tolerance for a wristfold of less than 90° at the top for a really good swing to be possible. So there are oceans of golfers who play at the game using the illustrated grip with swings that are atrocious for that reason, and often not even their teachers uncover the underlying problem! Their lifetime misery of 'struggle-golf,' contrived compensations, and inconsistency can be traced to the omission of *that single detail.*

Other "basics" besides these also contain their own critical details that are just as pivotal, subtle and elusive as those mentioned above, and they too are hardly ever addressed. I hope you will respect their incredible importance as they are pointed out and be conscientious in dealing with them as I advise. *Precision in execution*, from the very first moment those things are presented and made known to you, is the place where your golf future is determined. In the last analysis you will have only yourself to blame if your game is inconsistent, confusing, or unsatisfactory! And so, by reason of their subtlety and the fact that you may not realize their importance when they are presented (they sit there innocently without enough fanfare to draw your attention to their significance), I will identify each one when it is introduced. I will also include the reason why it *is* a critical detail, so that by understanding why yourself, you can make the subtle adjustments it requires in order to build a swing that fits *your* body. Most of these adjustments are not visible to a teacher or observer. No, NQR won't work! Install the details with great care and absolute fidelity because of their non-negotiable pivotal importance. Without them a good swing, center impact, or consistency just simply is not going to happen!

There's another bonus in this approach. It is this: dealing with those details *at the outset* simply enables you to learn to play golf well in the shortest time. The alternative is that the more you try to do something with inadequate and inaccurate technique, the more your practice is doing you harm. In effect you are learning to do it wrongly forever, thereby putting yourself into a frame of mind from which you will never realistically be able to make improvements. *Deeply embedded and, eventually, involuntary responses, usually cannot be changed.* This is a double-edged sword! 1) Compensating a fault to make a bad swing work reinforces the compensation, often leaving the original fault in place and requiring an extremely difficult accommodation for it, and 2) **believing that the compensation you are making is a normal part of good swing mechanics,** so you may well spend the rest of your golfing life using and embedding it ever more deeply, never aware of the *much* easier and more consistent procedure you could be using that would give better results if the original element had been addressed correctly to begin with.

Another trap: one of the worst things you can do is to hit golf balls before you have the correct habit of just how to move the golf club. Haste and impatience to get out and hit golf balls, where some may be struck fairly well, can easily do you considerable harm! I frequently tell pupils during practice, "It can be a pitfall to hit good shots; you'll think you're doing well!" In other words, a good shot will immediately reinforce whatever procedure was used to produce that shot, and your subconscious will not care at that point if it was from an inferior procedure. *The reinforcement of that good shot is far too narcotic in its effect on you,* and at that point your concentration can easily shift from dealing with a critical detail to a frame of mind in which you wish to repeat the feelings and motions that you happened to use for that shot.

This is not to pretend that a ball well struck *with* good mechanics isn't a joy and an appropriate reward, and that you shouldn't relish and profit from the reinforcement it provides. But this is to put you on notice that if you got away with it using less than optimum mechanics, you might be missing a lot of the "good stuff" and embedding a less effective procedure. It is rarified air up there, folks (skillful ball striking), and it doesn't take as long to get there as is generally believed if you practice right. But if you ignore the critical details and bash balls without discretion, you will not get there. You will make the *most* progress if you do not have any opportunity to hit anything but whiffle balls for at least a month while you ingrain critical details.

Okay, my rant is over. I can hear my wife in the background snapping at me, "Why don't you tell them how you *really* feel?" Please consider and act on the things written here, dealing with each one with full attention and accuracy, and after that follow the order in which all the other information and instruction is laid out before you. If you do these things, you will get to your goal faster than with any other program you can imagine.

My Apologies to the Lefties

Until the English language comes up with words that work for both righties and lefties that enable swing instruction without confusion, I apologize to the lefties who will, of course, have to make the usual accommodation for what I have reluctantly had to write as though my readers are all right-handed.

Notes

What's Covered in This Book?

This book contains the following things in the order, the manner, and detail that will enable you to achieve efficiency in the shortest possible time:

1. What IS the golf swing— exactly how does it work? What is its essence? How can we envision it as a self-sufficient whole, in which the mystery of its apparently complex parts dissolves, revealing a coherent simple underlying reality?

If you understand exactly how a good swing works and what it consists of, you can cooperate with, and profit from, the "things you will be instructed to do" since you will be doing them to accomplish a purpose, and not because someone *says* "Do this." I use the metaphor of a jigsaw puzzle to make the point. Much instruction is piecemeal, where you attempt to follow steps, tips, or parts of a whole, but where you do not have an overall picture of what you are trying to accomplish. I want you to see *the whole picture yourself,* and <u>then</u> you will understand why you do what you do, how the steps and tips and parts make it work, and how you can adjust and tweak the parts to fit your own body and strengths. Your practice will be seeking to accomplish the whole entity, and you will be shown how to fit the parts by your own common sense in the process, instead of feeling confused and vulnerable to every tip that comes in your direction, eager to read the latest magazine in search of **"THE SECRET"** that eludes you.

To acquire an understanding of the essence of a perfect golf swing, you will have to experience your club and body in motion. A child needs to be moving a bit on his bike before he will sense how to maintain his balance, and that is something he needs to experience for himself. He will not be able to say, "I've got it, Daddy!" before the bike is actually moving. He will not be able to feel it or react to it, as he must, until he senses how the bike behaves in motion. The feedback from trying to balance will guide him how to manage it. So it is with all the drills here, especially the first one. To gain a correct sense of the core essential or heart of a perfect golf swing (i.e., of the late, powerful release, and how it is generated) *you will have to do the drill exactly as it is given to you, where you will find out how it works.* * *And if you do it perfectly and reinforce the feelings and mechanics with many repetitions of it day after day after day, it will become as second nature to you as is walking, biking, and swimming, none of which require being learned a second time.* And a grasp of the core issue, a correctly executed release, becomes the basis for everything else about the swing that

---

* My video, *5 Minutes to a Perfect Golf Swing, 10 if You're a Slow Learner* features this drill, and because of its fundamental importance, it is the first instruction given to *all* of my academy pupils. Since it illustrates the swing 'in real time motion," many people find it much more helpful than words and still pictures alone.

follows— power, direction control, clean impact, and ultimately, deep joy in the game. It is fairly useless to proceed without a picture of how the swing works, and we see golfers who 'practice' day after day and never make any significant progress for that very reason. I have already mentioned my own experience of seeing pupils with no organized or logical plan for development of their skill simply because they lack the compass and central issue of what it is that they need to perfect, to say nothing of an awareness of the details to be installed along the way.

One of my discoveries about how we learn is that our grasp of a whole picture goes a long way to filling in its parts correctly. Most of us could memorize the *Gettysburg Address*. And in a short time we would be able to reproduce and correctly write down every single letter and detail it contains as originally written! We would automatically allow for the appropriate space between words, we would capitalize and punctuate as appropriate, and we could probably reproduce the entire document with just about everything correct— all this despite the fact that it contains *thousands* of individual "parts." And we are able to do this precisely because we conceptualize a larger picture— an entity— a whole *to which the parts belong. Grasping the meaning, the essence, of that whole picture* (while looking at the picture, not the separate parts) *is what gives us the ability to correctly fill in the parts.* Contrast that with asking someone to memorize a series of unrelated letters, commas, spaces, periods, and capitalizations, etc. The task of memorizing a string of elements where you do *not* know their inter-relationships, or where it does not *have* a unifying theme or meaning, would verge on the impossible.

2. How to use your own body and your golf club to be *able* to swing with the most consistent, efficient, and powerful means available to you

After you grasp the essentials of a perfect golf swing, in order for you to be able to execute that swing with *your* body (as contrasted with copying a model, likely with different strengths even if that model's build appeared to be the same as yours) you will be told step by step *exactly where* you will position your body, *exactly how* to hold the club, *exactly where* to move your hands and arms, *exactly how* to swing the club to the ball for perfect impact, perfect direction and distance control, and *exactly how* to do this with consistency and power. It doesn't matter what body type, strengths or weaknesses you have, because how to make a good swing is based on *principles* that I tell you how to apply to yourself, and in following them as you see explained, you will automatically fit your swing to yourself (for example, bend over enough for *your* arms to hang down freely from their sockets in front of *your* chest). Some elements of your swing may appear to be different from how they look in other good golfers, but they will be identical *in their structural relationships and in the functions they facilitate.* There are many human achievements that have been shown to prove the concept of "form follows function!" This is one of them.

3. You will be given a series of drills that will show you how the different elements of your swing work and what their role is in the overall picture. The drills will cover all necessary motions, exertions, and their timing and sequence, from which you will naturally generate *your own* perfect golf swing.

The purpose for every drill will be clearly explained, as well as the way to practice it for obtaining the maximum value from it. They will cover every element of the swing. The necessity and advantage of doing drills first and establishing good habits, rather than *only* hitting golf balls, is because of the way the motor and nervous systems of the body learn. This is true for two reasons: a) no one "gets the knack" of biking in the first day of trying, or walking in the first month or two of life; and b) the golf ball is far too seductive of your attention *and it takes your focus away from the task at hand* when you go to the range or the golf course and encounter it sitting there 'innocently' asking to be walloped. Without you realizing it, your entire agenda has just been shifted from "make a good swing!" to 'HIT THAT SUCKER.' *So what really happens when you go to the range or the golf course before you have correct procedures fairly well ingrained is that you freeze your learning, perhaps more permanently than you imagine, at whatever level it is when you suddenly have a ball to deal with.* As I point out in the first chapter on page 5, our brains operate in linear mode. So if you change your focus from learning how to swing well to hitting a golf ball before you have a pretty good and basically correct procedure, you essentially forfeit any opportunity to advance past the point where you left off, and you likely begin to embed procedures with flaws in them.

4. Since problems arise and mis-hits are a normal part of the learning process, you will be given complete information about impact, the reasons and cures for mis-hits of every conceivable kind, and enough understanding of cause and effect to be your own teacher and coach.

Instead of having to seek every new golf tip or suffer the pain of confusion when problems arise, your ability to correctly diagnose and eliminate the causes of bad shots will become part of your every day repertoire. So whenever a problem arises during practice or while you are out on the course, you'll immediately be able to make the necessary adjustments before your next shot.

5. You will be taught how to handle what is called "the short game" in a brief time, instead of having to depend on a sense of touch alone, something that normally takes a long time to develop.

Learning to putt, chip, and pitch with accuracy is normally thought to require considerable practice and experience. Refined skill certainly does, but getting the right start does not. People expect that it takes 'touch,' acquired over a long time, for accuracy in the short game, and for what we call 'getting the ball in the hole.' But the instruction here telescopes months or even years of practice into a short time by using two simple tools at hand, talents *which you already possess in abundance* (you just haven't related them to the golf club and its use!) and some common sense physical principles ('the laws of physics') that become clear and obvious as soon as you see how *they* apply to a given situation. The significance of this is enormous, since two thirds of the scoring in golf occurs *in* the 'short game,' and to get a handle on distance control at the outset is no small benefit!

Dealing with sand and the rough

The last area I cover is a much larger part of golf than we normally think about because we tend to operate in denial. We handle the rough and trouble shots reluctantly using whatever imaginative solution we come up with at the moment out of necessity. But we don't have a strategy or positive sense of what to do. It is hoped that the information here will change that for you, so that instead of dealing with inevitable problems in fear, that you will be able to handle them with confidence and success.

Repetition You will find that some subjects are covered several times as you move through the book. It is because of how they apply in different contexts, and to fail to include something I said before in a different place would be to omit showing you its importance to the particular subject where it is brought up again. So I ask your indulgence. It is my preference to say something too many times and from too many different viewpoints than to say too little. Hopefully in doing so I can make what are often complex issues understandable to everyone.

Notes

Chapter One

First Things First

Preliminary Items

There are several things you need to consider even before taking a golf club in your hands, because *they* could make the difference whether you will eventually succeed or not. They are:

- **Using Your Head** There's a lot to understand before you start swinging.
- **Misperceptions and Realistic Expectations** What are the *real* issues? Are things what they seem?
- **Equipment** The importance of choosing clubs that eliminate any need for possibly 'fatal' unconscious compensations that you will make and embed into habit if they don't fit you properly.

- **Optical Concerns** Things about your eyes and eyeglasses that can affect your ability to hit the golf ball at all, to say nothing of hitting it accurately.
- **How To Go About Learning** How to cut years from your journey and pain from your effort.
- **The Role of Instinct and the Subconscious** The "IRS" and its Agent, "T-Man."
- **Should I Play Golf Right-Handed or Left-Handed**
- **How to Profit From the Materials in This Book**
- **The Basic Principle of How to Swing a Golf Club**

Using Your Head: "Golf is 100% mental. The other 50% is mental!" (The bad arithmetic is intentional, in order to emphasize the most important thing, which is understanding what you are doing as opposed to seeking to do based on feelings by themselves.)

Golf is a thinking man's game, not a brute's sport. Skill is information applied with care, and a good score is not acquired by bullying the club, the ball, or the course. But let me make another point as well. I have just witnessed an incredible piano performance by an average-looking 21-year old Chinese artist, a demonstration of skill that could easily rank with performances we have heard from the greatest pianists the world has ever seen. His digital skill is phenomenal and his musicianship is clearly world-class. I say this to make the point that great talent is not a bit visible by observation of someone's appearance, size, body language, or anything else. It is hidden until its application comes to our attention by performance.

Such is the skill level we witness on television from the world's best professional golfers, who are greatly gifted with talents that can't be seen from appearances, such as keen eyesight (a universal of baseball players), an exceptional sense of balance, very good natural hand/eye coordination, and acute sensors in their muscular system like those relied upon by the blind to recall spatial positions and distances (called "proprioception"), among others. The Buick Open Invitational of 2003 is currently being played as I write, and the precision and execution of shot after shot of these plain looking men is so astounding as to take my breath away, exactly as did the piano performance I just mentioned. Their consistency challenges the credibility of *anyone* who has ever aspired to a life playing professional golf.

But all of us *can still play great golf and enjoy scores at or near par at distances matching the level of our strength.* Obviously we can not all be as precise as the professional competitor simply because we don't have the time or talents to reach their level, but by using good sense instead of muscles for the majority of what has to be done, we all can play well. And I love the following anecdote to make this point.

About 120 years ago a European socialite was hosting a party for musicians, and among those invited were two world-famous pianists (Josef Hofmann and Anton Rubinstein). When she greeted the first one, she noticed that he had quite a small hand. And when she shook the hand of the second, the small size of *his* hand caused her to remark, "Gentlemen, I noticed your small hands. How do you manage to play the piano so well with such small hands?" Without pause, one of the men answered her, "Madame, what makes you think we play the piano with our hands?"

Misperceptions and Realistic Expectations

One of the most unrealistic things you can do is to take a bag of clubs, some balls and tees, and start your golf experience by going to the first tee of a golf course to "play 18 holes." Why? Because of the considerable amount of information and skill needed to make that experience even remotely meaningful. It is a bit like placing a piano in a nursery where children, knowing nothing of how it works or how music is made, are allowed to bang on the keys*. The naivety of trying to play golf immediately, before acquiring any training or background in the things brought out here, is forgivable only because "it doesn't look that hard" to the uninitiated. And of course, golf can be "played" without skill, but the experience of mis-hitting consistently takes its toll on joy or pleasure from the effort.

The reality is that there are actually five distinctly different things that you need to understand and develop somewhat to play golf with satisfaction. They are:

- how to make a good *swing;*
- how to hit the ball on the sweet spot *with* that swing;
- how to control distance and direction;
- how to manage yourself and your game to score well; and finally,
- how to diagnose and correct mis-hits.

*When I teach golf, I often use metaphors and illustrations that occur to me from my background in music as a pianist, a music-major in college, and a piano teacher.

Keeping these areas of concern separate from each other while we learn is important because of the *way* we learn most of what we know, which is to say, linearly, meaning one thing after another. In other words, we mortals can really only learn anything when we address and deal completely with each thing before proceeding to another. To do that, we must turn our focus on and *absorb each detail,* one at a time, and after *that,* gradually put the whole thing together.

This way of learning is not just "for dummies." Such a one-at-a-time process recognizes how the human mind works, as borne out by the phenomenally successful sales of the *How To For Dummies* books that are popular precisely because so many people see themselves as 'slow learners' and therefore seek help from someone who will help *them.* The alternative is 'overload,' which happens when we have too much on our plate at any given time. Like the computer: when we give it more tasks than it has the capacity to handle— IT CRASHES! Besides that, the same as when you build anything substantial and omit any supporting element in its foundation (or use a defective one), the whole thing will collapse or fall apart as soon as it is stressed. So our process is five-fold.

1. Building a good swing

Before you work with golf balls, you need to learn how to make an efficient motion with the golf club by itself— what we call "a good swing." You first need to know how to make a consistent swing well capable of producing clubhead speed. I call it "going into the shop and making an Iron Byron" (the name given to an actual mechanical golf swinging apparatus used for testing golf equipment) that you will later use to hit golf balls. It is appropriate to make a good machine! You will be using it all your life— don't you want it to be the best available? There are obviously several critical details to be addressed in this process.

2. Learning how to hit golf balls in the middle of the face of the golf club with your 'swinging machine'

Suppose you went into a shop and made a good, or even *perfect,* swinging device, and you decide to take it out to the range and try it out. Or pretend that you are the operator of an "Iron Byron" machine. You set it 'here,' put a ball down 'there,' put a club in the clamp, and take a swing at the ball with it. Whoops! You have a problem! IT MISSED THE BALL COMPLETELY. Why? Oh, you didn't put the machine IN THE RIGHT PLACE!

Why am I shouting? Because, dear reader, *this* issue, i.e., *exactly how the machine needs to be adjusted and placed relative to the ball for consistent centered impact is one of the most overlooked and, for that reason, harmful omissions of golf lessons. Generalized instruction without telling you how to adjust 'your machine' for the variable situations that exist in real golf is insufficient. The operators of sophisticated swing devices need training. And so do you: YOU NEED TO KNOW AND UNDERSTAND HOW TO MEASURE AND ADJUST your body, your grip, your feet, and your club, just to hit the ball.* As mentioned above (and specifically as concerns **impact**), the failure of instruction to address specifically **how to create quality of impact and what to do to remedy an impact fault** again puts on the *pupil* the burden of discovering the subtleties and elusive facts that make great ball striking possible. Note how I continually talk about that concept, perfect *impact;* obviously it is a fundamental concern. And the problem is partly because it is natural and perfectly understandable for both the pupil and the teacher to blame ball-striking faults on the *swing*. But in fact an Iron Byron and your perfect swing can both just as easily mis-hit a ball for one or more of several reasons *other than swing mechanics*. These include:

a) Failure to measure correctly from shoulders to ball to enable solid **dead center** contact— after all, it is located about five feet away from your head (where a miss as little as 1/4th of an inch can be significant), and at impact your body is in a *very* different position than it was at setup;

b) Failure to deal with physical changes that occur as you warm up that require you to *vary* your setup from moment to moment (this will be clarified later); and

c) Failure to control the swing so that you *can* make the clubhead go where you want. **Things are not what they seem,** and it is precisely because there *are* several "secrets" to doing this that if you know them make all the difference in the world!

Here's an observation about human nature and how we think. When we know the answer to a question, we say, "That's easy." When we do not, our experience is "That's a hard question!" But the truth is that no question is hard or easy. You either know the answer or you don't. So a good swing or good impact is not hard *if you know the details* involved. Either one can be *very hard* if you don't. Which is to say, ultimately, it has nothing to do with "hard" or "easy;" it has *everything* to do with **having the particular information applicable to the issue, and then simply using it to accomplish the task at hand!** The difference between golfers who achieve significant skill and those who remain struggling with higher handicaps is ultimately in whether they know what the details are, and when they do, whether they bother doing them— i.e., at that point, in the choices they make. We can choose to pay attention to the details and do them right or we can ignore them because it's more fun hitting golf balls. It is not 'hard' except for those who make it hard. Quite a concept, isn't it?

This bears emphasis right at the beginning of this book. Good golf is a choice, not something for which you need great talent. If you ignore the details and drills in favor of trusting your existing procedure or your own smarts, you might do well. But the evidence is that there are too many things that can go wrong. So I contend that if you are meticulous and have respect for the details enough to check and double check and install them exactly as they are laid out here, your success is virtually guaranteed. This is a point Ben Hogan tried to make fifty years ago, namely that you need to do things exactly right and that if you do, you will play good golf. It is still true, although he himself did not spell out most of the necessary details that I discuss in this book.

3. Direction and distance control

Direction control: When we do manage to hit a golf ball dead center on the clubface, we still have not handled the business of being able to direct the ball to where we want it to go. And while the *process* to accomplish reasonable controls is easy, *precision* is another issue. I recall the 2002 PGA Championship that ended in a three-way tie on Sunday afternoon and required a playoff Monday morning to determine the winner. After a couple of hours on the practice tee, the three men arrived at the 17th tee where a check for a million dollars to the winner, generous endorsement contracts, and fame and status were on the line. Well, long story short, after the first two golfers hooked their drives into the woods on the left, the third golfer did exactly the same thing. One million dollars at stake, sudden death, and all three are in the woods with their drives— three of the best golfers in the world. Easy game!

I retell this event to underline how difficult precision actually is. This is the place for us to repeat and emphasize a significant reality about this game (which may have been given that name precisely because golf is "flog" when spelled backwards), namely **how** diabolically sensitive it is to minute adjustments and impulses, and that **it is the golfer's job and joy to find out what they are, learn their ramifications, and thoroughly deal with them, in order to achieve any consistency at all.** "Crime and Punishment" is the fitting title to a book that I may write some day to tell about the disproportionate consequences of wins, losses, and disasters in golf tournaments arising from tiny misses, some as small as an inch on the green, an 8th of an inch on the clubface, or a bit of deflection by a breeze. I mention this particular event in the very first chapter of this book on how to learn to play golf to illustrate the sensitivity of minute differences. If I could be in your face and shout in your ear to make the point, I would say to you what I say to my pupils, using the idea of the popular phrase 'God is in the details,' **"Your success or failure is largely determined by extremely small details and adjustments, precisely how you do things, exactly where you put and move your hands, arms, body, and your club, and how you manage yourself."**

And as I just said, it is not usually the obvious visible elements that affect the quality of mechanics and impact the most. It is more often the *incredibly tiny and invisible* adjustments that affect timing or impact or alignment or some other element of the total input of a given swing. The difference between Jack Nicklaus and someone conscientious and obedient to good instruction but of significantly less skill can be summed up in one comment, assuming they both use 'the same basics:' the precision with which Jack respects, installs, and executes all of those minute details *in* his basics is what separates the quality of his golf.

Here is another common experience. Many golfers react to an errant shot with "Oh my gosh! That was terrible! What's wrong with my swing?" Oh, Kemosabe, there may be *nothing* seriously wrong with your swing. As a human being with less than perfect working parts, you will suffer mis-hits as a normal part of your golf, and they usually require no overhauls at all. Most errors occur due to the omission [from ignorance] of details in procedure as opposed to 'bad swings' or lack of concentration for the shot at hand, and of course a good number occur simply because *of* inattention or fatigue.

Now, back to the subject of direction control. While it occupies the bulk of the attention of the golfer when he is on the golf course playing for score, the actual process of *getting* control over it is relatively minor in principle. It is a lot easier to learn how to aim as compared to some other issues, and the degree to which the golfer wishes to acquire great precision may well be limited only by how much practice he is able to put in. Obviously, for one wishing to play professionally, accuracy is a very big thing. But consistency sufficient to 'keep the ball in the fairway' need not be a lifelong struggle. I will show you how to go about acquiring this skill in the shortest possible time, and you may be surprised how really simple it is. I will address aiming with precision both in the full swing and in the various areas of the short game.

Distance control: I will show you in Chapter Nine a procedure to achieve distance control that eliminates the need for months or years of practice to educate a sense of "touch" for the task. You will be able to learn it in a very short time with just a little practice. And given that iron shots to the green and less-than-full shots constitute about ¾ths of all the strokes you play during a normal round of golf, the ability to control distance is very significant. You will almost always find that your distance from the cup too short or too long is greater than the distance right or left of the pin! Knowing this and managing your practice to take advantage *of* this way to control distance can be seen, then, to give you a huge advantage over those who remain clueless exactly how *to* manage it.

4. Self and course management

After you have achieved some skill at ball striking and distance and direction control, you still need to learn how to use it to score well on a golf course. With experience you learn how to deal with different situations and problems you don't encounter on a practice tee, and in the process gain skill in course management. You will also find that the hardest part of golf is not the course itself, but rather making accurate judgments about what you are capable of executing as you play. Again, most of us get in our own way because of unrealistic expectations.

Smart golf involves making intelligent and sufficiently conservative estimates of how far, how straight, and how accurately you can strike a golf ball under the actual conditions on the course - from the tee, from the fairway, from the rough, from sand, from the trees, and around and on the green. I mentioned how unrealistic it is to expect a child to "make music" with a piano without training. It is equally unrealistic to attempt a shot over water requiring 200 yards of carry if your best drives are 225 yards, or to score in the 80s on a 7200-yard layout. If par is 72 for pros who drive 300 yards on a 7200-yard course, simple arithmetic shows that if you drive the ball 225 yards (¾ths of 300), a 5400-yard layout (¾ths of 7200 yards) is comparable. Men wince at the implications of playing on such a short track, so much shorter than that of 'the big boys,' because of the universal macho imperative, "If *he* can do it, so can I!"

5. Diagnosis, dealing with details

You will be given the tools to diagnose your swing, your trajectory and your impact, the reasons for mistakes and mis-hits, and the information that will enable you to make the appropriate corrections. And all that will be possible without the necessity of using video feedback or "golf tips," more lessons, or expensive swing and impact testing devices. Video feedback is limited in its ability to identify most of the *causes* of mis-hit shots! It *can* show you swing faults, obviously, and it is most valuable for that. But swing faults are not as often the cause of bad shots as are things too small to be seen on camera. In fact, there are a few simple things available that can give you more and better information than any of these, because they precisely and immediately identify your problems. These 'things' include the path you can make in tall grass, your shadow on the ground, a mirror or window in which you can watch your image from front and side, a bottle of builder's chalk powder (ordinarily used to refill chalk-line spools), masking tape, and even a tube of lipstick.

All diagnosis and correction requires that you first decide whether your bad shot was simply poor execution for that one shot, or one of a series of mis-hits indicating a pattern. And the specific information you must obtain in order to make a correct diagnosis is threefold: 1) what was the path of my club through the ball? 2) where exactly on the clubface did impact occur? and 3) what was my ball flight? With that information you will know how to make adjustments or swing changes based on cause and effect, both of which are explained and illustrated in great detail in these pages.

When a golfer poses the anxious question "What did I do wrong?" I ask him, *"Exactly* where on the clubface did you impact the ball, and what was the flight of the ball?" If you don't take advantage of the information that can be deduced from the behavior of the ball struck, the value of practice is questionable and significant progress is probably on hold. Statistics such as number of fairways hit, greens in regulation, or number of putts per round are relatively useless for the purpose of making improvements to your ball striking. They are interesting figures for *indicating* progress but of no help in how to create it.

Equipment

There are two overriding issues about getting fitted correctly so that the clubs you use help you to gain skill, rather than interfere with that process. They are the lie angle of the clubs and the feedback you must sense from the club*head.* These two things are the first "critical details" of this book, and why they are important will be evident in a moment. (There are other fitting issues such as length, grip thickness, and appearance that you will also address, but they are minor in comparison with these two.)

Quality component clubs that are fitted to you are less costly than most popular brand name sets 'off the shelf,' so getting the right clubs is not an additional expense. These two things affect how you will <u>unconsciously</u> adapt your setup and your swing to your clubs, either for good or for harm— possibly permanent harm— to your golf game.

A common perception is that tall people need longer clubs and short people shorter clubs. This is not necessarily true. The distance of your hands from the ground when you stand erect determines the length club that is normally the best for you, and this distance is often the same regardless of your overall height. "Standard" length clubs are the right length for most people, but if your hands hang higher or lower to the ground than the average person, *some day* after building your skill you may want to experiment with longer or shorter clubs. A woman's standard length club is usually an inch shorter than what is standard for men, and individual manufacturers differ in their shaft lengths while setting lie angles based pretty much on the average person's hand-to-ground distance.

It may surprise you that the actual weight of the head of a woman's club is often heavier than the same club in a man's set, and the reason it doesn't *feel* heavier is its shorter length. The 'swing weight' of most clubs is in a range that most people manage well, so when you are developing your skill, it is really not anything you need concern yourself with until you have a pretty sharp game and want to go 'to the next level.' (An analogy fits here: it doesn't make sense to use fine sandpaper on a piece of wood that hasn't been smoothed in a plane first.) And as concerns drivers, because the difficulty of hitting longer clubs is far greater than their apparent difference in length from clubs you can hit fairly well, it is not advised that you use a lengthened driver. Tiger Woods's driver is, I believe, 'standard' driver length.

The lie angle that you need to use is found simply by placing a piece of masking tape on the sole of your club (checking lie angle for the 4-iron and 8-iron will provide information enough for all clubs) and then swinging it back and forth at about half speed while standing on a wooden or other 'soft' floor (fitters use a 'lie board') and allowing the sole of the club to brush the surface. When making these swings, you need to stand as erect and relaxed as comfortable as you can and swing with your left hand alone. Let your arm swing down in front of you close to your body. Gradually bend your upper body forward while swinging until you have lowered the club to where it brushes the surface of the board and the tape gets scratched a bit. If the scratches are made anywhere except at the center between the toe and heel of the sole of the club, their distance from the center will show a fitter how much more upright or flat the lie angle needs to be bent to fit you correctly— the process reveals the swing plane that fits your body. Fitting for lie angle is critical because if it is *not* correct for you, you will either contort your posture, setup, and swing *to fit the club* and be compromised in developing your skill because of that or you will make inappropriate adjustments in your alignment, swing, and/or grip in order to produce straight shots. Similar to other details, even small deviations in the lie angle carry consequences out of proportion to the amount of error. An experienced golfer can adapt without harm to a little mis-fit, but a newcomer will not know how and will unconsciously compensate his stance, his motion, and his aiming to the detriment of his mechanics.

The other critical issue is that *the head of the golf club must feel heavy enough for you to sense and respond to it, because of instinctive and*

---

unconscious reactions generated through your touch and in your neuro-muscular system—for good or for ill. I emphasize this and urge you to take it seriously, because of the great importance of dealing with and using your own hidden athletic and neurological responses for good, instead of being victimized by them for harm.

Two things that stood out in my own experience help me to make the point. The first is about when I was a child and learned to play the piano on our family baby grand, which, as far as I knew, was a perfectly decent piano. Why wouldn't I believe that? But unknown to me for the entire ten years I used it, sometimes for hours on end, I had to force it to produce enough volume, nuance, and shading. I had no idea it was that bad an instrument and I simply unconsciously did 'whatever it took' to produce the sounds I wanted. As a result, I was unconsciously making permanent a way of playing that required a lot of tension and far too much muscular exertion. In fact, it ruined my ability ever to play with facility and ease for that very reason. Muscular tension that was habitual during my practice got embedded and permanently installed in my technique, and it effectively ruined my ability ever to play rapid complex passages. There are many children as young as 12 years of age who have more facility than I will ever have, and I attribute my deficiency precisely to the faulty instrument I used during my formative years. A golf swing and piano technique have a lot in common regarding hidden neuro-muscular responses, in that both require relaxed muscular 'readiness' for significant and appropriate performance.

I need to draw another analogy before recounting the second of the experiences on this point that stand out in how well they make the point. Imagine driving spikes into a block of wood using a tack hammer. Your struggle is considerable. Now picture driving those same spikes with a small sledgehammer.

What a difference! All sense of struggle is removed, the **hammer** does the work, and **you** are relaxed and efficient (which as just said is a fundamental pre-condition of your body to be able to produce significant clubhead speed). When you respond to the weight of your clubhead whether it is because the shaft is soft enough or the clubhead feels heavy enough, you will naturally tend to let it 'do the work' instead of forcing it as you would a tack hammer that gives less feedback to which you *can* respond.

My second anecdote on the subject concerns the best golf pupil I ever coached. He was given his father's golf clubs to use when he was growing up— no training clubs— hence he learned to play golf 'with clubs that were too heavy for him.' Well, folks, I have to tell you, this young man (20 at the time) was the best ball striker I have ever had the privilege of working with. His distance (300 yard drives, 175 yard 7-irons), his trajectory, his swing, and the precision of his ball striking were simply extraordinary. When he was tested for these qualities at a young age in the PGA testing trailer that follows the PGA Tour from week to week, his 'score' was **'third highest ever tested'** in characteristics that are considered to be the best indicators of the quality of ball striking, such as clubhead speed, centered impact, spin ratio, ball speed, and such things. I have absolutely no doubt whatsoever, given my own background and experience with a piano as mentioned above, that that young man's use of his dad's heavy clubs had an enormous impact on how he acquired his skill.

This does not mean that your clubs need to be heavier than standard clubs. It *does* mean that you need a *soft enough shaft* so that you *feel the clubhead sufficiently to sense and react/respond* to it, thereby training an essentially effortless and relaxed procedure, as opposed to one in which, unknown to you, you struggle because of insufficient feedback. A clubhead *can* be quite light if the shaft is soft enough, and actually a lighter clubhead can be swung faster and produce greater distance.

A few years ago I acquired a fairly expensive new driver that for half a year I could not hit successfully. One day the lights went on and I realized that I was struggling because it felt too light. Without having to change the shaft, I added some lead tape to the clubhead, changing it from a difficult club to 'the best club in my bag' for one simple reason, namely to enable me to feel the clubhead more easily. Before the weight was added, with insufficient feedback I could not 'find the ball.' When I added weight to the head, all sense of struggle evaporated. I could feel where it was located and I could time its motion and release, which allowed me to relax and swing with even greater speed and without fear or struggle. It enabled me both to let the club do the work and to make more accurate centered impact.

Optical Concerns

If you wear eyeglasses, you will have to deal with three issues that are quite significant for golf. They are: refraction (their ability to bend light rays is the reason *for* glasses in the first place), distortion, and depth perception.

Refraction: While the skin of our hands senses the location of the center of mass of the club*head* when we swing it (through proprioception – i.e., feedback to the nervous system about the location of our hands and arms, *and* of the clubhead), our *eyes* are the source of information as to the location of the *ball*. A problem with eyeglasses is that the lenses can actually deflect the light rays bringing us the image of the ball in such a way as to deceive us as to where it *really* is. The ball is about 5 feet from our eyes, on the ground. At impact the surface of a golf ball when it is compressed, and the corresponding surface of the clubface contacting the ball are both about the size of a nickel, so guess what! Your assignment, Mr. Phelps, if you wish to accept it, is to get *that* clubhead onto *that* ball while it is traveling at something approaching 100 mph *without any overlap between those two nickels!*

     To see what your glasses do, put them on and focus on an object on a wall in front of you. Move the glasses up and down. Notice how the image seems to move. Your head stays still, but the image moves as the glass in front of your eye is moved. If you are wearing glasses for golf, how do you know "which image to aim at" when you swing? A spear fisherman is aware of this phenomenon. He knows that if he aims his spear *at* the fish he intends to catch that he will miss it. It is because the fish *is not actually where it appears to be!* Remember how a goldfish appears to move when you look at it first through the side of the tank, and then walk around to the end and look down at it through the surface of the water? It actually didn't move, of course, but the image you see *does* move due to the refraction of the light coming to your eye from the water— your *perception* of his location changed because refraction bent the rays of light bringing its image to your eyes!

     If you have not subconsciously adjusted to the refraction of your glasses or contact lenses (many people do), you will possibly have to intentionally aim 'north' or 'south' of the ball when you swing to make centered impact. This is addressed in detail in Chapter Five.

Distortion: Recently during an eye exam with a new optometrist, when the subject came up that I was a golfer, the doctor chuckled and said, "Oh, you can't putt, can you?" My shocked answer was "What the heck do you think you know about my golf?" His answer was "Oh, I don't need to know about your golf. I know about your eyes!"

The upshot of this exchange was a couple of observations: first, that the eyeglasses I wore would distort the curvature of the surface of the ground, making it impossible for me to see slope and break accurately, and second, that my peripheral vision would not *begin* to allow me a true read on the line to the cup. Of course, the optometrist was absolutely correct; I have a lot of trouble seeing slope and reading greens correctly.

Another issue is having to use peripheral vision when putting. Having to wear glasses magnifies the problem that introduces, simply because there is a curved piece of glass between your eye and the target *on the side* of your normal line of vision. In the last chapter, I will show you how to minimize problems related to our eyes for aligning your putts.

Depth Control: There is a third feature of your eyeglasses that can affect your game due to the instinctive and subconscious perception of how *far away* the ball appears to be. Look at something about 5 feet away from you through your glasses and then remove them. Notice the change in its apparent distance. When you are about to hit a golf ball, if the actual distance to the ball is different from the distance you *think* it is, you could easily hit the ball fat or thin and never know why. The possibility that your glasses are playing tricks on you will not enter your mind. In such a case, you may have to learn how to ignore and over-ride your incorrect perception by a deliberate procedure that overrides your instincts— not an easy thing to do! I cover this issue later in Chapter Five, dealing with depth control.

How to Go About Learning

We humans need to think linearly when learning something new, meaning that we learn best when we address a single thing at a time, to avoid overload. On overload, we absorb nothing. When a detail is presented to us clearly and simply by itself, it is easy to grasp. So learning the details that make up a golf swing involves recognizing this and then dealing with the details in a logical order, one at a time.

There is another talent involved in our learning that we also need to use to learn how to swing a golf club, and that is the ability to grasp a concept and apply it as a whole in which the details are logical consequences of the concept rather than unrelated parts. Concepts that are involved in the swing include: a pendulum, which I illustrate by reference to a playground swing; gravity, which we experience in walking and in watching a tree fall; wheels, which are round when you look at them from the side, and straight when you look at them from the edge, and similar things. Understanding a concept for golf enables the pupil to grasp something correctly that would not be clear or evident from a simple "do this" type of instruction that omitted the logic or picture of why it needs to be done a certain way. So this instruction will cover both needs: the need to take one thing at a time, and the need to see the logic of things so that you understand what you are doing, in contrast with doing things out of blind obedience.

The 'IRS' and its Agent, "T-Man"

'IRS' is my acronym for identifying the role of the subconscious in golf, the Instinctive Reflex System of the human body, given to us by our creator to protect us from sudden danger. I flinch and duck instantaneously in the face of an imminent blow, reacting defensively far more quickly than I could by consciously thinking about the danger. The "T-man" – the agent *of* the IRS, is a *Tyrant* in his 'absolute' control over our subconscious, as he must be in order *to* protect us. (A few years ago it was popular to refer to FBI agents as "G-men"— government men, and U.S. Treasury— IRS— agents as "T-men.) HE WILL BE OBEYED. How many times have you, mid-swing or mid-putt had a spasm of sorts— found yourself flinching or twitching, or worse, even lurching in some inappropriate way? After the swing you might have become aware of what triggered it— such as a sense of being misaligned, or too close to the ball, or whatever. We have all suffered from this kind of last-minute change of mind.

So I will address specifically what the IRS and T-man can do to your golf swing, and I will show you how to avoid getting thrown off by them. Actually, you will see how to turn your whole nervous system to your *advantage* instead of remaining exposed to its sudden and unavoidable impulses. Ben Hogan observed that a good setup causes a good swing, and it is fairly well known to golf instructors how true that is. While it isn't the whole story by any means, it does correctly hint that when the body is in an appropriate athletic position for a powerful swing, *subconscious mechanisms will trigger efficient muscular responses* managed by that same somewhat automatic neuro-muscular system.

The following is a profoundly important reality that reinforces the critical nature of having the parts of the body and the club in the right places for an effective golf swing. And it goes like this: the position of your body parts relative to each other give information to your subconscious athletic mechanisms. When these parts are aligned relative to each other for maximum power and efficiency, your instincts are likely to recognize how to use them well and will do just that. But if your body parts and the club are not in good alignment, your subconscious *will contrive something— some action or exertions— whatever it can find— to fulfill the mandate of striking the ball regardless if the action is good.* In the heat of the moment, it will not stop to ask questions or give you time to readjust to a more powerful or appropriate position. A la Ben Hogan, *if the body IS aware of the availability of easy and powerful resources to accomplish the task* (which is what occurs when your weight, your hands, wrists, arms, knees, legs, and feet and the club *are* in the best positions relative to each other for the task), *it will call upon those powerful and efficient resources without question,* and in the process produce your most effortless shots. And how we relish *those* special shots that we bring off from time to time! Their taste and feeling remain deep in our memory with the permanence and authority of a narcotic addiction! So ultimately, your IRS can work against you or in your best interests, since your bad swings and your good swings *both get their impetus from the same internal human computer. Your setup* is where you control your input: the swing is the result of that and of your image of what you are actually doing when you do swing. Knowing that your swing is not something you can control in the heat of the moment by some kind of talent that enables you to override your own internal wiring will add to your respect for practicing correctly!

Should I play golf right-handed or left-handed?

While I believe the jury is still out on how an ambidextrous person can best decide whether to play golf as a righty or lefty, it is my belief that in taking up the game, the golfer should choose to play righty if he would kick a ball with his right foot, or vice versa. It is because the *leg we stand on* to kick is our "dominant leg," and more of the *golf swing's* natural controls and triggers are based on body turn on that leg, *the pivot leg*, than on strength or coordination of arms or hands. It is the leg a baseball pitcher, a hammer-thrower, a football or soccer player, or a tennis player stands on when executing. Again as in previous comments, I believe that subconscious athletic mechanisms in the human body are so important that a person should follow his own instincts about how he would kick a ball when choosing which way to go.

Feedback from people who do a lot of things "left-handed" but play golf righty, or vice versa, give me pause. Without any personal experience about it I can't speak with a conviction of certainty. But I try to catch a newcomer to the game when he is not influenced by my thoughts on the subject by asking him which way he would bat a baseball if he were given an opportunity to pinch-hit. If he would go to the left side of home base to bat righty, I would advise him to play golf righty. Or vice versa.

How to Profit From These Materials

Let me summarize what I wish to emphasize on how to profit the most from this book in order to reach your goal of good ball striking in the earliest possible time. It requires the following things:

1) Install all the critical details in your procedure **without compromise, from day one.**

2) Do not hit golf balls or imagine that you can go out and play golf very successfully while you are installing these things. As a matter of fact, if you *do* attempt to play golf or undertake hitting a lot of golf balls with inferior or incorrect mechanics, *you risk installing into your instinctive reflex system* anything faulty that you are doing.

3) Monitor everything you do with total self-awareness using mirrors, plate glass windows, your shadow, video, or the help of a friend to observe and feed back to you the information you would like him to get while you are swinging (such as, "Do I lift my back?"). And when you *do* undertake hitting golf balls, use the diagnostic information available to you to make your corrections, i.e., your divots, your path in the grass, and the exact point of impact of the ball on the clubface.

The Basic Principle of How to Swing a Golf Club

The first critical issue for learning to play golf, prior to any discussion of golf swing mechanics, is that your golf swing needs to be caused, made to move, and activated by independent movement and exertions in the hands and arms themselves--NOT by body turn yanking or pulling the arms! And the left arm must be in control, causing and leading the swing action, and aiming and aligning the clubface. The right arm **never** *controls* the club.

Body turn should never be the source of the power or movement of the hands and arms in the golf swing. The body exerts and moves in anticipation of the movement of the arms and reacts to support their independent motion and exertions. For example, shoulder turn will occur to make room, in both directions, for the motion needed by them. And the legs and torso will move and exert to supply counter-force and bracing for the necessary stability and balance required by the whole dynamic entity, moving in synch as the arms move. Such support acts in the same way that a child balances himself while he pedals his bike, or a shortstop uses his legs for a 'ready stance' in preparation for a ground ball. Unconsciously and "automatically." The golf swing is similar: while you *consciously swing the club freely with your arms and hands,* your body moves simultaneously and reacts sensitively as needed to maintain a solid base for their swing, without lifting, lurching, or swaying, and all body parts will be held firm enough not to give way or collapse. And your brain will learn how to balance and accommodate everything and to furnish body power instinctively, in a short time, *without any conscious help, if you just let it do so.*

Where you encounter instruction in the body of the book seemingly in direct conflict with this mandate not to use the shoulders to pull the arms, it is because we need such drills to train the intimate connection of the arms' swing to the body's support. Once learned, you will be able to rely on the body to cooperate appropriately without worry.

A body yanking the arms ("slashing" and lurching) leads to the most common problems in golf, such as coming over the top and the consequent slicing, pulling that that causes, all kinds of mis-hits, and coming out of the shot. It makes pure impact on the ball either impossible, or at the very least, precarious and erratic.

THAT, body control of the swing, is usually the culprit in bad shots! The good news is that a hands-and-arms-in-control swing provides for maximum accuracy of impact and direction, and minimum interference from body movement.

Chapter Two

What Exactly IS the Golf Swing?

A Theoretical Model

A golf swing is a composite of three different 'moving parts.' They are: 1) a platform that rotates horizontally,

on which is mounted 2) an arm that hangs down from the left shoulder and rotates around that shoulder like a spoke of another wheel, and at the rim, the left hand holds onto 3) a flail.

The platform that rotates horizontally is the golfer's hips and torso. When they rotate in the forward motion of a right-handed golfer, they pull the left shoulder around to the left.

My left shoulder moves perhaps a foot from 'backswing' to 'impact' position because of body rotation, as shown in the above photos.

The (left) arm rotates vertically around the shoulder, and motion of the arm moves the hand. The hand moves the flail lengthwise in the direction of the rim of the wheel. The flail is the golf club itself, a weighted striker. As the arm moves like one of the spokes of a tilted wheel rotating around the left shoulder, it throws the clubhead (the flail) by a lengthwise pull on the *grip* end of the golf club. What causes the club to move from where it was perpendicular to the left arm at the beginning of the downswing to where it is pretty much in line with the left arm at

impact is popularly called "centrifugal force." The clubhead catching up to be in line with the left hand, however, is simply a result— an effect, caused by how the *other* end— the grip end— of the clubshaft was moved.

The three photos opposite show how my hand itself swung all the way from above my head to down past my hips in its own circular motion, with the shoulder as the axis of its

rotation. The three photos on page 31 show the action of the flail in my left hand, which is the core or central essential of the golf swing. The first of those three shows the clubshaft (flail) perpendicular to my left forearm just before it got thrown forward, and the second shows an instant later how the shaft 'caught up to' my hand, in line with my left arm. In the third, momentum has carried it past where it was in line with my left arm.

Swing motions are results of exertions The clubhead gets motion and velocity from three different actions, originating in essentially two different exertions, what could be called power centers. Body turn (the nature of its exertion will be shown to you in the next chapter) makes the left shoulder move around at the same time as the left hand swings down (by gravity with help from the left arm). Force applied by body rotation transmitted to the butt end of the clubshaft through the arms contributes to its downward speed as well. The club gets moved *lengthwise* down toward and then along the target line as the left hand inscribes an arc whose center is the left shoulder, *and the force applied in that manner to the shaft causes a centrifugal release of the clubhead. There is no deliberate muscular exertion on the clubshaft in an attempt to speed up the clubhead.*

Again, the whole mechanism works as follows: the rotating torso moves the left shoulder around in a horizontal circle. The left hand traces a different circle around the left shoulder on a mostly vertical plane. And the centrifugal release and catchup of the clubhead occurs as an inevitable consequence of the pull on the clubshaft lengthwise.

These three "parts" need to be combined in a coordinated sequence of exertions and motions to produce an efficient and powerful movement of the clubhead. The good news is that all of this can be learned in a few minutes with a simple drill that you will be shown shortly.

Trusting my natural physical coordination Everyone walks. If walking had to be explained from mechanical models, it would be extremely complicated, probably more than the golf swing. But in reality walking is easily *doable* by everyone, even by the mentally challenged! So the golf swing is actually easier than walking *if it is undertaken correctly.* The real secrets for making your golf swing effective and accurate, as I have said, are in the details, not in some special gift of coordination lavished on some people and denied to others. It is interesting that some of the greatest athletes in the world in other sports— the most athletically gifted among us— do not play golf well at all! And my guess why is that they are so used to 'feeling their way' into successful athletic action they fail to discover enough of the subtleties of the golf swing, and not dealing with them cognitively means that unless they were lucky enough to have 'felt' all of them correctly from instinct, some of the essential details get omitted. Their confidence in feeling their way that worked so good 'up until now' virtually forecloses any willingness to stand aside and really look at the requisite details. Such is the situation for a large number of golfers with the same personal history in athletics, and it also explains the willingness of *women* to take lessons, as opposed to the reluctance of so many men with the attitude, "I'd rather do it myself!" But back to the subject at hand, reproducing the mechanical model in a human body.

When the left hand swings in a circle around the moving shoulder and throws the clubhead, the three moving parts (shoulders, arms, and clubshaft) combine to generate considerable club*head* speed. If I run at 10 mph on a train moving at 30 mph and throw a ball at 20 mph while running, the total velocity of the ball relative to the ground is now the total of 10 + 30 + 20, i.e., 60 mph.) So we need to know how to use the three parts of the swing mechanism we have just described in order to get the most clubhead speed from it.

At this point I need to introduce the word "fulcrum." It is that point on the shaft where it pivots *between* the two hands, i.e., about five inches down from the grip cap— under the thumb of a righty's left hand.

I prefer to think of the golf club as a "sling" and not a "lever" because I do not even want to *suggest* that force be applied to it as is applied to a lever (by pushing against the shaft), except in a few special situations. This book and philosophy of how to produce maximum clubhead speed with minimum effort and maximum repeatability does not permit treating the golf club as a stick with which to *hit* a golf ball. The clubshaft is a *connector* between your hands and the clubhead (it could be a rope, a strap, a shaft *or* a stick); you will not use it as a lever or rod against which force can be applied.

You can pull a rope so as to try to stretch it and thereby create movement in what is attached at the other end (the sling technique), but you can't press against it like a lever and accomplish anything meaningful. You can use a stiff golf shaft *either* way, and while some golfers may succeed by using the golf shaft like a lever, my approach and instruction does not use that basis or philosophy of how to swing a golf club. Readers invested in 'leverage golf' will not find that validated or explained in these pages. On the contrary, it is my hope that you will discover the much greater advantage of the sling, or 'flail' concept of swing, vs. hit, procedure.

Another device perhaps more familiar to our generation that illustrates the flail action is a weapon used sometimes by police to achieve control in dangerous confrontations, namely, numchucks. This device consists of two wooden sticks joined by a short chain or cord, and by using one as a handle and casting the other to strike someone, the user has a deadly weapon where the harm it can inflict depends on remarkably easy effort.

Each one of the three moving parts of the body in a golf swing requires different forces or exertions to move *it*, and in a good swing the three are blended and balanced to produce the greatest possible clubhead speed. Since any given golfer is limited by *his* strength, *his* range of motion, and *his* speed, it is imperative that he know how to use his own assets as efficiently as possible, as opposed to what someone else, with different gifts, would do. Differences from other people in strength and range of motion and other features are not only not obvious, they are invisible, so copying what you see someone else doing can be an incomplete or even harmful procedure. And knowledge what to exert (*exertions* are also invisible, so you can't know what to exert by observation!) is gained by first understanding how these parts work in a mechanical sense, and then by doing the motions to reproduce the function you are trying to fulfill, all the while fitting yourself to your strengths— experimenting with what feels comfortable for you. While you are becoming familiar with it all, you will need to repeat the motion many times until you "get it" in the same way the child grasps how to balance himself on his bike. Learning it is accomplished by doing drills designed to imprint the feelings and exertions you are using into the part of your brain that processes and stores that kind of information. The process is the same that we use to learn and remember how to walk, throw, pick up a fork, or to do anything physical. Our motions are sensory, neuro-muscular, and intuitive, and most of them are managed subconsciously.

Installing correct motions with a golf club requires something that may not be obvious, and that needs emphasis.

Do you remember how you learned to ride a bike? You didn't learn to balance until the bicycle was in motion because *motion created feedback to which you responded and adjusted, and in the process you discovered subtle adjustments that worked to enable you to balance and control your bike.* I liken our talent for grasping physical concepts to the computer command known as "Snap to Grid." It is what causes a playing card in a computer game of *Solitaire* to move (snap) to the exact spot on your desktop screen appropriate for it when a card is dragged and dropped near its intended location. I believe when a person's body and motion are close to what works most efficiently for the task at hand, there is a sensor in a part of the brain that recognizes, and then installs (snaps to grid) exactly what motion, position, exertion, or combination of them works best for it. Normal people learn to walk, bike, run, and so on with apparent ease. We learn these things from trial and error as children, during our formative years. The neuro-muscular system of the body figures out how *because* of that faculty, in my opinion. None of us take walking or bike lessons!

In the same way, learning to move a golf club correctly will occur largely while you are doing certain things with it and responding to it with subtle adjustments that you sense are appropriate while performing the actions, not from reading about them alone. Reading fails to give the feedback and the information that comes from doing it which you use to make your own adjustments. So, while doing the drills it is imperative to be doing what is right and what works best rather than to be embedding anything wrong and to misinform your neuro-muscular system what adjustments *to* make. This is emphasized at the outset here to warn you that 'muscle memory,' habit, is a powerful faculty, so please respect all of the critical details as they are introduced in order to make it possible to reach your own highest potential, and in the shortest possible time. To borrow from Dave Pelz, practice makes permanent!

Shaft plane There are many teachers who emphasize the plane of the shaft and who teach golf mechanics by reference to it throughout the swing. I do not. There are three reasons why I don't.

- The first is that your address position does not resemble impact position at all, rendering it irrelevant as a reference (different golfers have different preferences for their own setup, some using low hands and some with high hands). The only exception is that the clubface points at the target at impact in a good swing. Well actually *at* impact, the clubface is a bit open; at *separation* it is square to the target line.

- The second reason is that the sweet spot on the clubface does not lie on the shaft plane: it is actually a couple inches 'north' of the shaft as you look down at your club, in the same way that the center of the blade of a hockey stick is not in line with its shaft.

- And the most important reason is that **your left arm connects to your body at your left shoulder, and it is controlled by that shoulder when your torso turns and pulls it. Your right hand does not** *control* **the clubshaft; it only adds force to the swing where it connects to the club a few inches down from the grip cap. So when a club is swung** (as opposed to manipulated by the hands), **the left arm throws the clubhead, and all of the parts that exist between the left shoulder and the clubhead behave as if they were all on a single plane— a straight line— even if** there are bends at the points of connection, at your elbow and wrist. The wagon wheel with club attached pictured on page 28 represents the underlying physical reality of what occurs. The left shoulder is the axis of the wagon wheel. On the way from the top of the swing down to an instant before impact, the left shoulder, the left arm, the left hand, and the clubshaft and clubhead are all on an absolutely flat plane as you see in the down-the-line picture on page 41. An instant before impact, *rotation* occurs both in the left forearm and in the clubshaft in such a way that the left wrist and the hosel of the club both 'get out of the way' as the massive momentum of the clubhead itself swivels into the ball. If the left wrist could extend outward to where the shaft was 180° relative to the left forearm, and if the sweet spot of the clubhead were at the end of the shaft, there would be a straight line running through the shoulder, the arm, the hand, the shaft, the clubhead, and the ball. But those parts of the swing mechanism do not have that capability, so there remains some angle both at your wrist and at the hosel of the club at impact. Your left shoulder, your left arm, your left hand, the clubshaft, and the sweet spot of the clubhead are most definitely on that wagon wheel flat plane on the way *to* the ball; it is only the rotation of the left arm and club coming directly into impact that causes the left wrist and the hosel to 'move aside' as momentum continues to move the center of mass of the clubhead in an absolutely pure orbit with no wobble to and through the golf ball.

Bottom line: on the way to the ball from the top of the backswing to release and rotation into the ball, the clubhead, shaft, left hand, left arm and shoulder are all on that flat plane, and the flatness of the plane between the shoulder and the center of mass and the clubhead exists in the dynamic reality of what happens in a golf swing despite the apparency of bends at the left wrist and the hosel of the club!

For proof that these bends are immaterial, you may remember a golfer who played with a 'broken' left arm. For *many years* the most accurate driver of the golf ball in professional golf,

Calvin Peete, used a bent arm to hit the ball straighter than all the rest of the field— his fairways-in-regulation statistic was *always* the best on tour! He had broken his left arm in a childhood accident and it didn't heal properly, so he could not straighten the very obvious and marked bend at his left elbow. But other than limiting the distance he could hit the ball, that bend simply did not affect his accuracy. And it was in fact irrelevant, since the *physics of the swing mechanism of shoulder, arm, clubshaft, hosel, and clubhead are that the line from source (shoulder) to center of mass of the striker (the center of mass of the clubhead) simply must be a straight line,* whether or not there exist any bends at the connecting points.

How the hosel moves aside or gets out of the way as the club rotates into impact is easy to observe. Suspend a club out in front of you by holding the grip between your two palms with the shaft vertical, then rub your hands back and forth to spin it. Notice how the hosel rotates around the clubhead, while the center of the bottom of the club— the bottom of the axis of rotation— itself remains steady. The clubhead does not rotate around the shaft!

This demonstrates how the axis of the club runs from the grip cap down through the bottom of the clubhead near its center. The same applies to your left arm: as *it* rotates into impact, even though there remains an angle at the connection between your left forearm and the shaft (an angle that gets pulled much straighter by the weight of the club during release than the angle that exists at setup), the hosel and wrist *both* turn counter clockwise as the center of mass in the clubhead itself continues along its straight line of motion. *Both* the hosel and wrist 'duck out of the way' as rotation occurs.

The flattening of the left wrist at release is further evidence that a **right hand** or **shaft plane** interpretation of what happens is a misunderstanding of the physics of the swing. It is of course caused by the force of the clubhead pulling away from your left shoulder. As a matter of fact, and this point was made by Ben Hogan, although people thought he meant bowing the wrist was to be deliberate, which it isn't, your left wrist will *get* bowed forward somewhat due to the force you are applying to move your hand as fast as possible at the same time as your club's weight pulls out away from your body. But even those forces are not enough to form a *perfectly* straight line from left shoulder to ball. And of course, the line of the clubshaft is now more vertical than it was at setup due *to* this pull-out force from the clubhead. As I said earlier, any resemblance at impact to the original (setup) plane of the shaft is probably coincidental (if it exists at all) and it would be due to the limit of the range of motion in the wrist of the individual golfer and whether he prefers a low-hands (Azinger), neutral, or high-hands (Inkster and Lopez) setup.

Let me summarize: 'shaft plane' is irrelevant to the underlying dynamics of the golf swing. The left shoulder essentially throws the clubhead, whose weight 'tries' to straighten the angles that exist between the left shoulder and the center of mass in the clubhead. The right hand helps to push the left hand at the fulcrum of the flail, but it does not control the shaft of the club!

"From inside to out, to on-line, to inside again" Words similar to this are often used to describe the path of your clubhead as it approaches, strikes, and follows the golf ball during a swing. The truth is that such a path is simply an optical illusion based on the fact that your eyes are looking down on the top of your swing instead of from the edge of its plane. Your own eyes are above your shoulders, so that as you look down at your own club path, it appears to be curved. If you could see your swing from a spot between your shoulders, you would see a simple straight line—the target line, and the motion of the clubhead from *that* perspective would be along a flat, straight plane-line, not along a curve. It is the same as when you look at a wheel from down the line. So looking at your clubhead from any perspective *other* than down the line or on its plane of motion it appears to follow an arc. But looking at it from down the line, it moves in a straight line, and this is important for you to know because of how you will guide both your backswing and downswing.

More detail about your motions

Let's have a closer look at how our bodies accomplish the three different swing motions that we first considered in a mechanical model. (Again, my apologies to lefties, who I hope will be able to reverse these instructions without great difficulty.)

The motions of your legs and hips: The platform of your swing consists of your legs and hips, on top of which your torso sits and gets turned by your hips. Your body moves in a horizontal circle. It rotates around what I like to call a hinge, running vertically through your body up from the inside of your right foot during your backswing and up from your left heel during your downswing.

Your backswing moves weight towards, but not entirely on *to,* your right leg, and then before the downswing begins, a small movement and weight shift moves your weight, hence the hinge of your rotation, to your left heel and left leg, after which your torso rotates around *that* leg for the downswing. Your torso is, for this purpose, the portion of your body above your hips. And notice this: wherever your *weight* is located, the axis or hinge *of* that rotation will occur *there.*

Take a moment to experiment and discover how rotation happens, and how it feels to consciously, deliberately, rotate around each leg, *and* how rotation naturally occurs above wherever your weight is located. Stand first with your weight centered over your left foot, and then rotate back and forth. See how your turn occurs *naturally* around your left leg. Then if you shift your weight over to where most of it is on your *right* leg and turn, you discover that the hinge of your rotation is now over *that* foot.

These two pictures above show how this plays out in your swing. In the first picture, taken during the backswing of my left-hand-only swing drill, my weight is over the inside of my right foot, and I am rotating around my right hip. In the second picture, just before I start anything deliberate in my downswing, I have fallen to the left, my arms dropped a bit because of that small movement of my hips to the left, and I am now standing, and will be pivoting, on my left foot.

The motion of your left arm Your left arm is attached to the left side of your chest at your left shoulder. That arm rotates around your shoulder like the spoke of a wagon or bike wheel, on a fairly vertical plane, slanted like the wagon wheel pictured earlier. The path of your left *hand*, then, is circular like the rim of such a wheel. The *right* hand is, of course, used and needed in your normal swing, but for describing the structure of the parts, the left arm is the point of reference.

The motion of your left hand and the clubshaft The last of the three basic structural hinges around which motion occurs is your left hand, holding the clubshaft, with a clubhead attached at the other end. As I have said, it is not a lever in this model: it is a sling— the free member of a 'numchucks"— it could be a rope with a striker attached at its end. The dictionary describes a sling as a strap or string with a missile attached at the end that you fling by whirling the strap around your hand and then releasing the missile at just the right instant. The whirling action creates far more speed in the missile than the speed of your hand alone. There exists what scientists refer to as "a mechanical advantage" when you do this, which means that one kind of mechanical function is exchanged for another for some particular purpose. With a lever and fulcrum or a block and tackle, a small person can lift heavy furniture, tree trunks, or even cars weighing hundreds of pounds. These devices exchange length of motion using *light* exertion (what *we* do) for the ability of the *device* to lift *heavy* weight a short distance. The mechanical advantage of a *sling* is to exchange force in a smaller amount of motion (in the hand) for clubhead speed in a much lighter object (the clubhead). And then, when perfect impact occurs in the collision of that clubhead with a golf ball, it exchanges the clubhead's velocity and heavier weight for greater speed in a lighter ball. *It, the ball,* gets its total velocity in the air from its elastic rebound off of the fast moving clubface, plus the velocity remaining in the clubhead as the ball leaves its surface after a very brief instant of contact.

We seek "effortless power," but "powerless effort" is the result if we fail to arrange or to time all the working parts for efficient mechanical advantage. Our struggle in such an instance is not because it is hard to swing a club fairly fast. It is because at some moment in the whole action we are putting something— our hands, arms, feet, clubhead— *something* — some part of the swinging mechanism— *in the wrong place,* forfeiting mechanical advantage. And poor timing does exactly that, in that it moves the clubhead into the wrong place just prior to impact, wrong because it put the clubhead too much in line with the left arm too early, and its speed when collision occurs is much less than what could have occurred with a different procedure.

Innate talent Most of us tend to regard ability (knowledge how) to swing a golf club as a special intuitive gift given to super athletes (this is true for many of them), hence not given to normal folk like us. This is simply untrue! I say untrue because, as it says in the first chapter, it can be taught to anyone by illustrating the concepts for him, showing him the critical details that come into play, and having him build his swing structure by installing one thing at a time in just a few steps. Indeed, even the most gifted golfers need to deal with those same details, and somewhere along the line they have to learn them just as you and

I do! I mention elsewhere how many super athletes are not good golfers for the reason that they do not deal correctly with some of the critical details.

Some Structural Essentials

With the mechanical model in mind, we can now undertake making a golf swing 'from scratch.' So let's look at some of the details of the model so that we build our swing correctly.

The Flat Swing Plane and Straight Plane Line for Golf

As it applies in a golf swing, the plane, like the edge of a pane of glass or the edge of the plane on which a wheel spins, also has a straight edge. If you set that edge on the ground, it is a straight line. We use that line in golf, and we place its edge over the ball, aimed at our target. We call it the target line. It is, then, the baseline of the wheel of motion of our left armclub assembly. And the direction of the plane line remains the same whether the pane of glass stands vertical on that line or if it is tilted. I can roll a wheel along a straight line on the floor and it doesn't matter whether it is vertical or tilts to one side. Tilting the wheel does not change the direction along which it rolls. The plane of motion of a wheel is the center line of the wheel looking at it from its edge, while its plane *line* is the line it traces on the floor as it rolls.

The image of the wagon wheel shows you what details you need to deal with. The left arm is a spoke, the left shoulder is the axle, and the left hand traces the rim of the wheel. Since the plane of your 'wheel' must be flat, the motion of your hand must be a straight line accurately aimed at your 'target,' namely, along

the target line. So, THIS IS THE BOTTOM LINE OF
DIRECTION CONTROL: A GOLFER MUST AIM HIS
ROLLING WHEEL, THE MOTION OF HIS HAND, DOWN
TOWARDS AND THEN ALONG THE PLANE LINE, THE
TARGET LINE.

The Correct Use of the Flail

As mentioned, the clubshaft will not be treated as a lever to push
against. In great golf swings the head of the club acts like the end
of a flail, or in the case of a sling it acts like a missile that gets
thrown by force applied at the fulcrum. Its principle is nothing
more complex than twirling a cord with a weight on the end of it!
In each case, there is a flexible connection at the fulcrum and force
is applied at the fulcrum to throw the weight. Your effort
will be to try to *stretch* or elongate the cord (in this case, of course,
the shaft) that runs between the handle and the other end of the
device. So you will pull lengthwise on the grip end of the club in
an effort to move the clubshaft lengthwise in the direction of the
grip cap! With these two pictures side by side here, it is easier to
visualize the action and to sense the dynamics of it.

Since the path of the hand is an arc, in order for the hand to be *able* to pull the club lengthwise, during the downswing the clubshaft must be directly behind— at 90° to— the motion of the hand. The arm is rotating, the hand is moving in a curved arc, and wherever the hand is *in* the arc, the clubhead will follow directly behind until it does get thrown. So for this to work well, there are two important details about where the clubshaft needs to be positioned at the beginning of the downswing and for some time into it. *You must set the clubshaft perpendicular to the left forearm,* and *it must be on the same plane as the rotating arm.*

If the clubhead is not *directly behind your hand* as your hand starts to move, a wobble will be set up the same way in which a water skier is thrown somewhat sideways when he is not **directly** behind the moving boat that pulls him. There are two different 'directly behind your hand' places, as you may already realize: one is that the clubhead is on the plane of motion of the spinning wheel— on that flat plane, and the other is it must be tangent to the direction of the motion of your hand, 90° to the forearm, or spoke of your wagon wheel. So you need to make sure as you begin your forward/down swing that your clubshaft is on the same plane as the plane of rotation of your arm *and* that it gets placed perpendicular to your left forearm before the downswing starts.

The picture on the left shows the clubhead, the clubshaft, my left hand, my left arm, and my left shoulder all on the same plane. That plane clearly is parallel to my feet and its line on the ground is towards my target. The picture on the right shows the clubshaft perpendicular to my left forearm on the way to the ball. Release will not really begin until my hand is below my belt.

The Release, an EFFECT

At a certain point in the rotation of your arm around your left shoulder, the club*head* **will seek to "catch up to your hand."** This "centifugal" action is the same as that of the contents of test tubes spun in a centrifuge, where heavier matter in the solution gets thrown to the bottom. It is the same as how the tip of a whip "cracks" in the air: it gets thrown so rapidly (over 700 mph) that it breaks the sound barrier. And it is the same action as throwing a weighted lure with a fishing pole.

A *golfer* also needs to 'throw' *his* clubhead, and that is accomplished, as I repeat, by yanking or pulling the clubshaft lengthwise. In a short while you will learn how you can do that effectively and how you can actually manipulate the action to *time* that catch-up reaction for best results in hitting golf balls far.

The Necessity of Hand Rollover During Release

Due to the way our hands are attached to our forearms, it is not possible for us to accomplish a complete release of the clubhead unless we turn our arms to permit the clubshaft to continue forward during the release. The wrist's ability to bend is limited, and unless the wrist and arm are rotated during the release, the clubshaft gets "stuck"— the motion runs into a barrier that can cause us to injure ourselves, or more likely, to change the mechanics in a way that diminishes the action of the club during the heart of the golf swing itself. We have to accommodate the limited range of motion and the structure of our bodies by rotating our arms counter-clockwise a full 180° during the release interval. From when they approach the ball until after impact, the hands and arms reverse their position, and the clubshaft moves from a gripcap-faces-target position at waist level on the way to the ball, to gripcap-faces-directly-away-from-target at waist level after impact.

Your hands will be halfway between those two positions at impact, and it is surprising how a natural, unmanipulated roll *of* the two arms consistently returns the clubface to exactly the same angle relative to the target line when your ball position, timing, and grip are consistent. You will be shown how to make that position square *to* the target line in chapter four.

The Platform Torso Moves Sideways AND Rotates, and The Forward Press is the Initiator of a Good Swing

As said already, your torso acts like it sits on a *moving* turntable. For making your backswing, you will first use a bit of a forward press by moving weight over toward your left foot an inch or two, and then the 'turntable' of your legs and hips moves back a couple inches to the right and your hips turn clockwise. In a full swing, ideally the upper part of your torso should turn 90°. Before your downswing begins— actually while your arms are still on the way up— your weight should fall back over to your left heel (the turntable slides to the left) moving your hips leftward, *without any turn occurring*. And then after your hands begin their motion down plane towards the target line, your torso will rotate counter-clockwise to move and support the pulling of your left arm and pushing of your right hand and arm. And this motion is *in addition* to what is due to *other* upper-arm and pectoral muscle exertions pulling the butt end of the clubshaft downwards.

At the risk of appearing redundant and putting you to sleep as you read here, I have intentionally repeated this entire action here, from setup to follow through, **as a whole**, because the success of your swing is related to the trigger set off in your forward press, whatever final form it actually takes. There are subconscious athletic mechanisms that get activated *by* that initial movement, and without it the wrong muscles and actions will be called upon. Once you have committed yourself to any sequence of actions, efficient or inefficient, it is too late to change since that commitment governs what happens during the blackout of your swing. The forward press *is* the key for how to correctly wed your swing to your weight shift, and that is about as fundamental to the overall mechanics as any other element of good golf swings. Different golfers activate their swings in different ways, some of them quite noticeable. Jack Nicklaus uses a slight rightwards turn of his chin, Sergio Garcia likes to 'get into his zone' with multiple waggles of his clubshaft, and several including Mike Weir use a 'trial' half-backswing.

More about the backswing When your forward press creates the imbalance in your body and you fall back to your right side because of that imbalance, use that energy, your body's response to gravity, to power your backswing. Heave, throw, fling or swing (choose a word that seems to fit your perception of it) your arms and club to the right and up. Use *enough* energy— it will be considerable— but *only* enough, to get the club and arms to float to the top. I liken a golf swing to a mom pushing her child in a playground swing. She uses enough energy to propel the child all the way to the top but not more. If she were to use too much force, the child would be thrown over the bar. And notice that she *does* "shove" the swing away from her; she does not carry it to the top of its stroke slowly by lifting it and putting it there. In a golf swing you need to do the same thing, that is, you need to *swing* it with enough energy to get it to the top. Failure to use enough energy that the arms FLOAT TO THE TOP means that muscles get activated that should not be, and they might impulsively act first with less than optimum results. The procedure of a 'low and slow' backswing is wrong for that reason: placing the club at the top *does* leave the wrong muscles 'in use.'

The opposite problem is when the arms and club are given too *hard* a shove in this backswing throw, because then they need to be grabbed to *stop* them from going too far, requiring some unwanted exertions that will be shown later to be harmful.

A subtlety of triggering your backswing with a small weight movement to your left side is that *your body needs to move at the natural rate that gravity causes you to fall as contrasted with a contrived or forced rate. Your backswing is 'powered' by the body falling to the right after the forward press, as mentioned above and your downswing is led by the body falling to the left.* Falling from one foot to the other is exactly what happens in walking, so there is no necessity to learn how to do this. All of us have already learned to walk before we take up golf (unless you start before your first birthday). We simply need to know how to *apply* walking to the golf swing.

In the next chapter we will put these things into practice so that you can develop your skill with full awareness of why you are doing what you do, and in the process you will become your own coach and teacher for the rest of your life.

Chapter Three

Making A Perfect
Golf Swing

Alignment of the Parts

Now that we have seen a mechanical model of the golf swing
and understand its principles, we can start to build our own swing.
The instructions will enable us to fit it to our own body parts and
strengths by installing all the critical alignments, adjustments, and
relationships at the outset. In that way we will not have to come
back later to try to discover and repair embedded *mis*alignments.
The quality of a swing is dependent on the alignment of its parts
in a way that allows it to work efficiently when in motion. The
workability of *any* mechanical device operates on the same
principle, i.e., the correct alignment of its parts.

This instruction will unfold gradually. It is taught by creating a drill that reproduces the essential core of the golf swing—the release and impact section of a full swing—and it introduces the body parts and their roles one at a time. It starts from a "just before impact" position of the arms and hands, not the normal address position, for the reason that it teaches the release action first before worrying about addressing or trying to hit golf balls. The impact interval is the core of the golf swing, and understanding and getting it right before introducing other things is imperative. No golf balls will be introduced until the 'machine' we build is ready. The business of *using* it for hitting balls introduces more concerns, so we will save them for later, as well.

This chapter will show you exactly what to do in the swing, so after you have read all the instructions and understand the whole procedure, you will take your pitching wedge in hand, find somewhere to stand where you can swing freely and where there is a line on the ground or floor that you can use as a swing alignment aid, and then you will install the details into your procedure and swing away. Some of these details require careful attention and precision, and I urge you not to let anything slip by.

This first drill, the essence, the heart of the full golf swing, is the best training aid available anywhere. It is also the best thing you can do as a warm-up and preparation for practice or play. And it contains absolutely everything you need to do for a quality golf swing. (Yes, there is more that you will need to learn to embellish and complete your mastery of the motion, but 'genetically' it is all here!) As mentioned earlier, when you wish to advance and improve your technique, or if you get off track at any time, you do not need to go to later chapters or "more advanced instruction" to make significant progress or resolve difficulties. The solutions to your problems, the place where perfection may be found, and the best training aids available to you *are right here in front of you on 'page one.'* *THIS DRILL IS WHERE YOU DISCOVER, DEVELOP, AND REFINE, YOUR PERFECT GOLF SWING.*

How to Stand

Your feet: The first critical detail is the placement of your feet. It needs to allow *and induce* the torso to turn. After you have learned the swing and you understand how your stance affects it, some variations will be suitable. But for establishing and embedding the critical elements, you do well to start with the positions set forth here.

Because your feet need to be close enough together to allow your torso to turn freely, I suggest you place your heels about 12 inches apart for now, and to angle your left foot out a bit. This will tend to encourage and call upon your lower body to turn for the forward swing.

I have mentioned earlier that a body will normally select the most efficient resource for any physical action that the brain senses is available for the task at hand. With the feet fairly close together and the left foot toed out a bit, perhaps 15 degrees, you sense the freedom and availability of the lower body to turn. It is difficult or even impossible for many people to turn freely with their feet as far apart as is often taught, i.e., "shoulder width between heels." In such a position, since your subconscious is unaware of the power in your lower body because it is out of position for ease in turning, it will not 'volunteer' that resource. Too wide a stance limits the range of motion and full use of the amplitude available to the arms, as well as the underlying support for the the downswing. Since you need all the help you can get from natural athletic responses that require no thought, having your feet far apart works against you while learning. The lower body is just 'not available.'

Another benefit of having your feet fairly close together is that you will learn balance better than if your feet are further apart. You could not learn to balance your bike with training wheels on it— they had to be removed to allow you to sense its behavior, and to respond and adjust to it. It is the same with the golf swing: having your feet spread apart reduces and possibly eliminates feedback about how to balance yourself during your swing. You will be unaware that an entirely different set of muscles and exertions is used to swing in perfect balance than if you can use your feet as 'braces' from which to 'push off.' You cheat yourself by using *those* 'training wheels!'— feet wide apart.

Later, when you have developed your game and embedded this critical detail in your procedure (feet close enough to permit a free turn and to lead you to use rotation instead of leg thrust), you may prefer your feet further apart for stability with longer clubs, but by then you will have learned how to limit the width between your heels so you don't inhibit your lower body's action.

Balance front to back: Your weight needs to be evenly balanced between your heels and toes. That is how I am balanced in the photo below. This is a critical detail for the reason that any imbalance of this kind will seek to right itself as your swing gets under way, and the upper body (and with it the club) can easily move *several inches* closer to or further from the ball during the swing when the rebalancing occurs.

This is easy to discover for yourself, as follows. Stand with your weight forward on your toes. Now rock your weight back to your heels. Notice how much your upper body moves back. If you hold a golf club as though addressing a ball and rock back between your heels and toes, the movement of the upper body also changes the position of the club on the floor or ground out from or back toward your feet.

In the first picture above, I am standing with my weight forward towards my toes. In the second, I have allowed my weight to fall back towards my heels. As you can see, the clubhead got moved maybe **six inches** as a result of that weight shift. Six inches is *a lot of difference in club position due to something as subtle as your weight being 'back' or 'forward!'*

Here's a closeup of the club in the above photos.

True balance would bring my clubhead near the center between these two extremes, that is, where it was in the photo on page 61. Since the sweet spot on your club is only as large as a nickel, balance of this kind is obviously an enormously sensitive detail, and it will become clear to you in your practice how critical this is to your ball striking. The greatest ball strikers in golf have extremely "quiet" upper body motion throughout their entire swings, and their balance is why. And be aware that such absence of movement is not something due to *effort*, but to a *setup* procedure made into a habit. *A properly balanced setup eliminates the tendency for any shift of your body toward or away from the ball during your swing.*

Your knees: Bend your knees a little as you see in the photo on page 60. This allows your legs to move freely for powering the turn of your torso. If you bend your knees more than just a little, however, you will create stress or strain in the legs. Use the least bend that will still permit your to turn your lower body freely. Retain this knee flex throughout the swing so that you don't lower or raise the height of your shoulders while you are swinging. Many golfers 'push up' with their legs. They might do it during takeaway to help 'lift the arms' back away from the ball to start the backswing. Some do it at the top of the swing to help *lengthen* their backswing. And others will push up with their knees at impact in an attempt to 'help the club to lift the ball.' But any of these disruptions causes a deflection of the club from its proper path. Just as with balance, movement of the upper body up or down during the swing causes thin or fat shots proportional to the amount *of* such motion, whether from legs shoving, balance rebalancing, or spine angle changing. There is precious little room for error when you are trying to make such a tiny sweetspot on your clubface collide with a target the size of a nickel on the ball. So, *especially* with the ball as far away from your shoulders as it is (some five feet!), *anything* that can disrupt the flight of the clubhead to the ball needs to be totally eliminated. Deal with the details, I like to say, or they will deal with you!

I use the image of a draftsman's compass to illustrate the consequences of allowing your upper body to move during the swing. You can make circles with such an instrument again and again and as long as the stylus remains in one place and the distance between the stylus and the pencil is not changed, the circle it draws gets retraced over and over. But if you trace one arc and then move the stylus to a *new* place for the next, the new arc is also moved to a new place and the pencil cannot retrace the old one. Applying this analogy to your procedure for swinging a golf club, the stylus represents your sternum, and the pencil is the clubface. Therefore *any* motion of your sternum closer to, or away from, the ball during the swing moves the clubhead exactly the same distance closer to or further from the ball. Even a **one-half inch** movement of your body up or down as the swing gets underway is all it takes to absolutely ruin a golf shot and along with it, your enjoyment of the moment, simply because it causes impact a half-inch off center! I hope you will respect this critical detail as you build your technique, as nothing else is as important for good ball striking.

Your upper body: Tilt your upper body forward just enough for your arms to hang under your armpits in front of your chest.

Your hands must hang straight down under your shoulders. And the forward tilt of your body needs to be sufficient for your left arm to pass across the chest without obstruction. Anyone with a large girth (or a woman needing to negotiate her bosom) should place the left arm directly on *top* of the left breast, as this position permits free motion in the takeaway that is not possible if the left arm hangs to the left side of the chest.

This is one of the most important critical details of the setup— specifically that your upper arms hang freely and have room to swing past your body, but never by reaching out *off* your chest. Such a position is stress-free, and it means that during the swing when gravity acts on the arms to return them to the ball, its force and the intended path for the arms and club will not be in conflict— there will be no tendency in the setup that you will need to overcome in your search for the ball. One of the most common impact faults in golf is hitting the ball on the toe of the club, and it is usually caused by the golfer reaching out for the ball, moving his hands away from his body in his setup while setting his clubhead down. In such a case, the faulty impact is not because of something done during the swing. It is a fault caused in the setup *by* reaching out, because your arms *will* return closer to your body at impact, and the club*head* will return closer to your feet than where you placed it to begin with. When a longer club requires that your upper arms *cannot* hang vertically in this manner because the club is too long to allow for that, the correct thing to do is to raise your chest, while still leaving your upper arms on your chest. That raises the club. The reason for doing it this way is because your chest acts as a platform of support under your upper arms during the downswing, and raising your chest prevents them from falling when you swing down. If arms that were reaching out are allowed to fall, the *clubhead* swings closer to your feet, and of course if they were set up at the ball, you would have to hit the ball on the toe or miss it completely because the arms and club are no longer 'out there' where the ball is when they comes back to impact.

For now you will be using only the shortest club in your set, your pitching wedge, since it will permit your arms to hang straight down. These pictures show my left arm hanging straight down for a short club, and then for the longer club, my spine angle raised, which raised my chest, and again I mention that I need the support of that platform under my left upper arm for that longer club.

See how the angle between my spine and my arms is the same in both pictures: only the amount of tilt in my spine changed in order to accommodate the longer club. My hands have also moved further from my legs for the longer club, but only as a result of the change in my spine angle.

Just as was mentioned about knee bend, the attitude or tilt of your spine must not change at any time during your swing. People unaware of the importance of maintaining this angle will sometimes lift their back at one of three specific moments during the swing exactly as some do with their knees: 1) at takeaway, to help lift the arms; 2) at the top of the backswing, in an attempt to increase the amplitude of the swing arc; and 3) just before impact, in an attempt to help the club 'pick up' the ball. So maintaining the spine angle is as necessary as maintaining knee flex for controlling the path of the club to the ball and for retaining a constant distance from the upper body to the ball between setup and impact.

How to Hold the Club

The left hand: *This instruction of your left hand grip is the most critical detail of golf.* It is because it is the connection between you and the instrument—the golf club. And many of its requirements are unknown to most golfers because they are not taught. Chief among the omissions are how your grip must permit you to load your club for power, and how to align it properly for square impact on the golf ball. When these details are fully understood from correct instruction, feedback, and experience, you will discover that "There *are* no slicers [as one example]: *there are only misinformed golfers!*" Your left hand is your main communication link with the club throughout the swing for sensing its position and its weight and for responding to it, and *it* is responsible for directing it where it needs to go, possibly as fast as 100 miles per hour during a downswing taking little more than one second. This is a lot of responsibility, so for clarity and in order to cover the subject as it deserves, I will discuss the details of the left hand grip one-at-a-time.

First: The club needs to be held as far out in your fingers as possible and almost perpendicular to the bones of your hand so that the clubshaft can get to the top of the backswing at a 90° angle with the left foream. It will retain that position as it follows your hand in the downswing on the way to the ball!

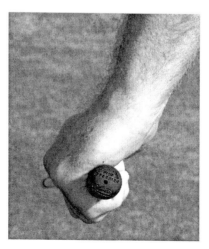

Notice the 'dish angle' between the back of my hand and my forearm. This angle needs to be maintained at all times throughout the swing, the only exception being that it will be pulled and flattened somewhat by the weight of your club as you swing through impact.

As a help to take up your grip properly, imagine that you are standing facing a porch railing in front of you. Place your left hand on top of this railing and grip it in your fingers, with the thumb "halfway" extended. This is how you need to hold the club. To achieve this position you may wish to use your right hand index finger to hold it parallel to the ground and parallel to your shoulders about waist high. The grip end will point to the left and the toe will be slanted back towards your chest (precision about this will be addressed later). Place your left hand as you see

pictured here with about half an inch of grip extending beyond the end of your hand. Squeeze your thumb and fingers a little, and make a note that the fulcrum is located between your thumb and forefinger— it is where the club pivots in relation to your left arm.

The reasons for taking the grip this way are critical, as I pointed out above.

1) **The left hand must be able to hold the shaft perpendicular to the forearm at the top of the backswing** in order to "load the flail" into the position from which it can deliver the clubhead correctly to the ball with maximum speed. At the top of the swing and during the early part of the downswing, the shaft must be perpendicular to the left arm and on the same plane **as** the left arm. Taking up the club in this manner makes this possible.

Here is a maxim that applies to all of the positions you encounter in fitting yourself to your club and to your own swing, namely, that if you can't get there *before* your swing, you won't be able to get there *during* your swing. Taking your grip this way makes it certain that you can achieve a full backswing wristfold (a term I prefer to use to avoid confusion with the specific and limited words 'wristcock' and 'wrist bend' used in much of the golf instruction literature).

2) **The club held mostly in the fingers permits a freer, more relaxed left wrist and forearm,** a condition that adds to the speed with which the club is *allowed* to fly forward during the release interval. If the club is held more in the palm, the release is likely to be inhibited by forearm and wrist tension. The *fingers* squeeze, but the wrist is otherwise relaxed.

3) A "medium" thumb permits the greatest range of motion for the average person, and its importance will show up when you go to place your hands at the ball at address, as follows.

Second: Placing the club down to the ball requires a small adjustment. After you take your grip this way, place your left hand and club down as though addressing a golf ball. It may feel different than what you are used to— you may feel that you can't get the clubhead down to the ball. Allow the club to shift slightly in your hand to ease getting it down there. Use the smallest adjustment that will allow you to accomplish both important things: a comfortable and relaxed address of the ball, and a full wristfold at the top of the backswing.

If you experiment with the angle of the clubshaft across your left hand, and if you make some very small adjustments in your fingers and the 'length' you extend your thumb down the shaft, you will be able to find a position that allows you both a comfortable address position *and* a full 90° degree wristfold at the top of the backswing. When I place the clubhead down on the ground, I keep my fingers as close to perpendicular to the shaft as I can and I extend my wrist down to its 'end of travel.' This takes up the slack in the wrist at address, it permits me to address the ball comfortably, and it allows me to make the full 90° wristfold at the top of my backswing.

Third: Rotate the club in your fingers to where its leading edge is square to the target line as you place the club down with your arm hanging naturally, as you see that I have done in the facing photo. (A toe-in-the-air position of the clubhead is correct at address, since during the swing the toe will be thrown downward by the force *of* the swing, and the clubhead returns to level.) The final adjustment of the clubface relative to the back of your left hand to produce straight ball flight is a detail that will be dealt with later when you are actually hitting golf balls. For purposes of this drill it is not necessary to be concerned about it yet.

Your right hand will not be placed on the club normally during this drill. You will use only your right index finger to support the clubshaft and to hold it parallel to the ground and parallel to the target line under your chin in your starting position. The reason for using the left hand alone for the drill at this time is to establish the correct framework or structure of the golf swing, a step which gets too complicated when the right hand is introduced at the outset. The right hand helps to produce power during the downswing, but it is not used for *controlling* the club.

Aiming Your Golf Shots Begins Here

All golf requires aiming the shot. It is the very nature of the game that aiming is a core issue, as opposed to baseball, for example, in which precision for where the ball gets hit is pretty much irrelevant. Most golf instruction tells you to align your *body* in certain ways for that purpose (parallel to the target line, usually), with the assumption or implication that it automatically takes care of directing the shot itself. This is not true. (I do not pretend that alignments of body parts aren't important— only that they aren't *sufficient.*) **You** align your shot! And you do it *consciously and deliberately during the swing itself by moving your hands along a line whose direction you have chosen for that purpose and that you will use as a guide in keeping with what you have read up until now.*

"The toy follows the hand that pulls the string!" The head of the golf club will move in exactly the direction your left hand is moving at impact because it follows your hand. So for this reason **begin** your golf experience by aiming the swing, and doing it in a way that will be uniform for every shot for the rest of your golf life, i.e., by using a line running along the ground from the target back through the ball, identified as the "target line." Your *backswing* is guided "through the magic of the left thumb" by tracing *a line under your chin that runs parallel to the target line,* using the tip of your left thumb to guide the motion of your left arm and the clubshaft. As your arm reaches parallel-to-the-ground you will rotate your left forearm slightly to aim your thumb and the clubshaft so that it seeks out the tip of your right shoulder as it continues in motion. For the downswing, you will direct the butt of your hand and the gripcap of the clubshaft down at, and then along, the *target* line, towards the target. So you use two lines: for the backswing, the line under your chin; for the forward swing, the target line, which is also the base line of the forward swing. *These lines define exactly how to direct your left hand and club away from and back to the ball for all shots, (for longer clubs the line "under your chin" is a bit further away from your toes).*

The Magic of the Left Thumb Illustrated

I demonstrate how I use my left thumb to aim my club in this next photo. It is aligned down the shaft, telling me where the shaft is pointed, and obviously it is pointed at the clubhead, telling me *its* location. I use my thumb for this drill, and for all my golf shots, to control exactly where I move my left hand, the clubshaft, and the clubhead. To get *back* to the ball I simply reverse my direction and aim the shaft, the grip cap and the butt of my hand back *down plane,* at -- and then along -- the *ball-to-target line,* and

through the golf ball. It all starts when my thumb directs the shaft in my backswing, aiming the butt end of the shaft and the grip cap at the target, with the shaft itself covering the line under my chin that is parallel to the target line.

In this drill without golf balls, swing back by tracing that line under your chin with your left thumb, and when your arm reaches the parallel-to-the-ground position, rotate your left forearm a bit and direct your thumb as though you were going to hit the tip of your right shoulder with it. Your club will then continue on a **slightly** slanted plane from there--a plane running from the base line of the swing (the target line) through your right shoulder. As your shoulder turns to the right in the backswing, continue to 'aim your thumb at your shoulder', (your thumb "knows where it is....") and ignore any *shift* due to the movement of your right shoulder, since placing the club into the correct place at the top is automatically handled simply by aiming at it with your thumb all the time.

This next picture shows me 'seeking my right shoulder' correctly as the backswing proceeds. My left hand moved STRAIGHT TOWARDS THE CAMERA until it got approximately as high as my belt, and then it continued on the slanted plane defined by my right shoulder and target line. *My left hand must not follow my torso turn around (to the left, as you view it here). It must move up from here as it continues, i.e., toward my shoulder.*

This procedure correctly places both that hand and the club where they need to be as I finish my backswing. *Where your hand and clubshaft and consequently the clubHEAD are at this point and where they continue in the backswing is perhaps the most important geometrical feature of correct swing mechanics. I can think of nothing more important than* *getting this right, and "right" presumes having things right in your stance, posture, grip and setup before you even start to swing that make it possible <u>for</u> you to get here, and from there, to the right place at the top!*

Now Execute the Drill

Make or find a 'target line' on the ground or floor and stand with your toes about a foot back from it. Tilt forward to allow your left arm to hang straight down from its socket while holding your club parallel to the ground and parallel to that line, and imagine a line directly under your chin and under your clubshaft. Place your shoulders, hips, knees, and toes parallel to that line and hang the clubshaft under your eyes so that it is between your eyes and the line

on the ground. Tilt your spine to the right just a bit by dropping your right shoulder an inch or so lower than the left. The first photo in this series, here on the left, on page 78, demonstrates the following details, all of which are critical. I have taken the correct left hand grip with my fingers almost perpendicular to the clubshaft, and my thumb is in what may be called a 'medium thumb position.' My left arm is hanging directly under my shoulder, my spine has a bit of a tilt to the right moving my hips a bit left of 'center,' my feet are fairly close together, my knees are bent a bit, and I am relaxed. My right index finger supports the club. I am about to 'trace a line under my chin' that runs parallel to the target line and my whole body is parallel to that line, including my toes, my knees, my shoulders, and my eyes. The reasons for the tilt in your shoulder and spine are: 1), it subconsciously triggers certain exertions and athletic responses for a good swing that would not be activated without it, and 2), it enables the arms and shoulders to remain "on-plane" during the swing— not from a deliberate *effort* to swing 'from the inside' but because they are in position to swing 'from the inside' *naturally*. It is a critical detail in principle, and you will later determine the amount of tilt you need by trial and error after getting feedback from actually hitting golf balls and noting the results and your level of comfort and ease.

The next step is to make the takeaway, transition, pre-impact and release motions to produce what is indeed the heart of every great golf swing. The drill will involve two parts, one to generate and load up the backswing, and one to make the downswing, a deliberate and specific act powered by the three different motions discussed in the second chapter, i.e., torso turn, left arm rotation around the left shoulder, and centrifugal release of the clubshaft. You will be given drills to develop each of these power sources in a couple of the next chapters.

The Backswing Procedure For This Drill

Here is the procedure for making the first motion—the backswing. The short version for executing the entire swing is simply to swing your left hand to the right tracing the line under your chin until your hand reaches the height of your belt and then swing back down by dragging the club as fast as you can, grip cap first, and letting it release through the ball. In the process of swinging, you will discover that most of the details laid out here will probably already be natural. But since the details are important and *not* natural for everyone, the following long version instruction is appropriate.

Start from the position shown on page 78, and then give the swing its energy by making a small forward press, or shift of body weight—a movement of the torso a couple of inches towards your left, just as I have done in the photo on the left here. Such a move will put you a bit off balance, i.e., you will have more weight on your left foot than your right.

Now "fall to the right", the same as if you were walking back to your right foot, and use the energy created by that gravitational force to throw (swing) your arms to the right and up. (I am often so energetic in my own swing that in my forward press I actually pick my right foot entirely off the ground, and the imbalance that causes provides *a lot* of energy that I use to swing my club back.) Trace the 'line on the ground' with your left thumb, and with your left elbow held firm but not rigid, 'push the shaft of the club' along that line. As you do so, retain the right angle that exists between your left forearm and the clubshaft, and also retain the dish angle of the back of your left hand. This is what I have done to get me into the position shown in the picture on the right on page 80.

Your arm will, of course, move in an arc around your left shoulder as its axis, and after it has moved about a foot or two, the clubshaft will be pointed upwards. As you move your arm to the right, turn your torso to "follow your hand" so that your navel continues to face your left hand as it did when you started.

Tracing the line correctly will direct the clubshaft on a bit of a slant as your hand gets up to belt high, because the turning right shoulder has now moved a bit around to the right from where it was originally parallel to your target line. If the club is allowed to continue to move up and you bend your left elbow, the shaft will hit you on the tip of your right shoulder. For now stop your backswing motion when your left hand is at the height of your stomach.

This is, for now, your total backswing. A swing limited in this way is sufficient to identify the core essentials of the golf swing. When it is time to make a full swing, you'll see that there isn't anything new to learn or to do except to turn further and swing higher. **Nothing is 'different' than this in a full swing; the full swing will simply be a bigger version of this drill—**

with greater turn and greater amplitude, and, of course, with the right hand in its proper place.

Let's take a picture of the position you should seek at this point of your backswing— as in the photo on the right on page 80. Your hips and stomach should be turned to the right, maybe 30 degrees— your shoulders a bit more than your hips. Your left hand should be no further away from the target line than it was at setup as viewed from overhead behind your shoulders. It should have moved to the right *without moving either closer to or further from an imaginary wall that slants back towards your shoulders from the line under your chin.*

The butt of the clubshaft should now be pointed at the target line with the shaft itself slanting upward so to a viewer looking from down the line from your right side, it will be on the plane line that runs between the target line on the ground and the tip of your right shoulder. Your weight should have moved *towards, but not fully onto,* your right foot, and all of the following angles established at the start should still be in place: the 90° wristfold; the forward tilt of your spine (your chest is no higher or lower than before); you have not pushed up with your knees (your left knee has folded in a bit towards the right); you have the same dish angle at the back of your left hand and wrist that you had when you took the club in hand to begin with; and you have kept the sideward tilt of your spine that you had at setup. Your balance remains centered pretty much on your feet— you are not in jeopardy of needing any rebalance between your heels and toes. (Obviously you are really not able to stop here and hold this position for long, but for clarity of instruction, I make note here of what you want your position to be for the moment that you are here.)

The downswing will actually begin in the same way as a child's playground swing turns around and starts down by itself— i.e., by gravity. Unless mom actually holds and stops the swing when it comes back to her, it starts to fall naturally. You also do well to cooperate with and use gravity for the timing of the start of your downswing in the same way, the reasons for which will be made clear shortly. And that brings us to what is for many golfers the most pivotal issue of their own struggles, namely,

The Transition

The transition from backswing to downswing *is* the crucial 'moment of truth' of a golf swing. In this specific instant all of the impulses, the automatic reactions, the subconsciously held mandates, the sheer panic and the emotional investment in 'a great shot' all conspire to make or ruin your day. Most people spend their golf life ignorant of, therefore unable to execute, the necessary sequence of events of this moment, to their confusion and detriment, and that is a shame. And here I will make another reference to music. Learning the transition move can be done in the same way in which an instrumentalist learns the notes of a melody, which will be played 'up to tempo' **at some later time**. Many musical passages are played as rapidly as 10 notes per second, but those individual notes are not learned or differentiated by the instrumentalist at that speed *while he is learning what they are. First he learns what they are, then he places them in the correct order, one at a time for certainty, and then he plays them very very slowly in sequence, attempting to establish the appropriate timing and rhythm, arriving at "concert tempo" only after considerable practice, diligent care, and comfortable familiarity.* (The whole world will know if they are played out of order in actual performance— a parallel to the golf swing in which even non-golfers can see the difference between good and bad swings. They may not know exactly *what* is wrong, but they will know that *something* is.)

Since the transition move is triggered by things occurring much earlier *in the takeaway*, I will start again at the beginning. The swing proceeds as follows: 1) the forward press— a weight imbalance— lets gravity 2) cause a fall back to the right side, taking with it 3) the backswing of the left hand only (in this drill) up to belt high during which some weight has fallen towards the right leg; 4) **and while the left arm and club are finishing floating up just before reaching the top of the intended total stroke, your body weight starts to fall back to the left. This leftward fall happens a fraction of a second before your hand reaches the top.** *After* the fall to the left, the left hand continues to the top and floats there quietly until gravity moves it and the arm *down, grip cap aimed at and then along the ball-to-target line.* Then the arm will pull down gently *and at the same time be pulled by the turning torso* as though stretching the clubshaft lengthwise. Body turn occurs during the backswing, but as the weight falls to the left and the left arm *begins* down, *there is to be no body turn either in the hips or in the shoulders for a split second. The left arm simply moves in a straight line down* and you need to wait before rotating your hips and shoulders.

These next two pictures show the difference between the 'top' of the backswing and the weight shift to the left that occurs before any intentional downswing. My left hip and left shoulder (and with it my head) have both moved to the left about 2 or 3 inches in this part of the transition. There is *some* movement down in the second photo due to this being only a partial swing drill that was caused by my weight shift. No rotation has begun, however.

How the Downswing Will Proceed

An instant after the left arm has started down, the hips and torso rotate to the left and pull the left arm. The key action here is that the hips **turn, the left hip does not thrust leftward.** But I repeat: the body's movement *to* the left prior to this rotation is not only in the hips. The entire spine moves leftward at the same time so that your head and the base of the spine move approximately the same distance when placing the weight onto the left leg. This is otherwise known as "retaining *that* spine angle."

And I need to make this point, which will seem to be in contradiction with what was just said and with what is taught by others who say to 'keep your head back!' But there is no contradiction. When you move your hips leftward to put weight over onto your left hip and heel, your whole body moves leftward with it, in unison. *And then when you rotate your hips after that, an observer will see that you moved your hips even further to the left than you moved your head due to natural athletic exuberance occasioned by the massive thrust of your turn. But you must not try to move the hips further left, because if you do so you will cause an inappropriate and excessive change in your spine angle that will 'leave the shoulders, arms and club behind you' to put you into a faulty impact position with the hands arriving too late. Such a swing leaves either a wide-open clubface and/or requires a mid-swing muscular effort to square the clubface, a compensation far too difficult for the average person to bring off.*

The concept of connection, or 'taking up the slack'
When loading your backswing, and during the transition, your body parts must be managed to 'maintain the connection of all swing machine parts by taking up the slack'— i.e., all of the parts of your body that exist between your left hand and your lower body. It is similar to the situation of a truck towing a car with a rope between them. Before the truck accelerates, the driver inches forward *to tighten the rope* so that there will be no jolt and so that the car may be accelerated smoothly. For the same reason you need to fully tighten your left arm and to fully fold your left wrist to take up all the slack as the backswing finishes, and then to hold your left arm firm as your body rotates forward. In this manner the power applied to the arm is not wasted or lost by anything being loose.

Then in the downswing, you have the responsibility of "bringing your arm and hand with you" as you rotate your torso to the left. You do this by 'holding firm' with your fingers, your left elbow, and in an actual swing your <u>right</u> arm as well. Thus your rotation applies the massive force of your body to the arms and hands, and through them, to the club itself.
Contrary to advice about using a light grip, for this purpose I like

to tightly squeeze the fingers of my *left* hand when I swing. I have discovered that *by doing just that, i.e., squeezing the fingers of my left hand, the ball goes further without applying any other effort whatsoever.* The firmness it supplies to my swing mechanism by that fairly effortless detail is a huge contributor to the energy I can get into the ball during impact. I consider tightening the left hand in this manner as another of the critical details of a great swing.

Another image is that of a rope running from your left hip to the left hand— up along the outside of your torso, out through your shoulder, to the hand. Your left hip has the responsibility of keeping the rope tight *until the ball is gone,* and to accomplish this your hips must continue to rotate during the entire forward swing. To let them stop prior to impact is to "shut the motor off before the finish line" of a drag race.

So Now Execute Your Downswing

The next two pictures show the downswing under way, and notice how my left hip has moved *further* left than when I started down, even though my *effort* is now only to turn the hips and to drag my club along the delivery line. The first photo captures my initial move and you can see that my shoulders have turned to the left. I still have a 90° angle with the clubshaft, and my hand is just about 'at the ball' with a fully un-released club. In the second photo my clubhead has released through *more than a quarter of a circle* at the same time in which my left hand moved less than a foot! And this late release is not due to effort of any kind. It is totally and purely due to the simple physics *of* release, in that the catchup simply **has to occur.**

The Release and Rollover

I need to expand on what I just mentioned. The release of the club is an inevitable effect. It is often misunderstood as though it were a deliberate action, requiring special effort. But that is the opposite of what happens in good swings. A good release is **caused by what came before.** A natural law of motion takes care of releasing the club if you don't do anything to prevent it, and provided the clubshaft was in the right position (still angled back at 90° relative to the left forearm **just prior *to* release).**

Here are four of the most common faults of golf swings that interfere with or prevent a good release: 1) failing to load up the backswing with a true, full, complete 90° wristfold at the top, 2) allowing the shaft to rebound or ricochet at the top, losing the wristfold before the downswing is under way, 3) shoving against the clubshaft with the right hand immediately at the top, or on the way down to the ball, in obedience to an instinctive desire to 'hit that sucker," dissipating its mechanical advantage long before it should be used; and 4) inhibiting the release itself with tension in the forearms or wrists and thereby preventing the natural closing of the clubface and catchup of the clubhead that a free release brings about. These things are mentioned here for completeness of the issue, even though the right hand is not on the club in its normal position during this drill.

The last two photos of this sequence show how momentum has carried my club and my body around to the left, and how I am balanced on my left leg as I finish, with my stomach almost facing the target. In a full swing the momentum would have been enough to pull me around to where my stomach turned even further than facing-the-target, and the clubshaft would hit the back of my neck as the club came to the end of its travel.

The IRS's most powerful weapon, the 'hit instinct'
A subconscious desire to **hit the ball** is for many people—
including many who are world-class athletes in other sports— the
barrier that prevents them from playing decent golf. It is for all
people the most subtle of the undesirable impulses a golfer has
to deal with. **It is driven by the misperception that the club
is a stick with which to hit the ball,** an idea so deeply
embedded that very few people will admit such a thing exists, or
who are self-controlled or patient enough to address and
overcome it. Even the word 'club' adds to the misperception!
Whatever it takes, people with this problem have no recourse
but to do this basic swing drill— especially as a partial swing with
the left hand arriving no higher than the waist— repeatedly and
routinely for the rest of their lives. Professional golfers do
something similar to this in their warm-up and practice every day
as **the** preparation for their day, often by hitting short pitches
before any full swings at all. Many start every practice or on-
course play by doing it again and again. Many review it at *or*
away from the golf course on a regular basis. And all are aware
that repeated reinforcement of an effortless and powerful natural
release must replace and overcome the hit instinct. The reality is
that most of us *do* have "this problem," so hardly any of us are
exempt from the necessity to do a similar drill daily for the rest
of our lives, to remain in touch with the subtlety of the timing
of correct release mechanics.

I wish to expand on this because of its pivotal
importance. The release is the action of the clubhead, having
been dragged by 'stretching' the clubshaft (the left hand pulling
the butt end lengthwise, perpendicular to the direction of the
motion of the hand) as it seeks to 'catch up' to the hand and align
itself with the left forearm. Looking at the golfer from in front of

him at impact, a viewer would see how the catchup of the clubshaft has brought it almost straight in line with the left arm.

Strobe photography shows that the hands actually slow down during release, but their change in speed is not because the golfer *tries* to slow them down. Actually he is trying to accelerate them! The deceleration is inevitable due to the physical concept of "conservation of angular momentum," where the lighter head of the golf club speeds up as its distance from its swing axis (the left hand acting as a wheel rim) increases. The total amount of momentum in the club remains the same, but its *location* shifts, the hands at the grip end of the club slowing down while clubhead at the other end of the club speeds up! This result can be ruined by any pressure applied against the clubshaft prior to impact simply because it uses up the mechanical advantage built into the mechanism **too early.** Wasting "release" before it is the best *time* for it means that by the time the clubhead gets to the ball it is actually moving only a bit faster than the hands instead of four or fives times as fast. This book is not the place for a complete explanation of the physics of the conservation of angular momentum, so I will let the following images speak to the nature of release: numchucks (already mentioned), a fisherman casting a lure with a fishing pole, and a line of skaters rotating around a pivot man where the last skater in the line is "thrown" from the chain of skaters holding hands with each other. And an image with several similarities specific to the golf swing is that of the Olympic hammer-thrower who rotates his whole body a few times to build momentum and then **THROWWWWS** the hammer **with a spin of his back.** And just as in great golf swings, it is not leg muscle that creates the rotation: it is the mass of the golfer's torso— his back and midsection— that in rotation creates the bulk of the energy that produces his clubhead speed.

This concept is a basic tenet of David Lee's explanation of the physics of the golfswing which he entitled *Gravity Golf*, and in which he identifies this principle of the 'counter-fall' of the body (falling backwards away from the ball simultaneously with torso rotation). Use of body mass to produce power will be introduced in the baseball swing drill in the next chapter.

Action of the Hands During Rollover

"Rollover," as already illustrated on page 53 refers to the motion of the planes of the two hands, of the forearms, and of the clubface. From their position before release all rotate about 180° counter clockwise during the release interval.

This drill will reveal if you tend to inhibit this natural rolling motion. If so, do it deliberately at first by twisting your forearms during the release motion in order to overcome whatever reluctance or resistance you may experience. After you have done it deliberately a few times it will normally occur without effort naturally from then on. During this action your left wrist must not be allowed to cup or scoop through the ball in any way. The force of the clubhead pulling away from you as the left arm and clubshaft travel through release will tend to flatten it (or even bow it outwards as the wrist arrives at the ball before the clubhead), but other than this inevitable *effect* you must never do anything deliberately either to bow *or* cup your wrist during any part of the swing. The planes of the clubface and the back of the left wrist need to maintain the same relationship relative to the left arm throughout the swing— in other words, your left *wrist* neither "opens" nor "closes" the clubface at any time by any independent action.

Some instruction uses the terminology "flat left wrist" to describe this requirement, but in fact the wrist may well be cupped in order to retain the correct position of the clubhead. The use of the word 'flat' is intended to mean 'consistent', not geometrically flat— straight line flat. There is a wonderful picture of Tiger Woods in his *How I Play Golf* that shows a cupped position at the top of one of his swings, and other golfers like John Daly who use a strong grip at setup also have a cupped wrist at the top. The cupped position is what occurs at the top whenever a strong grip is used and nothing is manipulated in the wrist or arm in the backswing. By the same token, a weak grip at setup shows up as a truly flat or even slightly bowed wrist at the top. What is important is not whether it is cupped or flat at any particular time during the swing but whether it *changes* from flat to cupped, or vice versa other than when it *is* pulled flat on the way to impact. This is a critical detail for the reason that any change *in* that angle is symptomatic of a manipulation of the clubshaft by the hand or wrists, and anything of that kind is disruptive of both the alignments of the hands and club, and of the buildup of clubhead speed to the ball. These three photos show in order an incorrectly flattened or bowed grip, an incorrectly cupped grip, and a correctly retained dish angle.

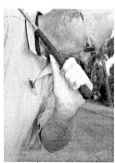

The Follow Through

What happens after impact is all effect, in the same way that once a bullet has been fired, its behavior is determined by what came before. We *interpret* our follow through to get information about what we did earlier in the swing. The positions which we pass through or arrive at are indicators of what happened before, and information revealed by our follow through will tell us a great deal about the quality and nature of the swing and of the shot. But trying to *do* something during the follow through is to give attention to something that will take care of itself. It is much more productive to attend to something much earlier in the procedure that *does* need to be watched, because giving your attention to the cause is more effective than looking back from an effect. I have never found that 'trying to do something in the follow through' causes me to do something different during a swing motion that occurred earlier. It may work for some, but I find it easier *to do the right thing to begin with, specifically by understanding and installing the right procedure deliberately.*

Faults That Are Revealed In Your Follow Through

Here are a couple of the more common indicators of faults in your procedure or setup that will show up in your follow through.

1) Whether you are in balance: your weight should be mostly on the outside of your left leg, your right heel having been pulled off the ground and your foot resting on your toes, with your whole body relaxed and balanced as your swing finishes. Any tendency to fall in any direction can indicate some unnecessary, inappropriate, or excessive exertions during your swing.

2) A left elbow bend during impact, which is known as a "chicken-wing." Such a position indicates that your torso turn stopped prior to impact— it should continue to pull and lead the left arm until the ball has been struck— and/or that the release was deliberately caused by exertions too early for efficient mechanical advantage, with the result that the arms *had* to fold as the club released too early.

The first of these two photos shows the chicken wing, caused by insufficient turn of the shoulders by the time of impact, requiring that the left elbow 'get out of the way' as the clubshaft comes into the ball. The second shows how a left shoulder turned out of the way holds the left arm straight until after the ball is gone. So a chicken wing is, like other features, an effect, a symptom of other procedural faults and it is not fixable by trying to do something about it specifically. Its cure is to change what caused it in the first place, in this case to continue the torso turn through impact until the ball is gone.

3) Your right heel is still on the ground or weight remains on the ball of the right foot as you go through the ball. This indicates a failure to shift your weight (actually, to *allow your weight to fall to the left*) before you *began* your downswing. It means that your swing had to rely on some contrived muscling instead of using the simplicity and greater advantage of gravity acting on your back to throw your arms into rotation.

4) An observer will be able to see whether you are lifting your chest or pushing up with your legs during your swing (causing a topped shot) and the fault is exactly that, i.e., lifting 'off the ball.'

5) A pull or pull-hook shot with a swing path to the left is caused by an "over the top" move, which is another error in the *sequence* of downswing moves. It means that you allowed rotation to occur and throw the arms out toward the target line before you committed the hands in a downward direction on plane at the plane line/target line. The resulting club path is from "over the ball" and then down— necessarily across the ball and left of the target. The correct sequence requires downward motion of the hands to *precede* rotation.

These are not all of the swing faults that show up in a follow through, but they are the most common.

A Review of This Routine and Its Purpose

You need to swing the club, to make the motions described and detailed in this chapter, *in order to get feedback* to understand what to exert. This half-swing drill is an excellent laboratory where that can be learned, and if you take time to get the full benefit of the drill by focusing on and sensitively tuning into how it feels and adjusting to make it all work smoothly, you will be taking the shortest road to acquiring your own perfect golf swing.

Imagine that you are setting yourself up for this drill while standing in a doorway with your shoulders parallel to the door frame, with the club hanging down parallel to and directly above the threshhold. Do the forward press as though bumping your left hip against the door frame, and then walk, rebound, or 'sway' to the right. Let your weight falling to the right produce the energy for the swing of your left hand up to waist level. By this I mean for you to move your hands to the right simultaneously with the shift of the weight back *toward* the right, where the large mass of your body falls in rebound from the moment before when you leaned to the left. The rebound is the source of energy for your swing back!

Then at the end of your backswing start the downswing by letting your body fall to the left, and you will then find yourself in a position to make a fairly energetic downpull of the clubshaft, even with a small backswing. The forward motion will consist of pulling the butt end of the club down and along the target line (imagine that you are going to drive the grip cap into the door jamb as hard as you can) while keeping your left elbow straight. In the picture on the next page I am 'driving the grip cap' into the side of my golf bag in imitation of the thrust I am describing here. I have also held the clubshaft with a finger of my right hand to prevent it from releasing because I do not want it to release until the last possible instant. Imitating this motion into an imaginary wall or door jamb while holding the shaft as I do here is a very good way to reinforce the late release and deepen your comfort and familiarity with how it should feel.

Obviously you will not be hitting a door jamb (you are standing where you can make a full swing freely), but swing as though you *were* trying to hit one and let the momentum you create cause the clubhead to release fully— both to roll over, and to catch up and pass the hands. Notice how I not only have 'retained' the full wristfold: I have actually *increased* it— made the angle between the clubshaft and my left forearm more acute than 90°, and this reinforces in my mind the flail procedure, the late release, and the core issue of clubhead speed, which is again, the tremendous mechanical advantage of throw-out action of the clubhead into the ball.

The faster you move your left hand down and to the left starting from that waist-high position with a full 90° wristfold, the more clubhead speed you can generate in release, and the more you will realize how exertion lengthwise on the butt end of the clubshaft produces both the release and the speed of the club*head.* Remember that you are attempting to stretch the clubshaft as if it was a rope, to pull it tight lengthwise. Yank that thing **hard,** and see "how hard you can hit the door jamb with the grip cap!" The faster the grip cap moves, the greater the release speed of the clubhead. In this action, you will quickly realize the necessity of permitting or even of *helping* the left forearm rotation for the action to finish smoothly.

A point needs to be made here that cannot be overemphasized, and it is this. The hands ARE FORCED TO SLOW DOWN DURING THE RELEASE INTERVAL AS THE CLUBHEAD SPEEDS UP due to a physical principle called "conservation of momentum." THE SIGNIFICANCE OF THIS IS THAT A SLOWER BUT STEADY, MASSIVE AND FORCEFUL DELIVERY OF THE BUTT END (FULCRUM) OF THE CLUB PRODUCES FAR MORE CLUBHEAD SPEED AT IMPACT THAN A FAST SWING TO THE IMPACT INTERVAL where the hands do not maintain their massive force as the clubhead catches up-which it does with incredible energy and speed. A chicken-wing is often the result of the collapse of the left arm at that moment, indicating the golfer's inability to maintain the forward movement of the fulcrum. So it is better to swing slowly with massive force through impact, than to swing fast to where that interval starts without massive support of the right arm and the right side of your body maintaining the velocity of the hands through impact. It is death to clubhead speed if the hands are allowed to slow down or to "back up" during release!

THE BASIC SWING DRILL

I have placed the eight photographs of my first drill together here
so that you can visualize the whole swing and install the instruction
from setup through follow through.

The Right Hand

As mentioned, the right hand in full swings is not responsible for control of the clubshaft, but for adding power and force to the fulcrum, which has a tendency to decelerate during release (as proven by the obvious difference in the distance you can hit a well struck shot using left arm alone vs. using both hands). Its force is not applied to the shaft, but to the pivot point of the shaft (the fulcrum), which actually is located under the left thumb pad. The base of your right hand doesn't act on, or for that matter even touch, the shaft itself: the *wristbone of the right hand* contacts the top of the left thumb, and it is its application of force *on the left thumb* that adds massively to the energy applied to the club.

In order to know exactly how to grip the club with your right hand and how to fit both hands together, consider how the hands connect to it and where it moves on the way to the ball! Its position is taken because of what is has to do long before impact itself, simply because it is too late to add any force at *that* time— force needs to have been applied earlier to build speed up *for* that instant. There is a distance of some three feet or more through which the hands move from the top of the swing until impact, and it is during this entire arc of motion that force needs to be applied. The speed of the club*head* is dependent on the speed of the *fulcrum* at release and impact, so you need to concentrate on how to accelerate the *fulcrum* on its way to the ball so that it *arrives* at impact moving as fast as possible. Clubhead speed is a function of *what happened to the club on the way, not due to something applied at the instant of collision!*

The base of the wristbone lies at the end of the right arm and it is connected to the right shoulder by bones and tendons.

Since the left thumb is on top of the shaft as the right hand arrives at waist level, the right arm is in a powerful position when the base of the wristbone is atop the left thumb so that all force available to the right side of your body may be applied to the club at that exact spot. The left thumb covers the grip at the fulcrum, so as was just pointed out, the right hand doesn't press against the club itself, but atop the left thumb. If you use a two finger overlap grip like Jim Furyk does, the point of contact of the base of the right wristbone will be quite high on the left thumb, above the last knuckle itself. If you use a ten finger grip, the point of contact will be down near or on the first knuckle. With any grip, however, the right hand must be above the left thumb, not beside it, and if you were to open your fingers without rotating your arms just to see how the palms relate to each other, you should find them at an angle, not parallel to each other.

These next two photos show how the hands drive the club into the impact interval of the swing. It illustrates why the

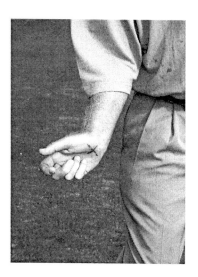

right hand grip needs to be taken as you see illustrated here and in the next eight pictures.

On the way to the ball the most powerful part of your right arm— the bone at the base of your wrist, is used to apply force.

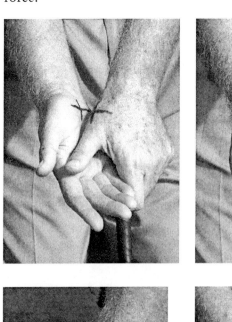

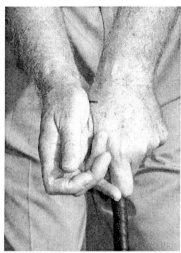

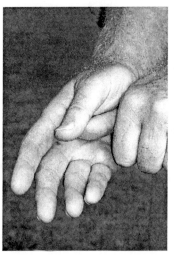

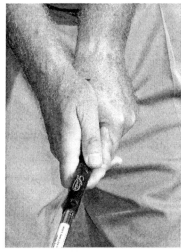

The Xs mark the top of my left thumb and the base of my right wristbone. I place the two Xs together and fold my left thumb into the pocket (in a manner someone compared to putting a hot dog into a bun). I overlap my left index finger with the little finger of my right hand. Such a grip is commonly called the Vardon grip.

In the grip pictured next, called a ten finger grip (women often find this grip enables them to hold the club more securely), the X of the right hand is placed down much lower on the left thumb, probably between the first two knuckles instead of above the second knuckle.

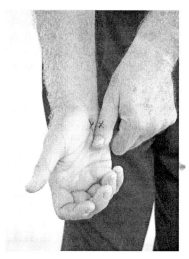 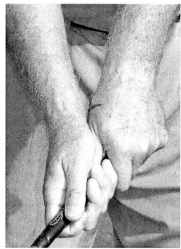

An angle between the two palms makes the wristfold at the top of the swing easier than having palms strictly parallel to each other, due to the greater range of motion of each wrist back against, rather than in line with, your forearms. Such an angle exists naturally when the two arms hang down from your shoulders when you are relaxed.

Notice the angles of my palms as they hang down. As I bring my hands up to waist level, I fit them into each other without changing the nearly perpendicular relationship between them that existed at the hanging position. In bringing the two hands together I fit my left thumb *deeply into* the crease or fold along the lifeline of the right palm.

The Application of Power from your Right Side

Having your right hand above the left as you come into the impact interval also **correctly places the right *arm* above the clubshaft on the way down to impact,** instead of beside it. Look again at the photos on page 103. If your right hand and the base of its wrist is not directly *above the clubshaft* as your hands move down *at* the ground, it is just not available to help increase downswing force on the fulcrum of the clubshaft and anything it could do to help speed up your clubhead is dissipated.

To maintain the position of the right hand on the club without inhibiting the requisite left hand wristfold, use the last knuckle of the right hand ring finger as a hook around the shaft and allow the pinkie to overlap (or interlock with) the left forefinger. *Place the grip of the club as far out in the fingers of your right hand as is possible and with the right hand high up on the left thumb.* Jim Furyk's two-finger overlap grip achieves this position naturally. In addition, to prevent undue stress in the right wrist, you must allow the fingers of the hand to run diagonally across the shaft so that the right hand can remain relaxed at setup and during the backswing. These details of the right hand are all critical due to 1) the sensitivity of the positions you need to maintain during the load up of the backswing; 2) triggers that you do *not* want to activate during the downswing; and 3) the mechanical alignments necessary for the most efficient application of the massive power of the right side of your body during the swing.

 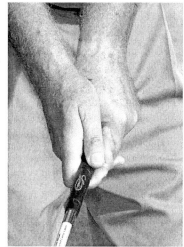

Now Do This Drill With Both Hands

You can now benefit from doing this drill two-handed, mostly for the purpose of incorporating the right arm thrust effectively. Adjust the position of your right hand so that it can thrust down on the top of the left thumb during the downswing— at the hinge or fulcrum of the clubshaft— to deliver the mass of the right side of your body onto the top of the club. Take whatever time you need to locate exactly how to put it where it can do the most good— directly on the plane of motion.

The drill done with both hands will be the same as the left-hand-only version except that now your right hand will be in its normal position. Be careful to maintain your 90° wristfold as you take up the club and move into the backswing. See if it helps to turn your body a bit to the right to give room for the right elbow to "get out of the way." **Make half swings only,** exactly as you did with the left hand alone, i.e., by trying to move the grip cap along the target line as before, to "hit the ball *with* the grip cap!" The reason for making half swings is that it will acquaint you with the feelings you will have arriving at the impact zone *with a full wristfold still in place,* the ideal, of course.

Instead of making one swing at a time, however, make continuous swings back and forth from right to left, back and forth, back and forth— continuously without stopping between successive swings. And there are a couple of things that you need to keep in mind during this drill. 1) Use a smooth rhythm without disruption, and in the changes of direction, wait for the downswings to start on their own. Allow enough time for the hands and club to fall of their own accord at the turnaround (in the same way in which a playground swing simply falls at the peak of its stroke). 2) Turn your tummy to the right in the backswing and to the left during the downswing *and sense how the rotation of the shoulders is needed to cooperate, keep pace, and move with the independent vertical motion of your arms and hands.*

There will be more detail in the next chapter about how to use body turn in its support in producing swing speed. This basic drill is where you can discover how to incorporate it specifically by using it to move the arms and club. You do it by coordinating it with the movement of the arms.

As said before, the arms need to 'keep up with' the body while the turn occurs: they will not remain idly limp and lifeless during the downswing to be left behind. Your backswing gently throws them back and up (with you controlling exactly where they go— by directing the motion with the left thumb), and the fall of the body to the left—*followed* by arms and club moving down and being pulled by body turn— pulls them down and forward. Making continuous swings of this kind is one of the most valuable drills in golf. It can be done anywhere, it requires no golf balls or driving range, and it allows you to focus on swing essentials and critical details. It is the process by which your body will assimilate a perfect swing, and if you are true to the instructions in every way, it fits your golf swing to your own body automatically.

What About Body Types and Differences?

There are whole books written on the subject of fitting your swing to your body type. The necessity of the right fit is to enable *you* to use *your* strengths efficiently. And after taking your grip to fit *your* hands (use grips thin enough to permit you to hold the club mostly in your fingers), the most significant part of that process is locating the swing plane relative to your spine that allows you to get the best blend of amplitude of motion and placement of your levers and joints— spine, arms and hands— that can produce the fastest clubhead speed of which *you* are capable.

There is a simple way for you to find this plane, actually, and is done by swinging a heavy club. If you tape some weight—say a half-pound or so—to the head of an old 8- or 9-iron, you can create one in a couple of minutes. It is one of the best devices available to teach you what plane will work best for you. Swing it back and forth continuously. And instead of trying to make the club follow a preconceived path, arc, plane, or orbit that you impose on it, swing it freely, unconcerned, back and forth continuously, and let it go where its weight tends to cause it to go. The extra weight adds to the momentum of the club to stay on plane, and its behavior **shows you** where it naturally wants to swing. Take note of where the hands and the clubhead move in your backswing, of the path it takes down and past follow-through. Swing it back *into the right place at the top of the backswing—namely beside and just above the tip of your right shoulder,* and then by using a down swing of the arms followed by a body turn to pull the butt end of the club, it will seek its own path based on your body, as long as you do nothing deliberate to the club except to allow this body action. Where the club then swings 'of its own accord' while doing this is critical information. Be attentive and make a note as where the clubhead seeks to go by itself in both the backswing and downswing when doing the drill in this manner **because that is where you will need to deliberately make it go as you seek to perfect your golf swing.**

Use a mirror to monitor your motion and your positions for comparison to the appearance and timing of swings you admire. Take delight in the exuberance of free, relaxed, easy, rhythmic motion, and make it your habit to swing freely on the same plane that you feel fits you best.

A Summary of the 'Basic Swing Drill'

This drill is your foundation. It is where you install the correct details of your grip, balance, stance, posture, forward press, weight shift, backswing (using your left thumb to take the club to the right place), the transition move, the downswing with its appropriate exertions of torso turn and arms moving in synch, and the rhythm and process of release. By reading your follow through you can evaluate the quality of your swings.

The next instruction will involve several other drills (ball striking comes later) to develop the elements that make up the swing and expand it to its full potential. It is hoped that you will retain everything taught here as you move forward to these other things.

Chapter Four

Drills for Developing Skill

Why more drills?

Drills are used when learning the golf swing in order to isolate and develop the correct motions and exertions, and to bring them to the point where they become natural and spontaneous. Using the example again of a pianist playing a passage containing as many as 10 consecutive notes a second or rapidly successive chords containing three or four notes each, three things become clear: 1) it is not possible to think your way through such passages during performance, 2) it *is* possible to internalize or train extremely complex physical motions to where they *can* be performed successfully with unbelievable precision and speed; and 3) unless the procedure is efficient at the outset, speed will never be possible later. And any musician knows that it takes years of practice of many different drills of various kinds, and hours of slow, note by note, chord by chord practice of the specific passages you hear him play, both to internalize the "entities" (certain kinds of groups of notes) as opposed to dealing with individual notes separately, and to reach the point where he is comfortable playing them for an audience up to tempo. This is the reason for drills.

But while the human brain is a computer of far greater capacity than I believe we can even imagine at this point, each one of us knows his own limitations, specifically of his need to *receive and take in one thing at a time, linearly,* in order *to* implant every one of the details correctly. ("For Dummies" books are enormously popular for that reason.) Another analogy applies here: when a motion picture is being created, the camera does not record motion: it records *still pictures, individual frames,* each one perfectly focused and clear. Playing those frames back in such a way that the *time elapsing between frames* is extremely small gives us the illusion of motion. And a pianist must correctly learn all of the notes, one-at-a-time, that are later to succeed each other in actual performance "up to tempo," where the time between notes is extremely small, far too short for anyone to be able to deal cognitively with each successive note or chord. So it would be out of the question for him to achieve reliable, nearly "automatic" performance, without those hundreds of hours of drills that embedded the fingering, the notes, and the chords correctly at the outset and that eliminated the need to think of each thing in the heat of performance!

We also have another kind of talent: the ability to visualize the larger picture, and in so doing, to grasp immediately all the parts that make it up. Even a child can learn the *Gettysburg Address* and as a result have the ability to recall all the individual letters, the capitalization, the spacing, the spelling, etc. In the same way, we also need to use our capacity to grasp an overall picture in which logic and the appropriateness of the parts and their relationships to each other "makes sense" and helps us to recall and reproduce those parts without struggling. While we are *learning* the parts, their relationships to each other, hence our ability to anticipate each in a timely manner, gradually unfold in the same way as happens when we are passengers in an automobile that makes the same trip every week. On the first trip we observe our route without concern about 'what happens next.' On the second and subsequent trips, we gradually come to be aware of what is about to happen— what building, what turn, or what object will shortly come into view, and so on. After a few such trips over the same roads, we can correctly anticipate what we will encounter and in what order things will unfold, not because we struggled to remember their succession, but due to the power of associative thought that informs us because of the repetitions. My grandchild of 7 recently gave me directions over several miles of busy suburban streets in a blinding rainstorm from the church to his house when we lost contact with the 'follow us' caravan after a wedding, for that very reason. He certainly had not "tried" to memorize the roads and turns: he simply **knew** them because *of* that natural faculty and the repetition of having made the same trip many times.

This is mentioned because if we are aware of how we think, we will be able to respect that process and learn efficiently. On the one hand, if we drill the *correct* motions into habits through repetition, we progress efficiently in the shortest possible time. But if we run roughshod over the process by bullying, forcing, or ignoring the linearity required and the specificity of each detail that makes up the whole, we disrupt the process and prevent the results we desire.

What Other Drills Do We Need?

Since a good golf swing requires 1) a trigger to set the swing into motion, 2) two main sources of power and a mechanical advantage we need to apply, and 3) structurally significant elements, drills will be given to ingrain each of those specific things. And as has been said, in order to learn to ride a bike *you have to get on the bike and ride it,* the drills need to be *experienced and repeated many times* for you to acquire the skills that you need. Tommy Armour, I believe, did not allow new pupils to hit any golf balls for a full two weeks. It was so that he could prepare them with drills, for the very reason that learning new physical skills simply requires repetition, feedback and response, adjustment, repetition, feedback and response, again and again. It is simply unrealistic to take up a golf club and expect good results without respect for this process. When I am asked "How many times should I do this — drill," I usually respond, "Five million. No, on second thought, six million!"

The Horizontal/Body Rotation (Baseball) Swing Drill

This drill is for the purpose of teaching you how to use body rotation effectively, to acquaint you with its considerable power and role in the swing as the foundation of everything, and how its *mass* is a contributor to clubhead speed.

Picture a merry-go-round rotating. If you look at its center or axis, it doesn't seem to be moving very fast. But if you look at its outer edge, its speed there can be considerable, due simply to the distance of the edge from the center.

When you swing a golf club, the "outer edge of your wheel" is your left hand, which is at a distance of two feet or more from its center of rotation— your left shoulder. And the clubhead itself is being thrown by *that hand* in a centrifugal release which multiplies the *hand's* speed by a factor of four or five. So body rotation is multiplied twice— once by the distance of the hand from the center— the shoulder is the axle and the hand is the wheel rim— and again by the release of the clubhead being thrown from and by that rim.

This baseball swing drill will use the same setup and procedure as the first drill of the previous chapter with just a couple of changes. Instead of hanging the arms down under your chin, you will hold the your hands and club out in front of your stomach, no higher than hands level with your stomach. The plane of motion of your left hand and clubshaft will now be perfectly horizontal, and you will swing the same as if you were going to hit a home run at a baseball pitched to you at waist level. You will be spinning horizontally, so extend your left arm like one of the spokes of a large wheel, with your left hand at the rim and the axle of the wheel running up your left leg. The clubshaft will be pulled directly behind your hand, on plane, and ultimately get *thrrrrrrrrrrrrrrrrrown* with considerable energy by your attempt to produce the fastest possible clubhead speed by spinning as fast as you can and throwing it. *Your hand will be moved by body turn alone, with absolutely no help from shoulder or upper arm muscles, which remain idle. Your arm needs to be dragged only.* Most people use exertions in the upper arms and shoulders to help the arms push the club to the left and forward, but this drill is designed to eliminate them because that kind of effort alone is not efficient.

For this drill, picture the following situation. You are standing with your shoulders aligned parallel to a target line, and you have a clothesline running from your left shoulder to the target. There is a carpet hanging on the line that needs to be beaten to remove the embedded dirt. You are to strike the carpet simultaneously with your left arm, the clubshaft, and the clubhead all at once as hard as you can, using only your left hand to hold the club. Extend one finger of your right hand to support the clubshaft until the forward swing begins. Notice that the object you are striking in this drill is not in front of you, but it is to your left— considerably left of 'a ball in front of your body.' This is to make you turn through, not just to, impact, and to introduce you to what could be the first time you ever made an appropriate use of your body in the golf swing. In a word, the body rotates *through* impact dragging the left arm (which is pulled tight onto your chest by the effort), and with your hand holding onto the butt end of the club, the clubhead gets whipped around at the last moment.

The first picture in the following sequence shows your setup for the drill, with your body perfectly balanced between your two feet. The second picture shows how you must move your hips a couple inches to the left and lean a bit on the left leg. This imbalance is a 'forward press,' the purpose of which is to create the energy that causes your backswing. As you 'fall' back towards your right foot, your arm is swung around to the right in unison with your body turn. The action moves your body weight towards, but not on*to*, your right foot.

The next picture on the left in this sequence was taken just prior to my full backswing turn, and my weight favors my right foot. It is clear that my body is pivoting over that leg. The next frame was taken just before I swing around to the left as my backswing turn is finishing, and it shows how I have intentionally allowed

my body weight to *fall back* to my left leg, where I wish to be *before* starting my forward rotation.

The next two frames illustrate how my body turn leads and pulls the left arm to and through the ball. My arm is being

dragged by my chest—I have done nothing in an attempt to move *it* forward independently, and the clubshaft is still at a 90° angle with my left forearm. My right heel is off the ground, and that is because my hip turn pulled it: I did not lift the foot or use it to push off. The hip action, turning ahead of my shoulders, also pulls the right leg forward. Release has not yet happened in the first photo since the object of this drill is to release into "a carpet hanging on a clothesline to my left!" And it is for the reason that I use this drill to train the latest possible release into my swing, to save the mechanical advantage of the wristfold for the last possible instant before 'impact.'

The two handed version of this drill

After you do this drill correctly using only your left hand on the club, add your right hand. It will provide massive help if you push the right arm and hand using the base of the right wristbone against the fulcrum of the club, which is under the left thumb.

This action is a 'piston-pushaway' from your right side. I often tell a pupil that even a small woman could shove a large man away from her and maybe even knock him onto his back by putting her right palm on his chest and giving him a sudden shove. That is the kind of force you have in your right arm when you use it that way (it is the same as the action of the arm when you do pushups!), and when it starts to apply its force to the fulcrum of an eleven ounce driver about half way down into the downswing, it can produce quite a bit of clubhead speed. These two pictures show the pushaway action of that right arm and how you can thrust the wristbone down towards and then along the target line to add considerable power to your swing.

During release, either with left hand alone or especially with both hands, you will need to allow, or help, the rollover of the wrists/forearms. If your left hand is swinging on a horizontal plane waist high, it will rotate from palm-facing-down at the ground to palm-facing-up at the sky as your hands move around in front of you. In a normal swing, the rotation is from palm faces behind you to palm faces outward.

I need to stress this critical point just made: during this drill use torso rotation **only** to bring the arms and club around, without any other shoulder, arm or wrist exertions. Realize that the turn is dragging your left arm and pushing your right arm and that you are not using any exertion in your left arm, any kind of twisting in either arm, or any slapping of your right palm, to produce the motion. For greater power, squeeze the fingers of your left hand. This will enable you to make a faster swing when your subconscious feels the security of your hold of the club in that way. It removes reluctance to swing hard from a subconsious fear that your fingers aren't tight enough to keep the club from slipping. But don't squeeze the fingers of your *right* hand!

I said before that a tight grip is contrary to popular belief that the hold of the fingers needs to be soft! There is a good reason for that common advice. It is because of the need to allow your wrists freedom to move without anything slowing them down. But you *can* squeeze your fingers without locking your left wrist. And to get the most out of your motions, also *hold both arms and your left elbow firm enough* not to collapse under the considerable force of the swing. By using hand and arm exertions as "firm connectors" only, the *motion* of the arms and club will be entirely due to body rotation and right arm piston-push. This is what you must seek to achieve. It is an action in which for the most part only "big muscles" do big work and the lesser ones (in the shoulders and hands) simply hold on. In that role, the smaller and weaker muscles are 'relieved of a responsibility' too great for the job at hand (i.e., moving the club), and ultimately *you* remain much more relaxed, and in that state, capable of much greater speed. As mentioned, a sudden thrust with your right arm pushing away can be powerful, and doing such a thing introduces neither tension nor strain.

Another point needs to be emphasized here. I consider it a fundamental mandate of golf mechanics that your relaxation and mental approach be the same as that of a child of five or six playing mindlessly in the leaves with his friends— exuberant, joyful, spontaneous, alert, alive, and carefree. Tension can be an extremely subtle burden, completely hidden from the golfer suffering from it and damaging to a good swing, so let the record state that I consider such an attitude to be a critical detail of the golf swing and of the whole business of playing the game. It remains a game; your mind and body remain alert and responsive, exuberant, and joyful, and at the same time you manage your mechanics respectful of the criticality of extremely small adjustments that are the difference between good shots and atrocious mis-hits. With a little patience and respect for how we learn, you remain relaxed, and in actual play you must be willing to accept whatever results occur as opposed to fearing them and letting tension work its way into your subconscious that seeks to manage your swing to try to prevent them! Then, using feedback from your shots, make the indicated adjustments in your procedure or in your setup for better impact **for the next one.** A free and relaxed simplicity produces results far more satisfactory than motions that are contrived and tense because you try to manage impact conditions during the swing itself.

How To Do This Horizontal Body Rotation Drill

The baseball swing drill requires that you start with your body perfectly balanced between heels and toes. You find your balance as shown to you previously by simply waiting until your weight has stabilized naturally and all rocking in your upper body or tendency *to* rock, has simply stopped before your takeaway— your wait could be as long as a second or two! This pre-takeaway balancing is a critical detail, for the reason that **any** change of your upper body's position from **or** towards the ball occasioned by your weight centering itself during your swing will cause a mis-hit off the center of the clubhead. It is critical in that even *one half-inch* of upper body motion translates into a one half-inch mis-hit— sufficient to miss the green. And a one-inch mis-hit— caused by an inch of upper body motion (an amount still too small even to be visible to an observer)— results in a disastrous shot.

Hold the clubshaft out in front of your body with your left hand only, parallel to the ground and to the target line, using the index finger of your right hand to support the shaft. Trigger the backswing by moving your whole upper body, hips and torso as a unit a couple inches to the left by leaning a bit toward the left leg, placing more of your weight on your left foot. This will create an imbalance which you are to use as "energy" to initiate the backswing. It means that in order to initiate your torso turn you are to let your weight fall back *toward, but not onto*, the right foot. Keep the clubshaft level all the time, and turn your hips and shoulders as far as possible, at least until your back faces the target. And here is a subtlety that is particularly important. **Before you reach the end of your backswing turn and while you are still turning, since you only leaned toward, but did not** stand on, your right leg (you are off balance again), you are to move your left hip and torso as a unit a couple inches to the left and allow your weight to fall back to your left leg! THEN you make your forward swing— i.e., after 'waiting long enough' for gravity to cause your fall to your left foot. This forward swing effort will originate in your mid-body/hip turn, which will drag the torso and the arms, and it may occasion the left hip moving a bit further to the left. Do not attempt to thrust the left hip further left, but realize that to an observer it may appear you are doing it on purpose because he will *see* your hip moving more to the left than your head.

The Fallacy in "Keep Your Head Behind The Ball"

When the ball is played mid-body, your head is minimally behind the ball already. When you drive a ball, it is even more behind the ball. A *ny* self-conscious or deliberate effort to keep your head behind the ball is misplaced. It remains "behind the ball" as a natural consequence of the hip rotation powering the swing; if it is done deliberately it creates an exaggeration and a caricature of good mechanics.

The critical part of the transition, the weight shift

One of the most elusive elements of the golf swing is this shift of weight back to the left that ideally occurs *during the backswing*, and which in most golfers takes more time than they are willing to allow. Since impatience causes the golfer to start his forward swing before his weight *has* fallen to the left, the swing is ruined in several ways and he remains unaware why. The act of falling onto the left leg is called "walking," and all of us have an intuitive sense of the harmony and beauty of those swings in which the golfer cooperates with that natural phenomenon (we call it great tempo, rhythm, or timing) as for example, in the swings of Annika Sorrenstam, Ernie Els and Freddie Couples. It is quite different from the haste or less harmonious rhythm of those swings which ignore or fight against it. When a golfer says, "I swung too fast!" in response to a poor effort I often correct him with "No, John, a fast swing is what you want. You didn't swing too fast: you swung too *early!*" The necessity to wait until your weight arrives on the left leg before body rotation— i.e., for rotation to occur when you are on the front foot, is a supremely important element for using available power. It is a fundamental in other sports as well, such as in serving a tennis ball, in the hammer-throw in the Olympic games, in soccer, and in throwing a ball.

Some golfers use a fast tempo naturally, in keeping with their metabolism and personality. For such people, the same principles apply and are not in conflict with their quickness. My advice to them is to use a very small amount of lateral movement of the hips during the backswing. In this way they really place very little additional weight to the right, and are able without effort to get back onto the left leg before their forward swing in the same manner. Tom Watson and Nick Price are classic examples of golfers who manage a quicker tempo perfectly, and neither one of them moves his body much at all.

A golfer who has trouble making a weight shift onto the left leg for the forward swing should do drills where he swings the club using his left hand alone while standing on the left leg alone. By using the right foot only to help maintain your balance and standing on your left foot while making uninterrupted continuous swings back and forth, you can overcome the reluctance you probably experience to shift to the left leg and train yourself how it feels to swing correctly with your weight on the left side. While doing this kind of a drill you may discover that you never have made a proper weight shift in the past and for the first time in your life discover how such a swing feels. It is quite a different feeling from a swing in which you push off with 'anchored feet!'

Do This Drill As a "One, Two, THRREEEEEEEEEEE"

The heart of this drill is to train body turn for unconscious support. It is common when people first do it to use their left arm to move the club and to neglect the full turn of the torso. Therefore this additional step will make the drill more profitable.

Do the drill first with left hand only, to a count of three. On count 'one,' swing around from a full windup without allowing your left arm to come off your chest at all, and stop the swing when your hips are facing almost straight left, your shoulders are facing somewhat to the left, your left arm is straight out towards where a ball would be in front of your left breast, and *with your left wrist still fully cocked and the clubshaft parallel to the target line. Stop completely in that position and check to see if you have correctly arrived there, as follows: was your arm carried by the chest only, and still in position laying on the top of your left breast? Are your hips turned fully facing the target? Are your shoulders at least 45° degrees towards the target? Is your 90° degree wristfold still in place with the clubshaft completely "unreleased?"*

The next picture shows how you should look when you stop at the end of counts 'one' and 'two' and run through these details to see if you are doing everything right.

After verifying everything, repeat the swing you just did, i.e., on count number 'Two.' Again stop when your left hand has gotten around to in front of your face, and check again on all of the details just mentioned, to see that you did in fact use only body turn to get to where you are, and that no release has occurred. If you find that you did everything right this time *then* do count number "THREEEEEEE," with an exuberant, full all-out swing as hard and fast as you can manage with the intention and energy to knock all the dust out of that imaginary carpet to your left. As you can see, your exuberance and the position of that 'carpet,'

positioned a full 90 degrees *further* to your left than where a ball would be, will generate a very generous and complete lower body turn. You will discover while doing it why I advocate that you leave your feet fairly close together for now. It will also make you aware of how much more you can separate them, if you wish, to produce greater speed in your swing. Turning your lower body far enough so you are *still* turning through impact, one of the objects of this drill, requires that your feet be positioned to permit it, and unless you correctly train hip rotation in the early steps of your golf experience, you might never get the best use of that important resource.

A Summary of the Baseball Swing Drill

Here is a recap of the sequence of motions of this drill. Once your body is balanced and quiet, lean to the left by moving your torso a couple inches to the left. Then while falling back towards the right foot, turn your torso to the right while holding the clubshaft level. Before you have reached a full torso turn with your back facing the target and while you are finishing your backswing, allow your weight to return (by falling) onto the left foot. Once you have arrived *on* that foot, spin your hips so that your whole body rotates around to the left, dragging your arms and the butt end of the club in the very firmly held fingers of the left hand. Once underway in this forward motion when you do it with the left hand only, the right hand that was supporting the shaft can drop away as it will no longer be needed, and rotation has pulled your left upper arm against your chest. Hold your elbow firm. Your hand will be dragged substantially by the rotating chest pulling your arm, the butt end of the club will lead, and if you use a lot of effort, you can really throw the clubhead and clubshaft *and your left arm* into that imaginary carpet hanging to your left.   At this point it will become clear to you why your knees are bent a bit, your left toe is angled out, and your feet are fairly close to each other— i.e., simply because that stance facilitates and even *induces* your hip rotation— the central driving motor or 'locomotive of the drive train' (hips, torso, arms, hands, clubshaft, and finally the caboose— the clubhead).

When getting ready to play a game of golf, doing this drill is an excellent way to prepare yourself for the exuberance, the rhythm and timing, the freedom of motion, the exertions that drive the swing, and for warming your body properly. Swinging a weighted club or two clubs at the same time slowly in this manner is also an excellent way to *strengthen* your golf muscles, and the feedback from heavier resistance is quite valuable.

The 'Chest Throws the Arms' drill

This exercise is simply what it says. Take a horizontal backswing like you did in the baseball swing drill, using both hands, and make your arms and club move solely by rotating your upper body as fast as you can. Try to throw your arms, at the end of which a golf club happens to be attached! Use the fastest upper body turn you can. In the process you will discover how the lower body needs to lead. And it will give you a more complete understanding of the sequence of the hips leading, the upper body following effortlessly, and of the power of this procedure to whip the clubhead around *at the very last moment, when it is supposed to release into the ball,* all simply because your torso moved fast and dragged everything with it.

The 'Pick Up the Wrong Foot' Drill

This is a simple **continuous** back and forth swing in which you lift each foot in succession entirely off the ground as you swing. In the backswing, pick up your left foot. As you go to swing forward, pick up your right foot. Raise each foot several inches off the ground as you do this. Its purpose is to make you comfortable with the weight shift that occurs during an athletic swing, even when there is very little visible motion of the hips to the right and left. Some pupils tend to get stuck on 'flat feet,' resisting weight shift at all, and others sometimes shift onto the *wrong* foot. Do not stop between swings. Set up a continuous back and forth, back and forth action, and repeat the drill daily until you find that your weight shift has worked its way into your swing without thought, where it feels totally natural.

This is how this looks.

The 'Arm Swing' Drill— "chopping with an axe"

Exactly what the arms do in a golf swing is often neglected or unclear. There are schools of swing philosophy that seem to be at odds with each other, namely that it should be "a body swing" in which the arms and hands are passive, versus "an arm swing" where the body reacts to and 'follows' the arms.

Actually, all golf swings are a blend of exertions that produce both motions, and someone's personal experience of his own swing are what color his convictions of what works best, hence what he might teach others.

I believe it best if you understand and familiarize yourself with both sources of power and speed (body rotation and arm action), and by doing the drills you will in time *unconsciously develop* a harmonious blend of all of the available resources far better than you will be able to do by cognitively managing them according to a formula received from someone else. That is the point of drills: they tap into the human body's capacity to "snap to grid" and fix upon what works most harmoniously and with the least effort to accomplish a skill.

The baseball swing drill acquaints you with the power in body rotation to produce clubhead speed. *This* drill will acquaint you with the speed you can achieve from your arms alone. Some people neglect this resource because they are unaware how much *distance* the hands travel from the top of the backswing to the ball, during which time on the way to the ball the arms can contribute considerably to their hand speed at impact. The "top of swing" position of our hands can well be as high as, or even higher than the top of our heads, while at impact the hands are only a couple inches above our knees. This distance is several feet! It makes sense that we avail ourselves of whatever help we can get during this considerable amount of time *by deliberately exerting muscles that can help pull the hands and club downward* as long as they blend harmoniously with the rest of our motions.

Before going further, I need to mention that some people do well to ignore **any** down arm exertion, and simply allow gravity to drop the arms and club into place for the forward rotation of the body to complete the down/through swing. Any conscious exertion of the arms can well disrupt the harmony and physics-perfect nature of a swing which originates from a center (your back) and has no interference from smaller muscles that are located between the center and the clubhead— exertions that have a mind of their own. But for golfers who wish to take advantage of additional help from the arms, this drill shows you what to do. Pictures showing the sequence of this drill begin on the next page.

Use the same posture, foot position, and knee bend as you used in the baseball swing drill but instead of facing the ball, turn yourself, including your feet and hips and shoulders, 45 degrees to the right of normal setup position. If you were facing "3 o'clock" ("12 o'clock being the direction of the target) for the baseball drill, turn so that your whole body is standing facing "4:30," including your legs and feet. Stand fully erect, and using your left hand alone for this swing, make a small additional right turn with your upper body during a backswing up and to the right of your right ear. Let the clubshaft drop down and touch your right shoulder blade. Then starting with the clubshaft fully cocked in your left hand, yank the butt end of the club down at the target line with all the force you can. Pretend there is a log running from your left toe out across a target line quite close to

your left foot. Pull down with your arm and rotate your shoulders to the left. Yank the club down as though you were chopping the log WITH MASSIVE FORCE!!!!! Picture your left arm and the club as one spoke of a huge bicycle wheel, and visualize that wheel rolling along the ground towards the target. Trace the target line on the ground and make the wheel "roll" along that line. Direct that wheel— your arm and the 'axe'— deliberately along that line with your left hand. CHOP HARD!

     Use the rotation of your shoulder to pull your arm, and at the same time pull down with your arm itself, and try to create tremendous clubhead speed. You need to pretend you *really are* chopping a log. Stand tall enough so that the club cannot reach the ground as you swing, and as your arm passes your left side, allow or cause it to rotate 180° as you did in the previous drills. Turn your whole body forward enough to follow your arm in its motion all the way as it finishes the swing. The motion should be a blend of the arm pulling down and of the body rotating.

Explore how to get the most out of your chopping arm by itself, and then see how much more clubhead speed you can get by synchronizing the shoulder turn with it. Again, note how your back must remain facing the target for a considerable time during the downswing to take advantage of the downward exertions in the arms.

Do the Arms Push or Pull?

There is confusion and misunderstanding about whether the arms pull or push *besides* **whether they** *get* **pulled or pushed—** which is different. In a horse and buggy rig, the *wagon gets pulled* by the straps attached to the horse's harness, *but the horse pushes the straps* on his chest to do the pulling. A golfer can push in the same way by pushing against his left thumb with his right arm, yet the club*head* is being pulled by that action. So the correct answer to the question, "Is the swing a pushing or a pulling action?" is that the arms themselves do *both* pushing and pulling!

There is another distinction also because they have two sections. The *upper* arms pull down— the elbows move from above the shoulders down to the chest— in the same manner as they are used in an overhand swim stroke. The *forearms*, however, when the two arms straighten, push out away from you! The unfolding of an arm in an attempt to straighten it requires that the forearm push away from your shoulder! So, the whole story is that the upper arms pull and the forearms push.

When your upper arms come down, they return onto the top of your chest as you pull them down *toward* you. And then when your forearms unfold, they are pushing *away* from you. So your arms do both pulling and pushing. (Piston-pushing with the right arm and hand was already introduced in the last chapter.)

This axe drill also reveals some important information about the way the arms move relative to the chest that you need to be aware of in order to manage the direction of your swing path. Namely, since your left arm is on the left side of your body, it must swing up to the right and down to the left of your shoulder line! When your left arm comes down from the top of your swing and passes your stomach, your left hand does not

move parallel to your shoulders at the start-down. And since momentum requires that it continue in the same direction as it started, the left arm must move from *in front of the right side of your chest to behind your left side*, on a line that runs *left of the plane of your shoulders* as it moves from top of swing position back down to the ball because it starts out in front of, not beside, your right breast.

You can experience this if you make a one-armed swing without turning your torso while you face the target line in a normal address position. Your left hand *must* move "across the ball" *on a line that runs to the left of the target.* A shot hit with this natural motion might be called "a pull," and if your actual golf swing does move to the left across the ball, the common perception is that you swung "over the top." The "problem," then, of pulling or swinging "over the top" might well be simply the golfer's lack of managing *his setup and his downswing sequence* to accommodate this natural path of the left arm. So now let's take a closer look at this especially critical area of golf swing mechanics.

Good golfers often correctly comment on how they need to hold the shoulders so that they do not turn until the downswing is underway. They also stand with a noticeable tilt of the shoulders when addressing the ball— with the right shoulder lower than the left. It is also often heard that by the time your club gets back to the ball that your shoulders again face the target line. These comments are confirmation that *the natural leftward motion of the left arm in the downswing has to be accommodated at setup and during the downswing sequence so that the club will not swing to the left of the intended target line.* And that leads to the following conclusions and some more critical details.

1) A right-shoulder-down tilt at setup is necessary in setting your torso so that the forward motion of your left arm can be down the line. If there is no tilt, if the shoulders are too level, your arm's natural motion will be to the left of the target.

2) The downswing **must** begin without any torso rotation at all so that the very first motion of the arms and club is *down-plane and on-plane*. The very first motion of your forward swing commits the club to *some* direction, so of course you want it to be on the correct path at the outset because it can't change direction once its path is committed.

3) **Both** arms themselves pull down in order to take advantage of *their* role in producing clubhead speed (they will chop at the same time as the rotating shoulders drag them). In some swings this pulldown will begin after gravity alone has allowed the hands to start by simply falling during the weight shift onto the left foot. The initial fall or pull-down is immediately followed— in a 10th of a second or less— with the hips and shoulders rotating.

4) You need to rotate fast enough so that the support for the arm motion is fast and powerful enough for the force and speed you want from your arms.

5) In order to access the full resource of their ability *to* produce clubhead speed in this downward motion, it is necessary to swing the arms all the way to the *top* of their available range of motion. This is accomplished by doing two things: by standing as erect as you can at address with your arms hanging freely, and by turning your *stomach* in the takeaway as far as *it* can turn. Determining how much forward and sideways tilt that is best for your own

build is accomplished by experimentation. It is a good idea to try various postures until you find what feels good and works the best for you. I know of no hard and fast rule for anyone to follow other than to experiment. Use ease of swing, naturalness of motion, and clubhead velocity and direction control as the standards for establishing your decision in these details.

A fairly erect posture coupled with the turn of the entire torso makes it possible for the hands to attain their highest possible back-of-swing position. Your hands need to go high above your right shirt pocket to achieve your largest arc. When observing great swings, especially in younger, more flexible bodies, both women and men, we often see hands as high as several inches above the top of their heads. And history has well established how "high hands action" played a part in the phenomenal golf swing and tournament success of Jack Nicklaus and Colin Montgomerie, to name just two outstanding examples. Other well known examples of an erect upper body include Freddie Couples, Davis Love III and David Toms.

6) A full shoulder turn with your back-to-the-hole is necessary on full shots to achieve a position in which you *can* direct the chopping and arm motions down-plane and on-plane. Your hands move from above your right shoulder down to, and then past, your left hip, in a slanted path that started with hands near your right ear and then out away from your right shoulder. The elbows return down toward the ribs, the hands move away from your shoulders, and the path of the butt of the club is to the left of your left pants pocket. Your hands cross your body on the way to the ball, they do not move perpendicular to the spine as in the baseball swing drill where the "ball" is waist-high.

ЋЋ ЈessingleЋ

7) To achieve a full back-to-the-hole position of your torso you may have to place your feet closed to the target line, i.e., with the right foot drawn back an inch or two and angled to the right a little. So instead of "trying to turn sufficiently for a good backswing," you simply accommodate the limitations of your own range of motion by adjusting the position of your *feet* at setup so that you *can* achieve the necessary full backswing turn without strain. I have you place your feet close together in these drills not only to accommodate the forward swing range of motion desired, but because that also permits more *backswing* amplitude. I am an enemy of golf instruction language which says "try to....." because you don't ever need to "try" to do anything! You **can** do things if you put your feet or your spine or your hands or your fingers or anything in a position that *permits* you *to* do them, and then **you simply do them!**

8) This brings up the subject of the "X factor," the idea that if you restrict your hip turn in the backswing while allowing the shoulders to continue until they have turned as far as they can, that somehow you load up a spring-like coil or tension that is allowed to "snap" back to help power the forward swing. This is a misperception, in that the human body has no elastic properties of any real significance. What *is* meaningful is that *all the slack be taken up* between the connectors that run from the body up through the torso, the arms, the left elbow, and the hands, so that when the backswing *is* complete, the "rope between the towing car (the hips) and the car to *be* towed (the clubhead) is tightened and all slack has been removed." At this writing, Annika Sorrenstam is considered perhaps the greatest woman golfer in the history of the game, and pictures of her prodigious swing (producing 285 yard drives fairly routinely) show that her hips

have turned almost as much as her shoulders at the completion of her backswing. Her "X factor" is not what has been stated as the "ideal" of about 45° between the shoulder turn and the hip turn— in her backswing there is a very small difference in the amount of rotation of her shoulders past that of her hips. During the *downswing*, this angle is increased due to the natural action of the torso leading, but in *achieving* her backswing, she does not hold back her hips from their nearly 90° turn to the right.

In any downswing, since the hips lead the shoulders, that tends to increase the angle between their two planes, but it isn't something requiring any thought or concern. It is observed and is an effect, not a deliberately contrived action, and like many other visible elements of golf swings, it happens *simply as a result of other things*. If a golfer attempts to cause an X factor and to worry about whether he does hold back his hips to create a 45° difference of plane between hips and shoulders, he is actually distracted from a much more important concern, which is simply to turn as far as he can while remaining balanced and in control of the motions and sequence of the downswing.

The Start of the Downswing

This drill highlights and draws attention to several critical details and their significance in the golf swing— regarding what you need to do in your setup and during the swing. Unquestionably the most problematic areas of golf include slicing, pulling, coming over the top, and the pull-hook. And it is for the following reason: golfers with such problems fail to deal with how the left arm *gets started* in its downswing. This information I am about to discuss here is in addition to what has been mentioned just above.

The last drill showed you how your left arm swings across the body diagonally from top-of-swing to impact *and that it is pulled by the shoulder rotating around to the left*. Therefore the left arm and hand *follow the shoulder; they never lead.* For this to occur, before you start forward your *back must face where you wish to pull the arm— specifically, your back needs to face the hole. It is because a hand up in front of and above your chest that will be pulled down to the front of your body toward your knees must move on a plane almost perpendicular to your shoulders! And to repeat, this is not only as you start down from the top, but for a very long time during the downswing.* The significance of this is that *both in your setup and during the early parts of your golf swing, you need to be facing away from the target— you need to be in a position where your shoulder pulls the left arm and hand down the target line, not to the left of the target line!* This is evident in the axe drill, where you intentionally stand facing 45° away from the ball to begin with.

If you face the *ball* and swing your arm, it swings to the left of the target. If you face *to the right of the ball sufficiently,* you can find a position where your arm and club *naturally move toward the target— on-plane down the target line.* I mentioned how over-the-top, pulls, and slices were the most common problems experienced in golf swings. It is because the golfer's upper body *is simply in the wrong place before and during impact,* **a position which prevents a down-the-line movement of his left arm and the club in his hand.**

The solution to the problem is not to "try" to do things that are contrary to the shape and structure of your body. The solution is twofold: 1) as said above, take an address that allows for the shape of your body and limitations in your range of motion; and 2) correctly manage the *sequence* of the elements of the downswing to permit your swing to be on line at impact, instead of to the left. A slice is often due to the path of the club cutting across the ball to the left because body turn dominates, with a square-to-the-target clubface (or an open clubface— a slice curve on the ball is *always* due to the clubface open *relative to its line of motion*). (A 'pull' will result if the clubface is square to *that* line to the left, and an 'over-the-top swing' is simply the characterization of any swing whose path *is* moving to the left instead of on-line.)

Summary: The Significance of All of This Entails Several Items

1) As said above, you may need to stand at address with your right toe angled out a bit, with the right foot drawn back a bit from a normal address position, and you may wish to put your feet closer together than you are used to, all of which allow a fuller backswing turn. The point being that *if your body is in a position at setup that prevents you getting there during the swing*, namely, to a full backswing with your back to the hole, <u>effort</u> will not overcome that limitation and enable you to do so during your swing!

2) You may need to address the ball with your *shoulders* a bit closed.

3) You may need to stand more upright than you are used to, in order to access the range of motion that is sufficient for your mid-body *to* make the full backswing turn of the torso.

4) You will unquestionably have to practice carefully, and ingrain, the correct sequence of motion of the entire swing, especially as concerns the *forward* motion, initiated by the body's gravity-induced fall back over to the left foot.

Chapter Five

Using This Swing
To Hit Golf Balls

I have already pointed out a few things that are important to keep in mind as you go to the range to practice. I remind you that the information that you need to apply to cause good impact or distance or direction control will be quite different from the things you are concerned with for making a good *swing,* assuming you continue to do what you have learned to do. Impact usually involves different issues than swing mechanics and the two things must be kept separate in managing how you practice.

The significance of this is that regardless of results, so often dependent on extremely small adjustments rather than swing faults, you must continue to use the *swing* procedures you have learned. Control of impact and direction is handled by *adjustments* in measurements, and in things in your setup, grip, stance, posture, and by details that are mostly handled before the club is moved at all. The adjustments are based on common sense, geometry, and eventually, on feedback from your practice, in the same way in which a child adjusts his balance, exertions, tilt, and steering when learning to ride a bike. (In that case, adjustments are handled subconsciously; in the case of golf, they are usually too subtle and numerous to be handled subconsciously, and I will shortly explain what they are and what to do consciously and deliberately to correct mis-hits.) *Adjustments* are what enable you to put your swinging machine (i.e., you and your club!) in the places relative to the ball that will permit the orbit of the swinging clubhead to go through the exact spot where the ball is sitting. Remember, that exact spot is about the size of a nickel! You are not to search out the ball or change your mechanics during the act of swinging at it. You need to find out where to put you and your club **before you swing** so that the club *will* go through the ball place and be square for impact nearly automatically, with only a bit of guidance or aim of your actual swinging motion while retaining the in-swing controls you have already learned.

The second consideration is that you will be deeply influenced to use a different swing than the one you have been practicing in the previous drills. Your IRS (Instinctive Response System) will seek to substitute old habits, feelings, and unconsciously driven impulses because the existence of a golf ball in front of you will cause you to surrender control to *it* when taking your swing. "Why can't I hit the ball with my practice swing?" is a frequent complaint, because of the uncontrollable "hit the ball" instinct that most of us experience. You too will be blinded by, and give in *to,* this instinct, unless you make the decision not to surrender to it, but instead choose (your golf swing *is* a choice!) to 'live within your means," that is, to swing slowly at first with small swings and easy shots where *you* remain in control of everything you do.

But in *addition* to a tendency to change your focus and swing because there is a ball there, as soon as the first ball is mis-hit, you probably will question your *swing,* (and may even your very soul, as though you are inferior somehow) and find yourself trying to change an in-swing action or motion to remedy the problem.

Unfortunately many of us have a tendency to mistrust and abandon our correctly learned mechanics and automatically assume that the problem with a mis-struck shot lies in something we are doing during the swing. Our first inclination is to believe that our "swing" was at fault because of the unchallenged presumption that swing mechanics are the be-all and end-all of impact or trajectory problems— an error that is reinforced by almost all mainstream golf instruction. It seems that such an interpretation of bad shots is the norm and by omission, there are no other explanations!

But blaming all ball flight problems on the swing is a great disservice to golfers. In fact it probably does more harm than anything else in the way it leads them to seek answers to their problems in the wrong place. Anything else that can do harm to a golfer's correct understanding of cause and effect doesn't even come close to the damage caused by automatically blaming his swing! But thankfully the truth is very different from that. **The truth is that if the swing is fairly good, the remedies for your mis-hits are almost always found in relatively small adjustments in your setup and in measurements established between you and the golf ball.**

A third point is that you must *observe and interpret exactly what happened* for each shot, so you can determine whether it was something in your *procedure* or your *setup* needing adjustment. The information you need for that is covered here next. And the most important *diagnostic* information for solving impact problems exists in two simple but important things, one of which an observer or even video replay will not be able to tell you: a) **exactly where** on the clubface you made contact and b) what was the ball flight. The point on the clubface where contact occurs can be determined by dotting the ball with a spot of lipstick or some builder's chalk. Chalk is applied by pressing a moistened ball atop the neck of a chalk line refill bottle and shaking dust onto the spot. When you scrape the excess directly back into the bottle, what is retained in the dimples will mark the clubface with a clear imprint of the ball. Place the ball so that the spot of chalk or lipstick is far enough below the equator for the loft of the club you are using, and in the path of the club to the ball. Grass itself will often make a readable mark, or an imprint made on some tape on the clubface will also work if moisture

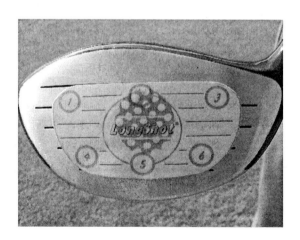

isn't present to obliterate it (I use label tape, masking tape, or impact tape for this purpose).

The photo was taken after a drive with impact tape affixed to the clubface. Builder's chalk will usually make a mark as clear. The trajectory of the ball includes *all the behavior of the ball,* whether it dribbles along the ground, flies appropriately high for the club in hand, gets skied, goes straight with no spin, or to the left or right curving *thereafter* either to the left or right.

Reading and Interpreting Impact

When any impact occurs, feedback is available from it and information is there to help you, and it falls into three specific areas that will be explained to you, each one with its own specific remedy. The common reaction 'I just hit a bad shot' is useless for leading to improvement. Impact and ball flight is essential information because it will tell you what corrections and adjustments you need to make— there just is no other way to find what they need to be. By paying attention to and using that information, you transform what would be wasted time (bashing balls) into efficient practice and improvement. Most people waste that resource and spend years squandering volumes of information simply because they do not know *how* to use it.

Here are the things you need to look at:

- **Direction of the ball,** whether straight or curved, and whether its initial direction and any curvature is to the right or left of the line intended. Terms that apply for shots curving left are 'hook' and 'draw' (a mild form of hook); and shots starting straight left are called 'pulls.'

Shots curving to the right are called 'slices' or 'fades' (the mild form of slices), and a shot starting straight right of the intended line is called a 'push.' Combinations are possible— namely pull-hooks and push-slices, pull-slices and push-hooks— names given because both features are present: a pull that also hooks, and a push that also slices.

- **Depth of the clubface in its impact on the ball**— the height of the path of the clubhead relative to the position of the ball, resulting in impact at, below, or above the optimum "center" of the clubface. Impact too high on the clubface is called 'fat'— the club path is too low. Such swings usually result in the club striking the ground before the ball. Impact is called 'thin' when the club path is too high and the lowest part of the clubface strikes the ball. The ball flight of thinly struck shots is lower. Both fat and thin mis-hits cause loss of distance.

- **Path control**: this is about whether the path of the clubhead is closer to or further from your feet than the position of the ball on the ground, causing collision on the toe or heel. Both types of mis-hit also cause a loss of distance and some directional problems, in proportion to the distance of impact from the center of the club. It helps to compare how a club in its path toward the ball is similar to the behavior of an automobile on the highway. Heel or toe impact occurs because you are 'driving in the wrong lane.' Two things are relevant about being in the wrong lane on a highway and that apply to a golf swing: 1) you don't instantaneously change lanes while driving— you get to a different lane gradually, and being in a wrong lane at any time was caused by something that happened much earlier, and 2) momentum of your car tends to keep you in whatever lane you *did* get into earlier. In the same way a club does not change lanes on the way to the ball in a violent instant: it gets to another lane gradually having been directed there *much earlier in the swing, by things done long before collision with the ball.* The lane of travel of your clubhead is dictated by intentions and exertions that exist long before the club is anywhere near the golf ball!

ADJUSTMENTS AND FIXES

Direction Control

Of your concerns, direction control is the easiest to diagnose and deal with, so the following information will give you a jumpstart for handling it.

The Path: Your *swing* must be directed along the line you choose (using a line drawn through the ball to the target) *by controlling the movement of your left hand* to and through impact, as taught to you in the third chapter. The advice, "the toy follows the hand that pulls the string," was given to help you picture how to move your left hand with precision, therefore to control the clubhead that follows in exactly the same direction. Then, *if the swing of the clubhead is correctly moved along the target line by tracing that line with your left hand,* the ball will also be propelled in that direction if it is struck in the center of the clubface and if the clubface is square to that line.

The Clubface: The clubface needs to be perpendicular or square to the direction of the path of the clubhead at separation of the ball from the clubface. (There is some closing of the clubface during the 5/10,000ths of a second of what is called the impact interval while the ball rebounds from its surface.) How the direction of the clubface at separation is managed is often misunderstood by golfers of all levels of ability. It will be clearly explained here and in chapter nine.

Slicing: If the ball slices, we are called "slicers." If we hook the ball, we also tend to believe that *that* is an inherent or personal idiosyncrasy or characteristic "tendency" that we must live with, or take drastic steps to try to overcome. Or that it is a "fault" requiring major surgery.

Such perceptions are misguided— no, they actually are harmful! A slice is always caused— I will repeat, always— caused by a clubface open to the path of the clubhead at impact. *That occurs because, unknown to the golfer himself, the grip taken at setup had the clubface too open to begin with, despite its apparently square-to-the-target line at setup. What counts is how much the left arm turns naturally as it gets back to the ball. So the strength of the grip taken before your swing begins is the reason why the clubface is open at impact,* due to the structure of our bones and joints, and not to a fault occurring during the swing. Obviously some slices are pretty much guaranteed by a wild and careless across-the-ball path of the club *and* a too weak grip (one in which the plane of the left hand, or of both hands, is placed too far counter-clockwise relative to the plane of the clubface). But if the grip is not too weak when the swing path is leftward, the flight of the ball will be a dead left pull— not a *slice!*

For someone with a decent swing (not perfect, just passable!) as taught in the third chapter, wild carelessness is not the fault and it will not be the factor in habitual slicing. In such swings, if the path of the clubhead is along the target line and his ball position is appropriate for the club in hand, the golfer *simply needs to rotate his left hand clockwise a bit relative to the clubface plane at setup* (the *right* palm should always be facing the target at address), and then tweak/readjust that left hand position until the swing does produce straight ball flight. You are not to use a strong, weak or neutral grip as defined by someone *else*, whether in a book, magazine written by experts, or in personal instruction. *You need to locate, by trial and error, what is for you the grip strength that automatically does produce straight, no-slice, no-hook ball flight.* Contrary to much of what we have been told over the last 50 years or more, there *are* golfers who can hit the ball almost string straight and do not need to live with or favor a draw or a fade.

In finding what will work correctly for you, it doesn't matter so much how your clubface looks at **setup** itself. You don't hit the ball until the clubhead swings away from the ball several feet and then returns, during which round trip lots of changes occur. The unquestioned assumption that taking up a club and addressing a ball means that the left arm will return to the ball with the back of your hand facing in the same direction as you set it at the start of the swing is where the problem lies. That simply does not automatically occur. If your mechanics are sound otherwise, **it is an incorrect placement of the club in your hands before it is even swung to begin with that is responsible for the slice or hook. It is because you did not match the orientation of the back of your hand that occurs naturally at impact when you took the club into your hands at setup.**

In-swing happenings are so instantaneous and so dependent on pre-swing things, including the personal characteristics of each golfer's body, that what happens during the swing has *already been determined* before the swing started.

Things that cause problems during a swing that are in place before you swing include using your body to pull your arms, failure to select a target line path (resulting in a "coming over the top" motion and other disruptions), and the adjustments, angles, and mechanical relationships of the parts of your own body that you establish in your setup. To imagine you can do things deliberately while the swing is underway to fix something that was adjusted or planned wrong at setup is simply out of the question, and the answer to what adjustments normally *fit you* is not found in books or from instruction, but only from trial and error guided by the concepts here and by common sense in applying them.

As your practice gets underway, then, and if you have not been compensating (doing things during your swing in an attempt to manipulate results), and if you find you do have a consistent pattern of slice or hook, make an adjustment in the strength of your grip by rotating your left hand clockwise or counter-clockwise on the club to correct *that*. *After* you have found a grip strength that gives pretty good results, it will then be appropriate to consider how to handle mis-hits, and the following information addresses all of those concerns.

If I take too weak a grip at setup, the club will arrive open at impact if I do nothing during the swing to square it deliberately. To have *to* do something during the swing to square the clubface is atrocious golf mechanics. The first of the next four pictures show me taking too 'weak' a grip at 'setup' for my own natural swing, and the second shows that when my arm returns to the ball with that grip my wristwatch and the back of my hand are actually turned more to the right. It is how my arm arrives back at the ball if I don't do something deliberately in an attempt to turn it more or less than what happens naturally. So the second picture, at 'impact,' shows how the clubface is wide open. The next two pictures show the opposite situation, where if I take a grip that is too strong at setup for my own natural mechanics, the clubface arrives closed to the line of flight.

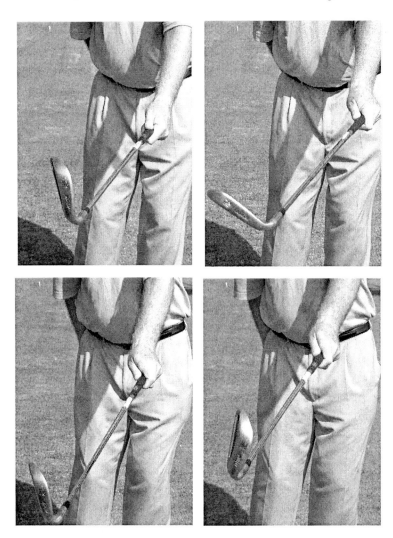

The correct grip for you will return the club square to the line on which the club is swung *because you found by trial and error* in practice just how strong or weak it needed to be when you did absolutely nothing to square the clubface for impact and your ball flight was straight. Your club arrives square without concern because of the adjustment you made before the swing began!

Hooking: This is, of course, the opposite of slicing, in that when the clubface arrives at the ball it is facing left of the line on which it is traveling, which would happen with the situation in the second pair of pictures above. This means that at setup the golfer must rotate his left hand around somewhat to the left on the club to change its alignment for square impact. This is what Ben Hogan says he had to do in 1946 to accommodate "retaining my power while curing my occasional tendency to hook." On this point a golfer may find that a grip that works for irons with the ball somewhere near mid-body at address requires a stronger grip than for drives played off his left foot. I often receive desperate cries for help such as "I hit all my irons good but I can't help hooking my drives!" and almost always the solution is that since the ball position is further forward for the driver, the arms *have naturally rotated further to the left than when the ball is further back in the stance.* Clearly then, using the same grip strength for straight shots with the driver as for the irons means it *must* arrive at the ball with a closed clubface. Weakening the left hand a small amount (Hogan's adjustment was a half inch turn) is all it takes to produce dead straight ball flight.

Sometimes the right hand can be the culprit. It is instinctive for many athletically gifted people to 'grab' the club with the right hand, and in the process rotate the palm clockwise so that it is quite a bit under the club at setup. During the swing the hand will naturally return to impact facing fairly square to the line of flight. The result is, then, of course, that the clubface is now pointed left of the target, and a huge hook is the result. As said, the right palm must always face the target when you place that hand on the club.

Depth Control

All beginners whiff (miss) the ball. All golfers struggle with fat, thin, toe, or heel impacts (toe and heel issues are dealt with under "path control.") But conventional instruction fails to address these things. It is a subject that, by omission, sends a message to the golfer that "You are a beginner or an amateur, you are not talented, good impact requires good hand/eye coordination, and you just have to spend whatever time it takes to learn how to hit the ball well. Or maybe you just don't have the ability! Instruction isn't intended to cover accurately striking the ball: it is *your* responsibility to figure out how to make good impact. Swing and hope. Figure it out. We all go through an awkward period and it is part of the learning process. Perhaps you are just a klutz anyway." (We are not told this in words, obviously, but the actual message is exactly that!)

Wow! What a shame! What a massive injustice! What a stupid and unnecessary waste! The *instructor* doesn't know what the problems are or how to instruct, so he puts the burden upon the pupil! Instead of being informed how to go about achieving centered impact, the golfer is left to fend for himself. The nearly universal result is that he spends his life in his struggles and his search. He studies everything he can, he asks friends, he inquires on golf forums, he watches golf broadcasts, he reads everything written by the best known teachers and golfers of all time, and he takes many lessons! But no one ever addresses it! And even if his search goes on for years, most likely he will still not find out what he needs to know. And he continues in the belief that since it is not addressed in instruction, that it *truly is* his responsibility to find out for himself, and that it is not something that *can* be taught. But as I said, this is a massive injustice, and it is just plain wrong, as you will see shortly.

The Two Elephants in the Living Room There are two common reasons for mis-hits (and a few other more subtle ones) that a golf pupil deserves to have been told in the first 20 minutes of his first golf lesson, or at the beginning of written instruction on how to hit the ball. This information belongs in "Lesson One." Its omission is equivalent to having being denied the password to your own computer— a simple thing in itself, but it must be correctly entered or you can't even log on! Golfers are more shortchanged in this area than in anything else, and I address it first, as you prepare to hit a golf ball, to enable you at the outset and then to embed "perfect impact" as your norm! This information will show you how to find the adjustments you need (that's what the issue is, **adjustments!**) *for* centered impact. You do not need to struggle blindly and helplessly for the rest of your life, looking for that most elusive and most satisfying element of the game of golf, namely solid, dead center, perfect impact on the golf ball! The following are the two 'elephants.'

1) Your Arms Get Longer During Your Swing When you are relaxed and take your club in hand to address a ball and correctly allow your arms to hang under your shoulders, it is natural and obviously appropriate to lower your sternum until the clubhead touches the ground, its sole level with the bottom of the ball.

But when you swing, the pull of your arms and club outward away from your chest occasioned by their weight swinging in a circular motion is considerable. In fact that pull is enough to "lengthen" your arms, increasing the distance from your chest to the center of the clubface by several inches! Not only does the club's pull straighten your left elbow. The left wrist flattens, its angle with the forearm straightens, and *your shoulders fold forward and inward.* Since your arms and the clubhead while swinging exert an outward pull a *lot* greater than their actual weight at rest, their combined force is enough to cause the clubhead to extend as much as 2 or 3 inches *further away from your chest* than the distance it was from your left shoulder at setup. The pictures on the next pages illustrate what happens.

In the first one, I am extending my left arm and club to the same length as I would when addressing a ball normally, but I am holding it up with the shaft pointed at my golf bag so that you can see how long it is from my left shoulder to the clubhead. Notice how the toe of the club is about six inches from the bag. The second photograph was taken without my moving *anything at all except* that I stretched my arm and shoulder blade forward to match how they get pulled naturally during a swing. Now the clubhead is nearly touching the golf bag. You can experience how your own arm, wrist, and shoulders 'stretch' by asking someone to try to pull the clubhead away from you while you hold your club out in front of you. The pull outward 'lengthens' your arm by several inches. Also, notice in the second picture how it also caused my left hand to raise up, more in line with the line running from my shoulder to the clubhead than it was in the first photo. This 'higher-at-impact' position of the hands is virtually universal in good golf swings.

The closeups on the next page show the difference even more dramatically.

2) At Impact Your Left Shoulder Has Moved Further From The Ball Than Where It Was at Setup When you address a golf ball, your shoulders are normally parallel to the target line with a small tilt to the right. During the swing, your upper body rotation turns your shoulders more to the left than their setup position. They *may* be *parallel* to the target line at impact (as viewed looking down the line)— more likely they will be open to that line— but your left shoulder *will* be higher, so it will be farther from the ball than its address position. If you don't let your back move toward the ball during your swing either by bending your spine down or by letting your knees bend more, since the left shoulder has rotated further to the left, *it takes with it the left arm, pulling the clubhead away from the ball.*

In the first of these two next pictures (p. 166) I am using a normal address position with a small tilt in my shoulders. My clubface is positioned directly behind the ball and I have extended my left arm and wrist as I normally would to 'take up the slack' before takeaway. The next picture shows how I arrive at impact. During my swing I did not change the height of my head, the angle of my back, or the flex in my knees. The only thing different in this picture from the first is the amount of rotation in my shoulders and the consequence of that rotation, namely that as my left shoulder got pulled a couple inches higher than it was at setup, it pulled the club off the ground by the same amount. That is a correct and natural result of the torso and shoulders rotating to and through impact, so the club *must whiff or miss the ball* because the shoulder is now in a different place than it was when I addressed the ball. I didn't do anything wrong at all during the swing. Natural action of my body parts *caused the club to return further from the ground than where I set the clubhead down to begin with.* As before, I did nothing during my swing to raise my head, push up with my knees, or change my spine angle. The pullaway of the clubhead from the ground is entirely due to the rotation of my shoulders.

The effect of this pullaway (as I call it) is of course the opposite of the effect due to the lengthening of the arms caused by the force of the swinging club, addressed earlier. So you might ask, "George, since the arms get longer and body turn pulls the club away from the ball during your swing, don't these two opposite effects cancel each other out?" And the answer is "Yes, for perhaps 20% of golfers, because in their case the two effects just happen to be 'equal' enough for a net difference of zero. But not for the rest of us, due to different body types, swing types, and range of motion. *Our* "net difference' is *not* zero."

There are several golfers whom we observe frequently on television whose accommodations for "measuring to the ball at setup" are 'unusual' and quite visible to an observer. Watch Juli Inkster and Nancy Lopez. Both of these superior LPGA professionals use the same procedure of lifting their backs just prior to takeaway. They extend their left arms and flatten their left wrists to full length as they raise themselves up a bit *to allow for the left "arm-club" straightening during the swing.*

In the first of the next two pictures I have 'addressed a ball.' In the second I am preparing for takeaway and I have raised my back to take up some of the slack that exists in my left wrist. During the swing that angle will not change as much as it would if I did not make the accommodation just before takeaway, making it easier for me to control the low point of my swing arc and minimize fat or thin impact on the ball.

(Sometimes during a broadcast the golfer will be reported to be using "high hands," but the raising up of the *shoulders* prior to takeaway is not mentioned, and *that* is what is actually happening, not an intention to lift the hands themselves!) Juli and Nancy begin their backswing after this adjustment. I do the same thing in my own procedure, and when I don't lift my shoulders high *enough* to compensate for the elasticity of my arms and shoulders, the result is a very ugly fat shot. But that is not the only reason for it: I need to create a 'measuring rod' (consisting of the left arm-club) that is reliable for measuring, using a length of 'arm-club' that is consistent. If I don't take up the slack during my setup in the same manner and in the same amount each time I swing, the length of my measuring arm-club (my extended left arm plus the length of my club) may well be inconsistent, and as a result I will have serious difficulties achieving centered impact.

Measuring for a longer club is automatically accommodated by the one adjustment and requires no change in procedure. Whatever the amount of elasticity in the wrist, arms and shoulders, it is the same regardless of the length of the club. Fairway woods and driver require slightly different measurement due to using a ball position more forward of that used for iron shots, and for the fact that a ball on a tee is higher than ground level. Measuring correctly for these clubs will be addressed later.

Why do I top the ball on the first tee a few minutes after I leave the driving range using the same setup adjustments I just used successfully on the range? Aha, another detail! In the period when you were not swinging a club, your body cooled off, and your muscles shortened a bit. The amount of "extension" that works when you are warmed up differs from what works for precision impact when you are cold because muscles are longer when warm. If you use the measurement to the ball that works when you *are* warmed up after your body has cooled some, you may well top your drives and make thin impact on a few shots for the first few holes. And it usually happens on those days when we start to play *without* warming up first. The amount of elasticity, as I call it, that exists in your shoulders, arms, and wrists is variable, and changes in temperature, long waits occasioned by slow play, and breaks taken mid-round need to be taken into account *even as you are playing*. All of these create a situation when you might cool off and your muscles would contract.

This fact is obvious when you think back to how far down you can bend while trying to touch your toes. There may be a difference of six inches in how far down you can extend your hands without bending your knees after you have warmed up and 'loosened up a bit' (even the words used to describe it are a tip-off of the nature of the issue).

Tension. There is another subtlety in this issue that you need to know so you won't create tension in your setup while measuring to the ball. When you *have* made a pre-swing accommodation in your arm and wrist to remove any slack and you sole the club, you may not have made enough of an adjustment to cover the flexibility of your *shoulders*, since *they* remain relaxed at setup and do not *get* extended or folded forward until the swing is under way. Since you don't want to create tension by *stretching*, simply address an imaginary golf ball closer to your feet by an inch or two—the amount to be found by trial and error—that compensates or accommodates your elasticity. Standing a bit farther from the ball automatically lengthens the distance from your shoulders to the ball, so you can handle the problem sensibly and comfortably this way. It is important to remain athletically 'ready-relaxed' for your swing, not tense. You might place the toe of the club at the ball, a bit 'south of the ball,' or some mark on the clubface or the hosel as a marker for the amount of adjustment that works the best. Do remember to remain perfectly balanced heel-to-toe as always. Then use trial and error to locate the adjustments that work best for you for centered impact. The accommodations *you* will need are personal, and again, they are not something anyone else can tell you.

The photo on the left here shows one way that you can address a ball to allow for extension, and doing it this way allows you to remain relaxed at setup. This setup could be used by golfers whose 'net difference between pullaway and stretch' is a *longer* left arm-club at impact than at setup. Allowing for stretch in some manner would be needed if 'fat' impact results from a normal address position. This is a procedure I have seen done by tour professionals not infrequently. It was an accommodation that Greg Norman used several years ago— he would set up 'too far' from the ball with his driver.

The picture on the right of the two is the opposite accommodation, and it is more commonly seen among professionals, especially on the tee. By placing the heel of the club at the ball instead of the center of the clubface, body turn pulling the shoulder away from its original setup position also pulls the club closer to the golfer's body. So if you usually hit the ball thin and wish to make good impact without having to dip or reach down mid-swing to 'get the clubface centered on the ball,' this setup accommodation takes care of the issue for you.

Is this really such a big deal, Hibbard? I have never heard of such a thing from any instructor or seen it in any book. Isn't it a bit finicky to get into *this* kind of tiny detail?

An anecdote will serve to illustrate this issue. Recently in a celebrity tournament when Greg Norman hit a ball thin and it landed a bit short, stopping about 15 yards short of the pin, he was heard to mutter "I hit it on the 4th groove!" (the center of mass or center of percussion of some iron clubs is located on the 5th groove up from the bottom of the clubhead.) Such is the awareness, sensitivity, and level of proficiency of great ball strikers, that they recognize *and are in control of* as little as 1/6th of an inch difference in depth between "pure" impact and a shot struck a bit thin! The miss cost Greg one stroke (two putts instead of one), and in a money situation, making such a miss *only once in 72 holes, one shot out of some 260 or 270 shots,* can cost the competitor hundreds of thousands of dollars, or even more! And at the level that most of us play, the difference in our depth control is far more than a groove or two.

I have frequently used that term, "depth control" in this book. By it I am describing our ability to deliver the club to strike the ball before hitting the ground, yet contacting the ball high *enough* on the clubface, at its center of mass. Ball speed is a product of clubhead speed *and mass*, so impact somewhere other than at the center delivers less than maximum mass and the ball will fall short compared with one well struck. If the club is too low as it arrives at the ball it hits the ground first. That obviously slows the clubhead down by itself, plus with impact *too* high on the clubface the collision delivers less mass to the ball. If the club is too high off the *ground* at impact (a 'thin' shot), the leading edge strikes the ball first and it and produces a shock in your hands (or you whiff the ball completely), and the resultant mis-hit from that kind of impact can range from a mildly thin shot (like Norman's) to one severe enough to dribble the ball only a few yards.

Making Adjustments

Different clubs need different adjustments. Accommodations for your driver and fairway woods must be different than for your irons, where both the ball position and the amount of shoulder/torso rotation differ, and because longer clubs require a flatter swing plane. If you experiment and take accurate account of the impact point on your clubface for the different clubs, you will be able to find the accommodations you need for them.

Because individuals are built differently from one another and their swings differ in timing and other details, some people's body rotation before impact is greater, so they may need more dramatic adjustments. As mentioned, many of them place the heel of the clubhead where the ball sits, especially for driving off a tee. Fuzzy Zoeller is the most noted example of this, as he stands *several inches* "too close to the ball" with the clubhead sitting on the ground 3 or 4 inches further from his feet than where the ball lies. His considerable upper body rotation naturally brings the clubhead back to where the ball sits. He certainly doesn't move his body or do anything compensatory during his swing to make that happen. Davis Love III, Ernie Els, and John Daly are a few of the thousands of accomplished golfers who place their driver *on* the ground, the ball on a tee a couple inches *off* the ground, and the *heel* of the club at the ball, as you see I have done in the photo on the facing page. It appears that my clubhead is two or three inches too far from my left shoulder to hit the ball on the center of the clubface, but the reality is that it takes that amount of accommodation at setup for impact to occur in the center of the clubface.

Path Control

Just as with depth control, which assumes that the golfer does not move the hub of his swing— his swing center— during the swing by lifting or dipping his torso somehow, the *path* of the club through the ball is also something caused or committed to long before the club gets to the ball.

I have already mentioned that the first thing needing attention for path control is the balance and stability of your upper body during the swing, your center of gravity resting quietly between the heels and toes, or possibly favoring a bit of lean onto the balls of the feet— whatever it is, it must rest there quietly! This is supremely important, and it rarely gets the attention it needs. And as always, to prevent a problem *during* the swing, you manage it by careful attention at *setup*.

How Balance Affects Impact Earlier I showed that if your upper body falls forward *even an inch or so* while you are swinging, your entire "swinging machine"— clubhead with it— gets moved forward and the path or orbit (the driving lane) of the clubhead *will get moved out further from your feet than where it would swing if your chest remained back where it was at setup,* like a car getting into a wrong lane on the highway. This causes impact either fat or on the heel, possibly even on the hosel itself, producing the ugliest shot in golf— the shank! *Inevitably.* And if your upper body falls backward even an inch or so during the swing, the clubhead *will be moved by that shift to a path or lane that is closer to your feet than where the clubhead lay at setup,* causing a powerless toed shot or thin impact with its inevitable shock and loss of distance.

Finding your center of balance at setup is equivalent to being sober before getting behind the wheel of your car before getting onto the highway! With an off balance setup— no matter how little it might seem to be— your body *must* rebalance— move— during the downswing. Good impact allows no room for even a little carelessness. Balance needs to be installed at address the same way as you take care of aim, grip, and the other things.

And here is how that is done. Your balance and stability are to be **found...located,** and that is done by patiently waiting, feeling, 'listening to yourself' and adjusting before you start your swing. It might take as much as five seconds or more after you have made your setup, before takeaway itself, for you to be able to know if your body is completely quiet, at rest, and if you are swaying at all. Stability is not something you control muscularly by "holding yourself" in a given place during the swing. It will occur as the result of eliminating any tendencies of your body to fall forward or backward during the swing because you didn't swing until you truly *were* perfectly balanced. Then your stability takes care of itself *during* the swing if you don't lunge. Once your swing starts you will be pretty much "in a blackout" and your swing will respond to the laws of gravity (which are friends of the IRS— for good or ill, in that you fight them and lose, or cooperate with them and win). If correct balance isn't handled at setup, i.e., if you are even a little off balance in your stance before you swing back, some forward or backwards fall *will* occur as your body 'rights itself' during the swing, and it will absolutely change your upper body's distance to the ball during your takeaway, transition, or downswing.

When you think you are ready to swing back, STOP. Feel in your legs, in your feet, in your sense of stability, whether your body is naturally at rest, or whether there is some subtle tendency to lean a bit. Are you absolutely still? Is there any tendency to lean forward? Is there any built-in imbalance that *will* right itself as soon as your swing is under way? Swing only when you are totally quiet.

Other Path Issues It is possible that a poor and inaccurate path to the ball is caused by a swing fault other than those already mentioned. The most common of these is a backswing that takes the hands and the clubshaft to the wrong place. This often happens because we are bombarded with advice to use a "one piece takeaway," to "swing from the inside," and other unquestioned or misunderstood 'mandates' that we attempt to obey. Unfortunately, most of such advice is incomplete or mis-guided, so what we do is not what we should do

If your backswing body rotation also brings your arms away from the target line (as you turn to the right in your one-piece takeaway), you will unknowingly create a tight, 'spring-like' condition in your upper body, shoulders, arms, and hands. This wound-up tension remains until 'permission is given to start the downswing,' at which instant that pressure in the right shoulder and/or in the right hand is released **outwards— towards the target line— instead of down,** and that is simply the wrong direction in which to commit your first movement! You will have no choice in the matter due to the amount *of* that pressure. If you happen to have flexibility such that you do not create pressure in going to a wrong place, the structure of your body simply will not permit you to start downward from there without the same result— namely an initial movement outward, rather than downward.

Once your upper body and/or your hands start out towards the target line instead of down, your "wagon wheel" will have to "roll" in a direction to the left of the intended target line just to hit the ball and even more significant, *the clubhead will travel in a 'driving lane' that is further from your feet than where the ball is located!!!* Pulls, heel impacts, and shanks are the most common results of the off-plane condition. And while Jim Furyk may be able to recover from a 'too-far-inside' takeaway, which he does by *remaining* "too far inside" during his transition downward, his procedure will not work for many of us who lack his control over his transition and whose body structure does not force his swing path outward as it would most everyone else.

The opposite problem (toe impact) can be caused by the opposite backswing mistake, namely swinging the arms and clubshaft too *high and too far forward of your body— i.e., above plane.* This is a situation of not taking the arms or turning the shoulders far *enough* around, *away* from the target line. When the position of your clubshaft at the top of your backswing is *above* the slanted plane defined by the ball/target line and your left shoulder, the club must come back to the ball 'in a driving lane' that is too *close* to your feet.

Summary Here's a short recap of these issues. Heel impact and shanks will be the result from a backswing of your hands and clubshaft too low, below the correct plane. Toe impact will result from *insufficient* slant of the club's swing plane— of the rotating wagon wheel— from a backswing that places the clubhead too high and too close to the target line, from which position it has to swing down too close to your feet. (Toe impact always produces the most common ball flight in all of golfdom— "short-right!" Heeled shots of course can be shanks, or often they are simply ugly low slices and of course they will also fall short.) And toe impact will result from an address position in which you reached your upper arms out from your chest, to which they return in the downswing.

The Importance of a Full Shoulder Turn Recently during the slow motion replay of a drive by Bruce Lietzke in a broadcast of a Champions Tour event, Peter Kostis commented excellently on the importance of a full shoulder turn, remarking that Bruce continues to excel at his game as he did thirty years ago and that his swing has survived that long because *of* his full shoulder turn. Peter's comment was dead on. He pointed out that many golfers fail to make a sufficiently full torso or shoulder backswing turn, hence suffer the inevitable downswing pull to the left. As I listened to him, I hoped that viewers would recognize the excellence of his statement and take it to heart. For those of us who cannot *make* such a turn easily because of a limit in our flexibility, the suggestion to flare our right foot and draw it back from the line, a tip also given in a *Golf Magazine* piece by Craig Shankland, will help. I believe that Davis Love III and Gary Player do place their right foot a bit further from the target line when driving, and John Daly's right foot flare is classic, so Craig's advice is valuable for everyone of us and does not apply only to people having a limited range of motion.

George: the title of this chapter is "Using this swing to hit golf balls." How come you're still yakking and we haven't even seen a ball yet? Here's the short answer. It's because when you build a tall building, you need a deep foundation. So there. Anyway, now you may start hitting golf balls with your pitching wedge.

Now With Golf Balls Take your pitching wedge using the grip you have been shown, and adjust the position of the club in your hand so that, for now, the clubface faces the target and the back of your hand (or your wristwatch) faces a little to the right of the target line. Use the setup, stance, balance, and all the other pre-swing details you learned in Chapter Three. Find a spot in front of the ball on your target line, draw a line through that spot and through the ball, and then with your arms hanging by gravity under your shoulders, *walk yourself to where your hanging clubhead lays on that line* (as opposed to 'reach out' to it). Use a ball position directly in front of your nose (for now), and sole the club even with the ball. Put your whole self (your eyes, shoulders, hips, knees, and feet) parallel to that target line. Then picture a line on the ground parallel to it under your left hand. YOU WILL TRACE THAT LINE, THE ONE UNDER YOUR LEFT HAND, in your takeaway, with your left thumb. Your clubhead and clubshaft will be on plane perfectly if you move your hand in that manner, because the direction the clubhead and shaft move is controlled by your left hand and your left thumb!

Before each shot, take up the slack in your left elbow and left wrist without introducing tension. Use ½, or at the most ¾ swings, and start hitting balls easily. Carefully sole the club even with the bottom of the ball, and swing away, making sure you do not change the angle or height of your spine. Remember to use a bit of a forward press to initiate and produce the energy needed for your short backswings, and wait for your body to fall *back to* the left foot before you swing down with your hands in the transition. *The object of this practice is to develop good swings. It is your duty not to alter any of the motions of your first swing drill just because there is a golf ball in the picture. Use short easy swings at first. Make whatever adjustments you need in order to create perfect impact with these short easy swings, based on feedback from the impact and trajectory of every shot. By using your shortest clubs at the outset you make finding the right adjustments as easy as possible— using longer clubs and hard swings at first pretty much guarantees that you will fail. Locating them is mandatory. This will be trial and error work and it is the essence of how good and effective practice is done! Want to be a good golfer? THEN DO IT THIS WAY!*

People often ask me "George, what swing aids do you recommend?" My answer is "Your pitching wedge!" And *this exact drill.* It is my warmup before every practice session, lesson, or round of golf, and it is what I advise every pupil to use in the same manner. It is **the essence of the golf swing at its best. It is the core issue of the perfect golf swing. It is the heart, the seed out of which all else grows.**

During practice or even on the golf course itself, allow mis-hits to occur— accept them— being careful not to steer or 'control' your club to the ball, but to use the **swing motion "through the ball place"** that you learned in your first swing drill. Let bad shots happen. Make adjustments **for the next swing** to correct any impact or direction or trajectory problems in the bad shot. Continue the process of hit, adjust, hit, adjust, until you have located the appropriate adjustment and its amount that *does* produce good shots. And here *are* the adjustments you will need to make for the various mis-hits:

- **Adjusting for fat and thin shots— depth control in action.**
  If you did not lift your body up away from the ball during your swing and you hit a thin shot, your shoulders were too high to begin with, at setup. So set your torso a bit lower to the ground. Locate exactly *how* high you need to stand to strike the ball and then the ground. To obtain certainty about the depth of the path of my club for any given shot, I put a tee on the ground a couple inches further from my feet than where the ball sits, pointed at the bottom of the ball, as a marker. I then look at my divot after the shot to see if the club *entered the ground* (not just clipped the grass) before that point. If contact on the ground was made before contact with the ball, impact was fat— my shoulders were too *close* to the ground, and my adjustment will be to stand a bit taller at setup. Let the record show, at the outset of your golf experience (if you have not already discovered it), depth control is the most sensitive and the most difficult part of perfect ball-striking. And in nearly 60 years of playing golf, I have never found a better way of dealing with it than dealing with it in this manner with extreme sensitivity to the distance I place my shoulders to the ground, using my left armclub to do my measuring! Be conscious of the elasticity of your body and the fact that your left shoulder is further from the ground at impact than it was at setup. By awareness of those two enormously important things, you will be able to make appropriate adjustments instead of living with what may have been your previous experience— namely frustration and

confusion. The devils you *don't* know are the ones to be feared, but now you *do* know of their treachery (i.e., why the clubhead doesn't simply return to where you put it at setup). Any power over you is now neutralized because you know both why you have the problems of depth control, and what to do about them. Physical elasticity and in-swing shoulder movement are a natural part of everyone's golf swing. They are not personal weaknesses that brand you as inferior.

- **Chunking your chip shots.** Around the green we tend to treat our ball striking with a different approach. We use more of a sense of touch than we use for full swings, so we often will allow our wrists and left elbow to soften in response to the sensitivity we wish to bring to a chip or pitch for managing the distance required. This softening of the left elbow, in particular, tends to have us lower our shoulders closer to the ground than if our left arm were straight, in anticipation of the shot. But it is a setup for chunking or shanking when the left arm *straightens by itself during the forward swing*, and the available distance between your left shoulder and the ground is too short for the length of your left arm-club! The inevitable result is stubbing the leading edge of the chipping club into the ground before contact with the ball! This is one of the most common faults in golf, and even if we have been playing golf for years, it continues to evade detection.

- **Toe and heel impacts— path control.** Toe and heel impacts are due to path problems. And as discussed, you first need to determine if your swing plane is sound, or whether your hands and clubshaft are arriving above or below plane in the backswing. You can observe your own swing in a mirror at your right side, and you need to use the tip of your right shoulder and your ball on the ground to define the correct clubshaft plane for your backswing. *Both* your left hand and the clubshaft must lay on that plane line at the top or on the way down, no matter what club you are using or the amplitude *of* your swing.

If that position is correct for your arms and club, the next detail to consider is your balance. Have you established a totally quiet body, eliminating any imbalance prior to your takeaway and then maintaining it during the swing itself? Toe impact can result from reaching for the ball by moving your upper arms away from your chest at address, because they return back down on*to your chest* during the swing due to gravity and downswing exertions. It can also result from an incomplete shoulder turn. And it can result from standing a bit too far from the ball *for impact* despite it appearing at setup that you are ok. Remember that body rotation pulls your left shoulder up away from the ground as you swing.

The angle between the clubshaft and your left forearm taken at address affects impact in a way that has not yet been mentioned. As a consequence of the straightening of the angle of your wrist as the club pulls outward from your body during the release interval, the clubhead also falls closer to your feet. This brings the toe into impact, not the sweetspot. Whether this phenomenon affects you or not will be discovered only by personal observation and feedback, so it is not a universal for all golfers. It is mentioned as one of the possible reasons for hitting your irons on the toe of the club. The remedy for it is to extend your clubshaft down more at setup in order to make its setup relationship with your left forearm as close to impact position as possible, and in *that* position, you eliminate one of the causes of impact out on the toe of the club.

I don't know of any short cuts to finding out which of these possibilities apply for remedy to toe or heel impacts (there usually are more than one). The remedy is self-awareness, adjustment, trial and error, and feedback. Let me suggest a simplification, however. If impact is on the toe, try standing a bit closer to the ball. If on the heel, stand a bit further from the ball. But be aware there may well be something else from among the issues discussed that needs to be uncovered.

- **Pushes, slices, fades and pulls, hooks, draws— direction control.** I have already elaborated on how the direction of the *path* of the club is easily checked by reading your divots or its motion through high grass. If you have handled direction of the club itself and you do swing it on line, shots travelling off line will not be pulls or pushes. Such shots will have to start on line or close to on-line and their variance from straight can only be due to an open or closed clubface. In that case, experiment with a weaker or stronger grip in the left hand. Also look at your right hand: sometimes it will be placed too far around to the right, somewhat under the clubshaft, at setup. This causes hooks because the hand normally returns to square-to-the target for impact. If that hand is too far around to the *left* of center, with the palm facing left of the target line, it will contribute to a slice. The best position for the right hand is always with palm-to-target. Use feedback to adjust, try again, adjust, etc. until your ball flight is straight.

A couple of tips and optional shortcuts

- **Pre-turn:** A backswing uses two distinctly different motions. One is torso turn, an action in the body itself, turning horizontally. The other is arms swinging, an up and down motion. Because of possible awkwardness in coordinating arm upswing while the body turns, I like to make a turn of my body to the right *before* I start my takeaway from the ball. I turn my torso, and with it, my forearms and the clubface, so that prior to the club moving away from the ball, the clubface has already been turned about 45 degrees open to the line of flight.

A 'pre-turn' simplifies everything for me because it makes the backswing a single direct motion instead of two different ones. Once I have pre-turned, the backswing becomes nothing more than an arm swing "up," with just a bit of additional rotation needed to complete the full shoulder turn appropriate to a full swing. It neither requires nor induces any manipulation of my hands or wrists, hence of the clubface, to get to the top. I also don't need to do anything consciously to complete or align my wristfold that puts the clubshaft into the right place. The simplicity of the motion automatically takes care of setting the hands correctly.

A similar pre-turn was a feature of Moe Norman's swing that Craig Shankland pointed out on a broadcast from *The Golf Channel* recently. So when I saw that the greatest ball striker of my generation used that procedure, I felt my own idea supported by some pretty authoritative sources and worth mentioning here for others who might like to try it. Feedback to me from some pupils is that it simplifies the swing for them, as well.

- **Directing the Clubshaft by the Left Thumb and the Gripcap:** This has been said, but it deserves repetition. On the takeaway from the ball, using the left thumb to "aim" the clubshaft towards the tip of the right shoulder, and on the way back to the ball, aiming the grip cap down at and then along the target line, you absolutely control where both your hands and the clubshaft need to go to remain on plane. The ball is out from your feet for longer clubs, but the left hand continues to trace that other line, a "line *under your chin*" (or under your hand for a longer club)— a line *parallel to* your ball-to-target line, as you take your hand away from the ball. And then as the clubshaft starts to rise, the thumb aims the shaft at the right tip of the right shoulder. From there the correct way to get the center of the clubhead back to the ball is to direct the grip cap of the club— i.e., the 'end of the cord' of the sling mechanism we call a golf club— directly down at, and then along, the target line. "The toy follows the hand that pulls the string"— the clubhead follows the hand that pulls the business end of the club— the other end! In fact, you can aim the butt of the club with considerable precision if you focus on a spot on the ball— ideally at '4:30' on the ball since you approach the ball "from the inside." (Focusing on a spot also helps to block out other considerations that have no place in your mind during a swing anyway.) Once the backswing has begun in the right direction by what you do with your left hand and when its continuing movement up towards the right shoulder has become habitual, there is no other mechanical swing thought that is appropriate other than to direct your downswing motion down-line. That direction, and an exuberant, free motion, constitute all that you need or ought to concern yourself with during the "blackout" that is natural and appropriate once a swing is under way.

Summary of Impact Issues and Adjustments to Make

The sweet spot on the club face of most irons is usually a bit closer to the hosel of the club than to the toe, and about 3/4ths of an inch up from the bottom of the sole. If you have taken up the slack in the left elbow and the left wrist at setup, if your swing plane is okay, and if you do not move your back away from or toward the ball during the swing, and if you mis-hit the ball, adjust your setup as indicated on the next page to find the sweet spot on the clubface for your next shot.

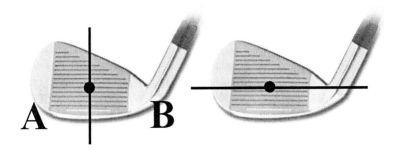

The vertical line in the first (left) diagram represents the center of the clubface between heel and toe. Impact toward the heel usually requires that you lower your spine angle at setup from what it was. This permits or brings the path of the clubhead on the way to the ball closer to your feet. Impact toward the toe requires that you raise your spine angle--the opposite--to move the club's orbit further from your feet. YES, SPINE ANGLE!

The horizontal line in the second diagram represents the vertical center of gravity of the clubface, and impact below it is said to be "thin," the remedy for which is to set your left shoulder closer to the ground at setup. Impact above the line ("fat") requires that you raise your shoulders at setup.

Impact at "A" requires to you walk a couple inches closer to the ball at setup; impact at "B" the opposite--i.e., you are standing too close and need to get your feet a couple inches further from the ball.

Pay careful attention to the 'length' of your left arm/ club unit, the amount of your spine tilt toward the ground, and the height of your shoulders, at setup. These are what you need to use as "base line standards" for measuring reliably for consistently centered impact, shot after shot.

Growing Little Swings Bigger

Progressing to longer, more energetic swings, and to longer clubs, requires patience and diligent self-discipline. The desire to 'test' your ability before you have developed it sufficiently will cloud the information and possibly leave hidden the reasons for mis-hits that **will** start to occur as you "get bigger." Lengthening a club, or adding amplitude to a swing, increases the difficulty of precision impact considerably, and if you take out *any* longer club at first and especially your driver to "see if it still works ok" without working up to it extremely gradually, you may have introduced any number of slight mis-adjustments from which it will be impossible to recover. The only way to "get there" is by gradual increments, because in tiny steps and small changes from club to club, the subtle differences and adjustments needed for precision can be discerned, whereas leaping to a longer club or greater amplitude in big bites tends to obscure their subtleties. Leaping ahead of your level of achievement is like starting integral calculus before you've learned multiplication— you will be in over your head. When that happens and you seek "tips" for help, they won't stick. You don't need another tip. You need to go back to the place where you *did* succeed, and then work your way up gradually. It is the only way to see what is needed.

Chapter Six

Gravity and the Pendulum

Cooperating With Gravity

One of the most important things that a golfer needs to know is how his body and his club respond to gravity in a golf swing. Since the laws of gravity cause a pendulum to swing at a consistent rate, grandfather clocks are made with them to keep time reliably. The golf swing uses pendulums— the arm(s), the clubshaft/clubhead, and, though it is not strictly speaking a pendulum, the body itself (an "upside down" one— it behaves similarly). I have made the point that cooperating with the laws of gravity, rather than fighting them, will work best. Walking itself operates efficiently for the very reason that we do cooperate with gravity!

We don't think of it that way, but obviously walking is simply falling forward to reposition our weight (the word for what we feel in the form of 'resistance' or exertion in our muscular system as a result of gravity) from foot to foot successively. Very early in our lives we learned how to manage our muscular responses and timing so that we can walk easily and relaxed, totally unconscious of how we so easily remain in balance. We also have learned to do it with the least amount of stress or effort by keeping our legs fairly straight. Our neuro-muscular system has instinctively learned how to use our weight shift and our limbs efficiently. If we had to be "taught" to walk and to anticipate and manage all of the intricacies walking entails, it would be an enormously complicated endeavor. But it was not like that at all: cooperating with gravity is something all of us learned by instinct long before any cognitive processes were at work.

This is a good time to clarify part of what David Lee means by his use of the term *Gravity Golf.* Let me make my point this way. If I were describing walking to an alien just arrived here from an entirely different universe than this one in which gravity is a basic, and if I chose to characterize it as "Gravity Walking" in my explanation, he could believe that I was describing a personal system, especially if a "walking teacher" down the road used a different approach called by another name, say "The Ten Step Method". But the operation of gravity in walking is not a personal system at all *nor is walking learned by method It is learned in response to a need to perform a function with our legs that enables us to move from place to place. It is discovered by the subconscious of a child as he attempts to perform the function and not in obedience to theories. Its underlying principle to which the body responds in order to accomplish the goal desired is simply to respond to the force of gravity by falling* from one foot to the other successively and timing the placement of our feet and the exertions that keep us erect. I make this point for a very important reason while on this subject, because form follows function, and learning to do something that accomplishes a dynamic action requires that we approach it not by mimicking visible elements but by understanding the underlying forces and dynamics and then applying them effectively, regardless of incidentals in their appearance (everyone's walk is personally idiosyncratic and different from everyone else's.)

In the same way, then, *Gravity Golf* is simply a name for the explanation of universally operative, natural principles that have a great deal to do with swinging a golf club efficiently, and by that emphasis it differs from teaching that ignores it, is unaware of it, or works against it. David did not invent gravity. He does not tell people to create it somehow. He *discovered its operation in great golf swings*, and for the first time in 500 years of golf shows how cooperating with and using gravity efficiently *does* make them great. (Isaac Newton's discovery of how gravity works in the universe was published in 1687. David Lee published how gravity works in golf swings in 1994. Given that scientists knew tons about mathematics and astronomy two thousand years ago, the fact that Newton's discoveries are so recent shows just how subtle this concept of gravity really is, and why it took so long for anyone to discover its function in *golf!*)

So, since the body *is* used to swing a club, and inasmuch as the arms and club are pendulums, to be using them on a daily basis unaware of how natural laws of gravity and dynamics operate for good or harm in how they are used is to be severely limited. How unnecessary it is to spend a life clueless about it, and thus to struggle and waste your passion and energy, when a simple explanation and a little sensitivity can "eliminate the mystery!"

The following illustration will do more for you than tons of instruction books and hundreds of hours of ineffective and blind ball bashing. Using the lessons it contains will help you to *find* your most efficient mechanics rather than leaving you in the dark, perhaps to manhandle the club, and if you are in competition with nature, you lose!

The Natural Behavior of a Pendulum

Picture Mom swinging her two-year old daughter on a playground swing. She gets the swing going easily at first. She instinctively knows exactly how much energy she needs apply to get it to swing all the way to the top (or however high she wants it to travel) *and no farther*, and then how and when to "help it" on each successive stroke to keep it in a quiet and exuberant orbit. Notice the following things about this swinging pendulum and how perfectly Mom manages it:

- Mom's stroke to get the swing just to the top and not too far is instinctive and unpracticed: she *just does it!* Obviously she doesn't want to throw the baby out of the swing with a violent heave that could propel the child over the bar! And her stroke is an energetic enough shove to get it up there, though brief and limited— she does not *carry* the swing to the top. She does not push the swing 'low and slow.' She **swings** it!
- She never "slams" the swing out of its smooth orbit with a premature or ugly jolt or "bump." Her stroke is gentle and gradual, while at the same time vigorous enough.
- She never had any lessons on "how to time" it or how hard to push— her instinct about *how much* effort to apply,

how to apply it, and *when* to apply it gently enough not to jolt the child, was innate. And she had this sense at the outset without training or practice.

- She pushes the swing exactly in the same direction as its arc dictates (not down, not up, but perpendicular to the chains), yet the seat and child go 'up' and 'down' as well as in a horizontal direction at the bottom of the stroke, simply because the chains hang down from above and the arc of motion of the seat is tangent to them. Our arms hang down from and are attached to our shoulders above them in the same way. Such a structure defines the travel of our hands in the same kind of arc as the travel of the seat of the swing, namely to a circular/orbital path around its fulcrum. Our shoulders are the fulcrum of our arm swing, and the hook where the chain connects to the bar is the fulcrum of the playground swing.

- When the swing reaches the end of a stroke and the child has floated as high as that stroke carries her, the chains are without (muscle) tension. They are, in fact limp and unstressed other than pulled a bit by the weight of the child in the seat. For a split second, actually, the chains, the seat, and the baby hover in the air at the peak of the up motion, waiting naturally to start falling back down by the pull of gravity alone, which will occur in a quiet and pure orbit, because no force is applied to disrupt it.

- When the swing reaches the end of a stroke, the down stroke takes more time to start than we may be aware of before gravity changes its direction. If you observe that moment carefully, you may be surprised just how long its turnaround takes. Realize that nothing besides gravity acts on the swing to cause it to start back down. And like the tree falling over that was mentioned earlier, its initial motion and rate of fall is extremely gradual before it acquires much speed or momentum.

- When Mom receives the swing set into her hands in preparation for its next movement or stroke forward, she does nothing initially to move it: she simply *receives and cradles it* in *soft receptive fingers*, in an instinctively gentle action which will in no way jolt the swing, move it out of orbit, or jam it. And she knows how long to wait without any practice or thought whatsoever before adding forward moving energy for the next stroke. Note here that I am not saying that there is no force acting on the swing except gravity. I am saying that her application of force occurs after gravity has set the swing into motion. Want to be a great golfer? Then treat your clubhead and golf swing the way Mom treats the playground swing, by waiting for it to start. *Then* apply your considerable force in a smooth manner.

A Drill to Learn Pendulum Stroke Timing and Efficiency

I'll take each of the above points and apply them to this drill one at a time, and I urge you not to minimize the importance of any of them. The first step is to create a moving pendulum with your left arm and club, because to understand your golf swing you need to use its vertical component (arm swing) of the basic swing drill, to which you will of course add the horizontal component taught in the baseball swing drill (body rotation) for your finished normal golf swing. After you have set the club in motion as directed and as soon as it is clear what to do, *you are to cause all motion of your arm and club through torso rotation, without any left arm exertion at all. All motion of your arm and club is to be caused by gravity acting on your arm and club, and the rotary movement of your shoulder, to which the left arm is attached. The pendulum is to get its motion and energy solely from weight and from torso turn pulling the fulcrum of the left armclub to and fro.*

Using only your left hand to hold the club, while you are bent over a bit take your grip as you did in the drill in the third chapter, and with your arm hanging straight down under your shoulder and the clubhead at least 6 inches off the ground (choke up a little on the grip if you need to), use a straight left arm and start swinging your shortest club back and forth, *continuously to the right and left without stopping between successive strokes*, no more than enough to carry the butt of the clubshaft to chest high on the backswing, and perhaps a bit higher at the end of the forward swing. The motion is to travel no further back nor no further forward than what you see in these next two pictures.

In your backswing, roll your wrist to the right about a half turn and deliberately with hand action fold or cock your wrist to get the clubshaft into a 90 degree angle with the left forearm. In

the forward motion, roll your left arm to the left a half turn and swing it forward allowing the release and a 're-fold' of the clubshaft to where it is again 90 degrees to the left arm. With very very gentle effort during this continuous back-and-forth swinging, maintain an extremely quiet orbit without jolting the club in the least, so that it behaves like the playground swing, without wobble, jolt, or interruption. And as said earlier, do not bend the wrist backwards to cup it more than its natural dish angle (the folding of the wrist may *seem* to cup the wrist but it must not *increase the amount of cup that existed naturally)*, nor try to flatten the hand into a straight line along the hand and wrist.

(A picture in Tiger Woods' book, *How I Play Golf,* clearly shows a dish angle at the top of the pictured swing, so you will be in good company if yours is also obvious.) Let whatever dish angle that exists naturally when you take the club in hand remain during the motion. It is critical that you neither scoop nor hood the clubhead during any part of its motion or allow any change in the angle of the back of the hand relative to your left forearm.

Some cautions: Nearly everyone getting started in golf applies far too much energy against his club shaft and to his arms, jolting the swing and the clubhead with the following results:
- The club wobbles out of a smooth orbit, and
- The clubhead gets heaved with some violence, and often too far, thereby requiring muscles in the hands, arms, and shoulders to become activated and engaged in order to stop it from whipping around and traveling beyond its intended "top of the swing" hovering point, causing a jolt and a wobble in the orbit before the downswing ever gets a chance to start! Don't think damage isn't done, at any level of play, when the clubhead gets thrown further back than just barely enough to arrive to a 'quiet top.' The tension-producing "grab" necessary to start a club back down will tend to knock it out of orbit and

cause a mis-hit, using up potential down-cock prematurely, and disengaging the body mass from the clubhead, the result being to deliver less energy to the ball on all three counts!

- Those who try to take the club back "low and slow" actually engage, and *leave engaged,* muscles that ought to be idle and relaxed at the top, since they "put" the club up there: they did not *swing* it up. *Putting* it there, as opposed to *swinging* it there, fails to trigger athletic reaction, where the whole body feels the weight shifting and responds unconsciously to that. In addition, this reaction is important for your subconscious mechanisms to install good motions into <u>habit</u>. The impossibility of thinking your way through a golf swing is obvious, and the solution is to tap into the same part of your brain as is used by musicians and others who need to be able to act virtually instantaneously with reliable precision, namely your neuro-muscular response system. I have mentioned your 'IRS' earlier in reference to your nervous system. It can and will work against you when you haven't dealt with details that need attention. In this case, you *need* to make it your friend for reliably embedding good and mostly automatic habits!

These things then require the following of you:

- Use sensitivity and "pendulum awareness" like Mom's with her swinging child. To master your swing, treat your arms and your golf club with sensitivity to their dynamic (i.e., "in-motion") natural behavior so that you can respond to it in motion, rather than to try to overpower your natural rhythm or the direction momentum carries your arms. When you swing simply and relaxed without making an effort to direct the club, it is more likely to find a swing plane by itself that is natural to your own body and fits your girth and your range of motion.

- Use this natural and easy motion therefore to find the swing orbit that does fit your body by letting your arms and the clubhead travel up and down as vertically as you can comfortably manage. It is because the most powerful and naturally recurring path our hands choose to travel (as for example, when instinct is allowed to control them) *is* on a much more vertical plane than most people use, one where the left arm especially is very close to the chest and where the arm may even press against the left breast. Let the pendulum's gravitational fall and momentum show you *where* it wants to travel and the *rate at which* it wants to move and release.

- Let this exercise teach you how your *hand* must travel *up* in the backswing with very little slant away from perfectly vertical. Body turn and left wrist rotation to the right are what moves the clubhead correctly *around* you in an actual golf swing where the plane is slanted, and where the clubshaft does not travel exactly vertically going back. The clubhead *will* travel in its correct swing orbit if you do not move your left hand away from 'the wall sitting on the target line' going back, because such a motion back from the target line more than just a little moves the hands and the club off plane!

- Don't use much exertion in your body turn at this point. Use only enough to provide the energy for this amount of arm and club motion, and attempt to eliminate exertion in your left arm or shoulder. Your arm simply hangs, your fingers hold on, and the club gets "thrown" by your turning shoulder. (You may need to help the release and the refolding of your wrist deliberately to achieve the shape you saw in the photos on pages 198 and 199. Do use deliberate and forceful forearm rotation if there is any question that you may be wrongly scooping *under* instead of correctly rolling *over* the 'ball.')

This exercise will help you discover how your swing is eventually going to be shaped and how it will fit your body. It will become clear to you as you simply swing the club in this way 1) how it wishes to move when unaffected by inappropriate exertions applied to it; and 2) how it will help you find an efficient and easy orbit if you are gentle enough with it to respond to its tendencies to locate what path it seems to swing the smoothest by tapping into the principles of timing that are explained here. It is just an exercise at this point: your final true swing orbit (where clubs are too long to hang directly under your left shoulder) will be on a more slanted plane, like the illustration in Ben Hogan's book of a pane of glass with its edge running approximately along the target line and through the ball, tilted and resting on your right shoulder.

You'll discover how it travels at its own tempo— ("the law of the pendulum")— and you either find it and cooperate with it taking its "own sweet time" in making its stroke, or you will have to fight it, and probably not come away unharmed.

You'll discover how long it takes at turnaround at the top before it starts to fall.

You'll discover that you don't need to yank it down from the top. You need for it to start down of its own accord by the action of gravity on it, and then you will assist it with far less effort (applied by torso turn) than you imagine is necessary (did Mom jolt the swing?).

The next step is to gradually increase the energy of your torso turn during the downswing and experiment to find out how fast you can swing the club using shoulder turn only, while your arm and shoulder muscles remain relaxed and idle, allowing only for enough firmness in the left elbow to prevent collapse. Feel yourself using body rotation to produce the movement of your arm and club, and continue to increase your body turn speed until you have reached your best effort— again without pausing between swings. The drill is done best as a continuous to and fro action without stopping. Jack Nicklaus years ago characterized *his* swing (golf *his* way) as the turning torso pulling the arm pulling the butt pulling the shaft pulling the clubhead, so there is certainly nothing new in this drill at all. My emphasis is to have you use it to isolate and clarify how the concepts of a pendulum and gravity work in conjunction with body turn as the energy that moves the clubhead.

The IRS Factor at Work at the Top of the Swing

Backswing energy and the 'quiet top' When you initially exert muscle to get your backswing started in normal practice and play of the game, you need to use only enough thrust, throw, heave, or swing (choose the word you feel is the best descriptor of that initial effort) to cause the club to arrive at its top-of-backswing position by floating there, but not enough that it has to be stopped from going too far back by muscular action— by any kind of grabbing, or with enough energy to cause the L wristfold to dissipate or flatten. As said earlier, do not take the club back "low and slow" if you want to accomplish the most efficient backswing preparation for the downswing, since it leaves exertions in your arms and shoulders until the top of the swing. *Those* active muscles signal to the brain "USE US!" But you don't *want* to use those: you want to have the downswing proceed by gravity fall and torso turn, for the most part, with the arms simply following the lead of the pulling shoulders. They need to be held firmly enough to keep them from collapsing during the forward swing, but *they* do not move the club. The opposite golfswing technique than that described here is the 'grab the club with two fists and swing that sucker' procedure used by many retired professional baseballers. Charles Howell, at half the body weight of a few of them, shows how erratic and inefficient that is by comparison, with his prodigious distance. Anyone wishing to play at tournament level will need to pay particular attention to this aspect of the swing, since subtle differences that can affect their scores by only a stroke or two over eighteen holes will determine their future.

How to "Build a Swing" From This Drill

After you have learned how not to *move* the club at all with hand, arm, or shoulder muscle, but only with torso turn and gravity, after you have learned to float to the top because of the energy that you created for the swing only at the *bottom third* of the backswing, after you have learned how long you need to wait for your body to fall back onto the left heel before starting your leftward torso rotation, after you have learned how to wait for the club and your arms to begin their fall down by gravity, after you have established a perfectly quiet "top" of swing behavior of the club (no wobble, no disruption of orbit, no "yank", jolt, or jerking of the club), and after you have learned how to help, not jolt, the forward motion of the club by it being pulled by the arm being pulled by the torso turn, then, do this, still with the left arm alone:

Put about five whiffle balls in a row in front of you, teed up, or sitting up in the grass. Before you strike any of them, get little continuous swings going back and forth (no bigger than the swings in the above drill), and make several passes at a spot on the ground a couple inches closer to your feet than where the first ball sits. Make continuous, uninterrupted "practice swing passes" at that spot in the grass, and monitor your motion during the exercise for any intrusion of tension, and to ascertain that you are doing what you're supposed to do. When you think you've got it right, without any break in the back and forth swings you are making, inch over during mid-swing to permit the swinging club to pass through the spot where the first ball sits, without adding any muscular action of the arms. Do nothing different in that particular stroke than you did in your practice strokes. To put it another way, if the club moves any quicker or starts forward earlier than it did in the practice swings, it is likely because "Yew hailped!" (the IRS factor at work again), and you muscled the club instinctively by virtue of the incredible trigger to your unconscious caused by the ball sitting there waiting to be walloped! The "hit" instinct in golf is a significant hurdle in trying to learn physics-perfect mechanics, and this exercise is another opportunity to address it. Without any break in your continuous swing pattern back and forth, back and forth, keep making several "dry practice swings" near where each ball lies. When your little *practice* swing is perfect, inch over to the next one and let your swing pass through *that* "ball place," picking up *that* ball. Continue this, and hit each one in turn. Do this exercise often and for several minutes each time. It is one of the best available to help you eliminate the "hit" instinct from your procedure and to enable you to use your most efficient, probably nearly perfect, 'practice' swing. Wouldn't it be wonderful if we *could* always hit the ball with the same swing we use without any ball to hit. Well, we can, and this little drill is one of the places where we learn how to do just that.

Using continuous motion back and forth, you will be able to tune into the dynamics of a swinging club and cooperate with its natural behavior. Let the club teach you. Stay with it until you can do this drill perfectly with no impulsive muscular actions at all from the time you start swinging until five, or even ten, balls have been successively struck in this manner.

The Right Arm

When you have learned what to do and can do it pretty well with the left arm alone, then it's time to do it with your right arm alone—the same drill, with all the same disciplines as above. But now choke down with your right hand and aim your palm at the target. Your right arm will be nearly straight as it hangs down, not bent as in a regular swing, simply because the left hand isn't on the club. Remember that when your right hand swings, your torso (I like to use my tummy) will "pull" that arm forward the same as it pulled your left arm forward. I find that using the image of my *tummy* for the forward motion a better swing thought than my shoulders because it is less likely to trigger the use of muscles in the shoulders in the forward swing. There is no muscular connection between the stomach and the right arm!

Do this drill with your right arm alone in the same way you did the left arm swings previously, and train both arms to equal levels of skill for the purposes that have been explained. After getting the motion down good without hitting any golf balls, do the same thing you did when you set up a row of whiffle balls and strike each of them in turn, as before. Again, monitor yourself to see that you don't swing with different exertions when you strike a ball than you used in the dry practice swings.

The drills you have been given so far have equipped you with all of the necessary mechanics of a physics-perfect swing. You also should have discovered to some extent how *involuntary* motor mechanisms operate, and it is hoped that you have come to see how you can overrule or eliminate destructive triggers and impulses. And you are learning how to manage the exertions that produce the best results.

Apply Your Skill to Ballstriking

Now go to the driving range and "put these things to the test." During that process, keep a close eye on things so that you don't introduce viruses and let them become part of your swing pattern.

It is quite easy for someone else, even a non-golfer— even a child in the family— to tell when your "strike-the-ball" swing is different from your innocent practice swings. It will not be easy for you to be honest about it, though, so it pays to have anyone's help. "Yew hailped!" is evident to any observer simply due to any difference in your tempo or in any muscling you "commit" in your forward swing. So I suggest that you do ask *anyone* to observe you now and then when you are doing the exercises in the last section— or at any time, actually— to see if you are helping your swings by muscling— i.e., whether your strike-the-ball swings are different from your innocent practice swings. And this is not meant to imply that your all-out full swings won't have great energy or exuberant effort: quite the contrary. You will not swing easy. You will need to *swing as hard as you can* most of the time. But you will be doing it by cooperating with the efficiency of the laws of physics, not by trying to *hit* the golfball with a golfstick!

The instinct to "hit" being so pervasive and damaging, I would really like to be able to eliminate that word entirely from my vocabulary, since words act upon our subconscious instincts and aid and abet the IRS factor of our game. I prefer to use words such as "strike", "throw", "sling", or something along that line. One picture David Lee gave me was to imagine that the ball is glued to the clubface on the takeaway and that the forward swing *throws* the ball off the clubface. Another instructive picture is of a Jai Alai player, whose curved basket, the cesta, throws the ball (the pelota) by means of a roundabout total body-turn-throw. There is no striking of any kind, just a huge arc body turn with an extended arm. And I'm told some players can hurl the pelota at 190 miles per hour, which is faster than the speed of a golf ball that will travel 280 yards. I'm also under the impression that a hockey puck is propelled with tremendous velocity because of the "pickup" action similar to that of a golf clubhead picking up a golf ball, so it is no surprise to me that many hockey players are pretty good golfers.

Chapter Seven

Leftovers

The drills described so far are designed to ingrain physics-perfect swing mechanics. They also show you how some motor mechanisms get triggered and how to avoid their interference, mostly by using procedures in which they have no reason to show up. Your body can't obey a "don't do!" command, so by doing something *else* where what you are trying to avoid isn't even possible, you totally avoid the problem. For example, if you are 'driving west,' you don't need to "don't drive east." In addition to this, if you listen to, feel, and do the drills with attention to the instructions and information given about each one, you will be learning exactly which exertions and body motions you do need, and you will achieve a great swing much faster than when you do drills without a specific purpose.

Other Drills for *Perfecting* Your Skill

There are two approaches to drills that give you the most *improvement* in the shortest time, and I think we profit from both. One is to work and practice in the manner you have already begun, i.e., with specific, careful, detailed building of your swing, installing the basics, and then working gradually from easy to harder while being meticulous about impact and mechanics as you build, understanding and installing basic movements, exertions, and procedures correctly. It is serious advice that any time you want to improve, do basics better. Don't skip to the last pages of the book for some secret that only shows up later. The secrets **are in the basics, and with the correct adjustments (the critical details) correctly applied and installed.**

The other is David Lee's approach where you "Throw yourself into the middle of the ocean and swim, darn it!" and you are forced to learn good mechanics by virtue of the simple fact that while you do the drills you can't even make decent contact without using efficient physical actions during your swing, something you can only learn from trial and error. It is exactly how we learn to walk— i.e., by sheer blind struggle, groping, feeling, and adjusting during slowly emerging insight. He developed his drills over a twenty-year period in which he refined how to communicate his *Gravity Golf* discoveries and principles, and there probably isn't a better or more focused golf swing program that will work better to put the ultimate finishing touches on a swing (both the mechanical elements and the precision of centered impact on the clubface). The drills teach by feel, and while you may look like an idiot when you are doing them due to mis-hitting the ball *badly,* their instructional value in your body is enormous. (Incidentally, please don't beat up on yourself at *any* time you mis-hit during *any* kind of practice out of a misplaced embarrassment any more than you would beat up on your child struggling to walk.)

About David Lee's Drills

His approach addresses the most important thing about the golf swing by destroying results whenever any muscular action is applied to the club shaft or bad timing occurs from impulses or motions that work against purity of execution. Exertions other than those produced at the center of rotation automatically cause a disconnection between your body and the club and it disrupts the clubhead orbit. Their effect is similar to a passenger in the back of a speedboat trying to pull the water skier's rope when the engines cut off. Such inferior *effort* in the golf swing is not only futile, it also disrupts the path of the clubhead.

Drills already given *do* incorporate physics-perfect mechanics in this respect. Power is generated at the center and carried out to the clubhead. The arms are moved by body rotation with wrists and hands just holding on and with minimal downpull exertion. The right arm extends in a piston-push. No right-to-left shoulder, arm, or hand exertions are activated for *moving* the club— they *are* used to retain resiliency and must be firm enough not to collapse or weaken during the violence of a swing that is asked to develop clubhead speed of 100 miles per hour or more.

There is another phenomenon that is operative and that is central to his approach, which of course is hardly unique to David Lee, and which may seem to defy the laws of physics. Actually the theory may be faulty, but execution as though it is valid accomplishes an important part of how you get to hit the ball farther. And it is this: a fast clubhead speed using a flippy swing of the hands will propel the ball with less velocity than a slower feeling motion in which **body turn pulls tightly connected arms.** It is like trying to drive a spike with a tack hammer. No matter how fast the stroke you use to try to do it, a tack hammer just won't deliver the force available from a 2-pound sledge, which DRIVES the spike without effort. Your body mass in the swing provides the weight behind it to lessen the experience of effort. Recall the struggle you feel using a club too light or with a shaft too stiff where you don't sense, hence cannot respond *to,* the clubhead itself. You have to force it. You are not able to "let the club do the work," as we are advised. Body mass rotating can be said to relieve the other muscles of considerable responsibility for providing power in your swing, and this is another reason for the apparent ease of the swings that we admire the most. Which leads to the next point before continuing about David.

The Physics of Ball Velocity, and the Mandate to Maintain Pressure Through Impact

The formula to calculate the momentum of a moving object (simply, its energy) is the product of mass times velocity, and the law of "conservation of momentum ['energy']" ($mv_1 = mv_2$) means that whatever momentum goes into the collision is what comes out— after allowance for less than perfect elasticity of the materials in collision, where heat is given off in place of bounce. This is why technology seeks to put harder materials into the face of drivers without making them heavier. Incidentally, given the *laws* of elasticity, it is impossible for a ball to rebound at a velocity faster than clubface impact velocity, so in all the concerns about legality of drivers, there is a natural limitation to the potential rebound velocity from your equipment. It's simply impossible in nature that *any* rebound can be faster than impact clubhead velocity. As a side note, due to this fact, it would be hoped, and it may come to be, that we shall soon see limitations on the elasticity of the *ball* used in legal play or in competition, as opposed to attempting to impose restrictions on the coefficient of restitution of the face of the drivers we use, simply because it is easier to establish industry standards for balls than to monitor and test hundreds of drivers.

There are two concerns, then, for the golfer in his search for greater distance. The one is fairly obvious, namely getting the effective mass of the clubhead into the collision, hitting the ball on the sweetspot (the center of percussion) of the clubface. There is simply more weight delivered from that point of impact than from anywhere else on the clubface surface (the *center* of mass in the clubhead is back from the surface). More effective weight going into the collision itself means the clubhead gets slowed down less during the impact interval. Ball speed relative to the ground at separation is equal to the sum of the velocity of the rebounding ball and the velocity of the clubhead. So a centered impact produces greater ball speed relative to the ground than an off-center impact. Less obvious, though, is the reason why one swing will produce more clubhead velocity than another that seems to have about the same tempo and speed that *does* impact dead center. It was brought out earlier that the trailing hand's main function is to "help the pulling hand" to produce and maintain clubhead velocity. The reason for this was mentioned earlier. Stroboscopic films of golf swings show clearly that when the clubhead enters the "release interval," the hands slow down considerably. And this is due to a physical principle that requires the grip end of the club to *back* up as the clubhead *speeds* up. You can experience this yourself by hitting balls with the left hand alone; you just don't get the distance that you can with two hands on the club. Therefore the right side of the right handed golfer must apply force to prevent whatever 'backup' or slowing down of the hands occurs, as much as possible, and possibly to *add* hand speed to the effort.

Secrets of Crushing the Ball

During the release and impact interval maintain the pressure of the forward movement in your hands. Let your body continue to rotate, let your right side continue to press, shove the right wristbone hard against the fulcrum, and then attempt to compress the ball with your whole body's mass, not just hand speed! And contrary to other instruction, firm fingers, a firm left arm, and some 'stiffness' in the arms contributes more to a delivery of the effective mass than is the case with too light a grip and arms too 'loose.'

This use of muscles for firming the arms is, as you can see, not the same as using the right hand or arm to manipulate the club *shaft*. The turning hips provide massive power to the torso and thereby to the right shoulder. The muscles of the arms and hands need to remain "rock firm" in delivering that force to the fulcrum of the club. Firm pressure there helps to maintain the forward motion of the "handle" on the way to impact, and the catch-up speed of the clubhead is much greater in a swing with "a lot of right side" in the action. This and a late release explains the ball flight of those golfers we call "sneaky long" whose easy looking swings surprise us with how far they do make the ball travel— "perfect impact!"

Specific Gravity Golf Drills

David's drills include the following (using a 6-iron at first), and eventually using every club in the bag, including the driver, even for one-armed golf swings:

- Striking golf balls with full swings and with the fastest body turn you can muster with right arm alone, and then with left arm alone, wherein you monitor shoulder and arm exertions to eliminate their independent action;

- Striking golf balls set out in a long row on the ground, not on tees, 10 or 20, say, and without setting up to or measuring by feel to the balls at all, walking up to and striking each one in turn. He calls this form of torture "no reference" drills, because they exclude your ability to call upon "muscle memory" (the "proprioception" sensors) of your body, a faculty he feels is not in your best interest in developing your skill. So he devised his drills specifically to eliminate proprioception as an aide and to require that your eyes alone tell you where the ball is. This develops confidence in your hand-eye coordination. And coming *to* trust your eye is tough, especially when you first try to do it.

Do you wonder if indeed your eye can find the ball and direct you to it? Picture Michael Jordan tossing a basketball flawlessly through the middle of the hoop while falling backwards from 30 feet away. All he has available to direct his hand *is* his eye and the incredible computer in his head that translates perceived distance and direction into muscular commands of great sensitivity and precision. We all share this capacity *in kind*, if not in degree. Our optical computers are extremely capable, and we can trust them and we can train them. We *must* if we wish to achieve any significant degree of skill in golf, since too many factors work against a purely muscular memory procedure (which is used by blind golfers, incidentally)!

David's drills are done standing either on both feet or on the left foot alone, with either hand alone or with both hands. He advises his pupils to train each arm/hand separately and to develop the weaker of the two to the skill level of the stronger. The discovery David made that caused him to identify his work as *Gravity golf* is that most of the body's effective swing energy comes not from muscle in the legs, shoulders, arms, or hips, but from action of gravity on one's whole body. At the top of the swing your back begins to fall backwards away from the ball, like a hammer thrower who leans backward against the pull of the hammer in his arms during his pre-throw rotation, and that same use of his back triggers rotary action in a golfer. The reason his head doesn't appear to move back away from the ball while he is falling is that the gravitational pull on his back is offset by 25 lbs. of arms and club whirling around and pulling his chest forward *towards* the ball, in the opposite direction. It is similar to what you would feel if I grab the head of your club while you lean backward and hold on. If you relax enough you will feel the pull of your arms in their sockets, as opposed to muscular tension, and my pull will equal the amount of gravity pulling you backwards.

More About Timing

Timing has already been discussed in explaining how a pendulum moves. In reacting to gravity, it falls gradually from dead still at the end of its stroke to maximum speed at the bottom, and then it slows down again as it starts back up the other side to its apex where it again "stops." Such is the behavior of the playground swing, turning around at the top of both the forward and backward motions from the simple force of gravity.

The time for a complete back and forth motion or "period," as it is called in physics, is fixed by the length of the pendulum and by the constant amount of that gravitational force, regardless of the amplitude of the stroke. That behavior is called "the law of the pendulum," and as already mentioned, it is why clockmakers used them to keep reliable time. The force of gravity at sea level is such that a falling rock *gradually increases its speed* at the rate of 32 feet for every second it remains in motion. (On the moon, that gain in speed would be only 5 feet per second per second!)

Now here is why this is mentioned again. We are unaware that the natural rate of the fall of a body five or six feet tall (with its center of gravity about 35 or 40 inches from the ground) is quite slow, and that the natural time for falling from one foot to the other in a golf swing is about a second.

This means if you are in touch with the natural behavior of your body in response to gravity, and if you wait for it instead of forcing or muscling it over to the left foot for the beginning of your forward swing, it will take something approaching a second from the time you leave your right foot in your backswing until you get back to your left foot for the initiation of your forward rotary motion! Who has that kind of patience????

Answer: Freddie Couples, Jack Nicklaus, Ernie Els, Colin Montgomerie, and virtually all great swingers, that's who! So the lesson here is that most of us simply need to wait longer before swinging down, in order to allow the body to fall leftwards and the arms and club to fall downward before applying rotary exertion to the forward swing.

And there is another thing about timing that needs to be mentioned. As a trained pianist, I am aware of our ability to sense small divisions of time and to act on cue with great precision. Nearly everyone would march at exactly two steps per second if you asked him to step out in military march time without giving it any thought. One hundred twenty beats per minute *is* march-time— exactly two steps per second. And we are capable of discerning extremely small differences in musical tempo, which an artist uses to communicate very subtle differences in sentiment or emotion. This is mentioned because in the process of developing golf skill a golfer often installs his own personal timing and starts his downswing at a very specific moment that he has gotten used to. Sometimes such a start down is too soon. Thereafter the habit he has formed says to him, "Start NOW!" and without him being aware that it *is* simply habit, he will start down at the time he trained himself to do so **even if he has not completely finished his backswing or fallen back onto his left foot for the downswing.** The results of a downswing that starts too early are 1) it occurs before the arms or shoulders get back far enough, and 2) it is initiated before body weight has returned to the forward foot for correctly hinging the rotary turn of the torso and hips.

Collapsing (popularly called 'overswinging') An opposite problem is also possible, namely a subconscious desire to make the biggest arc possible, resulting in a 'broken' backswing. How far anyone should swing is dictated by his own range of motion and not in imitation of anyone else. Some people allow a joint to collapse (the left wrist, the left elbow, or the right knee) or the spine or legs to lift out of their correct position in an attempt to make the biggest backswing they can. But any kind of collapse destroys the connections and integrity of your body parts, and it ruins any chance for an effective downswing. We need to accept and use our own *natural* range of motion. So when any parts of the body collapse in order to take the clubhead back further, connection and control is lost.

As for not making a full backswing, I recently had a pupil with considerable flexibility who stopped his backswing and impulsively started forward quite a bit short of a 90° shoulder turn. I challenged him to wait longer (not to swing back further) before his downswing. When he did that, namely wait longer, his shoulder turn was even *greater* than 90°, and that was for no other reason than he *gave himself more time* before he started down. It happened by itself not due to effort, but simply due to his overriding the IRS control of his mental clock, which had previously started his forward motion too early.

Setup for the Release Interval Drill

The basic philosophy of the teaching in this book is that things are done at **setup** to enable and empower the swing to create perfect impact "automatically" without in-swing manipulation or contrivance. So in this next drill the *release interval* of the swing is isolated, put under a microscope, and perfected. Once understood and executed well, the rest of the swing is simply a larger motion, not a swing in which something *different* needs to be introduced. So getting more power will not require or permit changing anything at all but simply making this little drill bigger. It teaches you by working backwards from 'impact position,' in order to show you *its* relationship to what came first. Instead of correcting something during a swing where commitments that work against you were already in place before impact, the drill is designed to have you install *only* such positions and procedures that *will* permit and induce the desired results.

In the process of working with this drill you will make adjustments in some details of your setup to make things work the best. One of the ways to find the optimal setup you need for a good swing and the position that permits good *impact conditions* (especially as concerns the distance between your heels) is to *find and stand in impact position without any motion*— just to "pose" in the before-release, just-before-impact stance that you will arrive at *during* a good swing. It is instructive to do this for several reasons, one of which is that if you can't stand there *before* you swing, you will not be able to get there *during* your swing. If you know how it feels to be there for impact, you will also find or accept it more easily during your swing because it is a familiar place to be! So do it now while you're reading this! Even without a club in hand.

That position will include the following details.

- All your weight will be on your left foot.
- Your hips/tummy will already be facing toward the target.
- You will start the drill with the clubshaft at 90° with the left forearm, with the butt end pointing straight at the target and with the shaft parallel to the ground.

The Release Interval Drill

The release interval of the swing is the most critical part of your total swing motion. This drill isolates the release **position** of the hands and clubshaft you need to experience, which teaches more than words, pictures, or demonstrations by someone else.

Without using golf balls at first, start with your body in the first position pictured, which I will call a preset, and from there make short continuous, uninterrupted, back and forth swings with no break at the top of either the backswing or the forward swing. Make half swings only, where your hands travel only as high as your pockets in either direction— no further— and repeat this portion of the swing over and over again. Move the arms and club with body turn only, and let the hands and club just *react*. Allow the club to turn around at the end of each stroke by the force of gravity only in the same manner as the behavior of a playground swing, and then add acceleration to the motion by using body turn. Be certain you attain a 90° wristfold at the end of each short backswing and that the shaft *refolds* after impact, the shaft extending downline directly towards the target, exactly 180° opposite from the top of its backswing position. You will be surprised how little motion it takes to fling the club heartily in this manner!

Start the drill each time *from* that pre-impact position with your hands under your chin, with the clubshaft parallel to both the ground and the target line. Remember to position your feet and lower body so that you can stand still in this position with your weight already on your left foot and with your tummy facing the target. This will require you to allow your right foot to be pulled up onto the toe, with very little weight on it. Be sure that your left upper arm lays on your chest (pecs), and it may help to press your upper left arm rather tight down onto your chest. Move everything simply using torso turn, and allow the hands to get pulled and roll in response. In this drill you need to do some things deliberately, and to learn of others from feedback. Namely:

- move your hands straight back away from the target and then up while your torso turns (do not let torso turn cause you to move your hands further back away from the target line);

- as your hands move to the right and then up, use your left thumb to direct the clubshaft along a slanted plane whose edge lays on the target line and whose surface lays on the right shoulder— similar the pane of glass illustration in Ben Hogan's book;

- coordinate arm swing and body turn through impact;

- seek to discover how it feels to be on the left foot only during impact;
- cause the butt end of the club to move down and forward first, and then watch how the 90° wristfold remains almost until impact because it was not released too early;
- experiment a lot, and decide how to place your feet, knees and lower body before you swing so that you "*can* get there from here," ('there' being in the desired impact position). Arriving at the setup position that fits your swing to your body will involve experimenting with how narrow or wide your stance ought to be, whether either or both feet need to be angled out, and how erect or bent forward your spine needs to be for a free swing.

The Concept of "Parallel Left"

We are told to set our feet and body "parallel left of the target line" with the line across our feet running left *of the green.* Other than just plain missing the point— we don't aim with our feet, we aim the swing (i.e., the shoulders do the swinging, not the feet) by directing the movement of our hands *at the target.* Reliance on the feet to handle aiming is insufficient. Parallel lines (railroad tracks) appear to <u>converge</u> at 200 yards. Or put another way, if we align our bodies and swing precisely at the <u>pin</u>, balls hit truly straight and parallel to our bodies will land 30 inches or so to the right of the cup, since the ball at address was some 30 inches from our feet. "Parallel left" is simply parallel. Also, ball position automatically aligns your shoulders, so use a spot directly in front of your nose for placement of the ball for iron shots, because it sets your body squarely for an on-line swing path.

Notes

Chapter Eight

Driving the Golf Ball, and Power

The most seductive aspect of the game of golf is not the ability to score well. The truth is that for most of the fifty million who have been drawn into its black hole, it is the sound we hear and the feeling of ease and the satisfaction we experience when we strike a golf ball solidly, straight, and far, that gives the greatest pleasure. We feel good after a round where we have hit good shots even if we don't score very well and lousy when we hit a lot of bad ones even on those days when we did manage to scramble to a respectable score in the process.

Most of us instinctively believe it is effort that produces distance. By now I hope you realize that precision of impact is far more relevant, in that a mis-hit of as little as half an inch—

itself due sometimes *to* trying harder— makes a difference in distance of up to 100 yards in some cases. We press and strain in the effort to try to gain that extra yardage, but tension and interference from wrong exertions disrupt our precision. Actually we gain *more* yards with less effort using better technique and rhythm. Yes, more effort applied correctly and with precision, once you *have* built your skill with care, will produce greater distance, because it creates more clubhead speed and makes centered impact easier. The pros hit the ball **very hard.**

At a recent Masters tournament, people noticed that Jose Maria Olazabal had gained about 20 yards with his driver since his last appearance. When it was discussed, he had not changed either his club or his swing nor was he swinging faster, but had simply made adjustments that enabled him to improve impact. Instead of hitting toward the toe, he was hitting the ball in the center of the clubface.

Small golfers whose distance is most impressive, like Sergio Garcia, Ben Hogan, Annika Sorrenstam and Charles Howell, among others, are certainly not known for having remarkable strength (not to minimize that part of their talent), but they are *all* known for their finesse, efficiency, and accurate ball striking. And everyone needs to accept their own limitations, which cannot normally be changed unless a physical fitness program is undertaken.. What we can and need to do, then, is be cunning in the application of the subtleties, in keeping with the quip, "Old age and treachery will overcome youth and skill!" (When I said that once during a friendly round, one of the more experienced codgers in the group interrupted me before I finished, with "Don't forget greed!") Treachery is simply another term for practicing and playing smart.

So let's review what features we already know are important for achieving our own maximum distance, and then have a look at a couple of others— in other words, let's consider treachery first, again.

Tempo and Rhythm

Your tempo is the total time for your complete swing, from takeaway until you come to rest at the end of a follow through. A few years ago during preparation for a clinic I attended, while teachers and participants were swinging clubs and warming up, an observer came up to me and remarked, "You must be a pro!" I had nothing on to identify myself as one of the instructors, nor was the staff separated from the guests. I wondered what made her make that comment, and after reflecting on it, it dawned on me the only thing she could have seen was how I was swinging slower than everyone else. It reminds me of how much the swings of Ernie Els and Freddie Couples are admired by nearly everyone. And in fact, it is due to their tempo and rhythm. Both the lady who spoke to me, and the general public, when observing golf swings like Ernie's and Freddie's, instinctively recognize and admire when a swing "cooperates with" as opposed to "fights against" the rate gravity causes things to fall and the laws of dynamic motion. Gravity does not make a tree fall instantly, whoom-bang! It be— ginnnns to fall ever so slowly, gradually picking up speed, which becomes serious gradually, and which produces its greatest speed, and hence massive force, as it gets close to the ground.

A body acts like a tree in two respects. Our *weight falls* from one side of the body to the other, and our center of gravity is quite high from the ground. Ernie and Freddie wait for the natural fall of their bodies to the left foot, before swinging down; they do not push themselves over to it. This is what distinguishes their admirable swings. Rather than shoving hard to the left with the right foot, they simply allow themselves to fall a couple inches to the left before the downswing, and that is caused by the imbalance of the body leaning toward *but not standing on* the right foot at the end of the *backswing*. Then, like the tree, the body's fall to the left is not hasty or impulsive. The pause or delay in falling to the left also resembles the float and natural turnaround of the playground swing which falls back to the ground after a quiet 'pause' at the top. When we try to imitate that with a golf club, we realize it takes more time than we are aware before it starts to fall back down.

Advocating such a tempo— i.e., one in cooperation with the speed of gravity, is not to advocate a *slowswing*. There is a big difference between the total time of a swing and its *clubhead speed at impact*. I realized once when I was cracking a whip that I made a louder crack when I *approached* the "snap" of my wrist with a *slower* arm motion than when I rushed my arm. In other words, the 'crack of the whip' was loudest when my 'swing' prior to 'release' was leisurely. When I rushed my arm on the way, the noise I created was less.

Often a golfer will mis-hit a shot and react, "I swung too fast." But the truth is simply that he swung too *early!* The ramifications of this will be made clear when you consider the geometry of the golf swing's arc around the pivot point in the body. If the weight is back toward the right foot, the hinge or pivot occurs around the right side. The club path is closed to the line of flight when the ball gets struck in that manner, resulting in the dreaded over-the-top slash to the left of the target line. And it results simply from swinging before sufficient time has elapsed for the weight to fall to the left foot, because if the wait time is sufficient and the body's weight *has* fallen to the left foot, the hinge or pivot occurs around the *left* foot and hip, hence the arc of the swing is down-the-line. It simply cannot *be* over the top from there. In view of this, **once on the left foot,** it becomes clear that not only is there no need to "swing slowly," there is every need or advantage to swing as fast as you can so as long as you remain in control.

Stance For learning your swing, you have been advised to keep your feet fairly close together, because this enables your lower body to turn freely, and it trains you to balance in the same way that removing training wheels from a bike is necessary for a child to learn how to balance himself. When you wish to launch long drives, however, a narrow stance may not allow you the exuberance and energy possible with a wider, more stable stance. If you find that by spreading your feet further apart that you can swing faster, by all means do so. You need to test how wide you can stand and still turn easily, and your stance is too wide if you experience a 'bump' getting over onto your left side in the transition (your weight needs to slide smoothly to your left leg) or if your lower body does not turn automatically and easily to lead and power you. Experiment with flaring one or both feet, also. A flared left toe permits more body turn for the forward swing. (John Daly flares both feet somewhat.) And a right foot toed out (to the right) makes it easier for the upper body to turn further to the right for a longer backswing. It is a good idea to experiment with your feet in various positions to see what feels the most comfortable and permits you the fastest and most effortless swing and sufficient freedom to turn your hips in either direction.

Rhythm is concerned with the timing of the movement of the parts of your swing relative to each other. Let me use another example from music to develop a point about the golf swing and power.

I can play the Star Spangled Banner "correctly" quite slowly, or I can speed it up a bit. Or I can play a 33 rpm recording at a 45 rpm speed. In each case the rhythm of the musical selection has remained the same— only the tempo was changed— speeded up. You know that it is the same piece. The temporal relationship between the notes as they are played is the same.

Now, suppose I am playing a melodic passage with a rhythm of "slow— quick quick slow— quick quick slow," and so on. I can change that rhythm if I want to simply by waiting longer after the 'slow' and hurrying, compressing, the 'quickquick' (it amounts to changing a half-note followed by two quarter-notes into a *dotted* half-note followed by two *eighth*-notes.) The tempo or pace of the whole passage remains the same, but both when the quick notes get started and how fast they need to be played before the next measure begins has changed. More time elapses before the first of them is played, but then when they do occur, the two quick notes take the total amount of time of what was, formerly, the duration of only *one*. The release of a good golf swing similarly should occur, not early in the swing (after two counts) nor slowly to the ball (like the two quarter notes), but later in the downswing (after maybe *three* counts) in a **very** quick-quick pace (like two eighth notes), *or even after the last count at the last possible moment in a nearly explosive acceleration* of the clubhead at the very last instant!.

This image of the timing of musical rhythm might help you to experiment with your swing. Consider swinging with less than full backswing amplitude and a slow downswing where you hold onto the 'L' angle of the clubshaft back from your left forearm, where you intentionally hold on without releasing until the last possible instant. Wait as long as possible, *then* release! It is easier to do this with short clubs, harder to do with a driver. But after you have done it with short clubs and short swings, it is instructive to *try* to do it with a driver, as well.

Another way to view this is to notice how much *distance the clubhead travels* before release begins. If a golfer's release begins early in his overall motion, speeding up the overall tempo speeds the club up only a little. But waiting longer before release can *by itself* cause or permit a much faster clubhead speed. How do Els and Couples and Howell do it? Aha— back to technique, that's how! So let's have another look at their treachery.

The drill in Chapter Three produced its *entire release* (from a 90° wristfold) *at the end* of a swing arc that began all the way up above your right shoulder. You made a full 90° angle at the top and it remained in place until after your left hand returned below your belt in your downswing. But by the time your hand had moved just a foot or two more to the left— to a point in front of your pants zipper, the club<u>head</u> moved from the height of your right shirt pocket to the ball— a distance of about 5 or 6 feet! And this happened naturally— as a result of what came before, not by some new action applied during release. You did not press against the clubshaft to make that happen. You did nothing to 'hurry the clubhead.' You simply pulled the *grip cap end* of the club down toward, and then along, the target line— and the release **just happened!** Understanding this phenomenon of natural release— as a result— is critical, and you manage and create it by installing all the procedures of that drill with care (cunning/ treachery), as opposed to ignoring their supreme significance by bullying the club with blind reckless exertions, applying force inefficiently.

The details, again:

- Take a grip that will permit the full 90-degree wristfold that you need to have at the top of the backswing.
- After an address which includes correctly measuring to the ball and finding a quiet balanced stance, set your swing into motion with a forward press—i.e., with a slight movement of your hips to the left.
- Allow your weight to fall back to the right in order to trigger a *swing* of your arms back and up. Use your left thumb to direct the clubshaft to its correct on-plane position at the top. *Lean toward* your right side and right foot, but do not move your hips to the right enough to fully *stand* on it, as your backswing proceeds.
- In your backswing, make a full torso turn (your stomach included) enough to get your *back* fully turned to where *it* faces the target.
- Be sure the clubshaft has achieved a full 90° relationship with the left arm, and be sure that you have taken up all the slack in your body and left wrist as your arms and hands float to their topmost position. While your backswing is slowing down at the end of its way up, fall back onto your left foot.
- Wait long enough for your body to fall onto the left heel (as opposed to hurrying leftward by pushing leftward with your right foot), and then let your arms fall **down** before any rotation occurs.
- Next, add rotation as seamlessly as possible— rotation of your torso, hips, and shoulders, which supports the

arms pulling down and around, dragging the club— while simply holding onto the grip, without pushing against the club*shaft*. Pushing will be done using the base of the wristbone of your right hand, moved by the right side of your body and applied to the top of the base of your left thumb, at the fulcrum. That point is the golf equivalent of the connection of the two arms of a numchucks, or the end of a fishing rod where the line feeds out.

- Direct your downswing with the left hand aiming the grip cap to and then along the target line while retaining your spine angle and knee bend so as not to change the distance from your sternum to the ball.

- What is known as a 'late release' will happen by itself if you do nothing to press against the shaft. All your exertion will have been applied to the fulcrum of the club as though you are trying to stretch the shaft and pull the clubhead lengthwise behind your hands. Any effort to help the clubshaft forward into the ball by pressure in or movement caused by the right *palm* will waste the mechanical advantage of release too early.

- Mis-hits are corrected *for your next shot, not for the shot you are making* by adjustments in your setup— and not by consciously steering or 'thinking your way through' your swing. It must remain the same as it was during your drills and practice. Use your learned swing, and make adjustments in your setup to fix impact faults. This kind of swing requires a different mental attitude than the "hit" mentality, in that you must overcome the IRS-driven compulsion to manipulate your hands or the club during your swing— this is what is called "steering," mentioned above. Trust your timing and release action by deliberately relinquishing control of it. Learning how to trust your swing will take care of itself when you have become accustomed to this approach. I like to say that your brain knows more than you do. Our natural coordination contains skill that works well without our having to think about the details that have been made into habit.

"Where's the Beef?"

A book on the golf swing without telling someone how to out-drive Tiger Woods and John Daly wouldn't sell a single copy, so I need to recount an incident that will help you to understand how to produce *your* most powerful swing.

I was working with a pupil (Bob) who had a background playing sandlot softball, a little tennis, and golf for a couple years. I asked him to picture himself in the following scene: he is five years old, playing in the leaves/pine needles in his yard with friends, mindlessly enjoying the exuberance of "being a kid," absolutely lost in the joy of play, as free and happy as he can imagine.

I asked him to make some easy, relaxed, mindless baseball swings (with his driver) at about waist level, with both hands, and then I challenged him to see just how fast he could spin around and yank that 'bat.' I asked him to forget everything technical and with the simplicity as that *of* a five-year old child to become "mindless," exuberant, un-self-conscious, and freely relaxed. "Bob, how fast can you swing that thing?"

Without strain, tension, muscling, inhibition, second thoughts, or steering, and after his body had paused at the back of his swing while he instinctively waited for his weight to load onto his left foot (which occurs when we *do* wait long enough for gravity to act on us at its own rate), Bob made a tremendously fast swing. His own natural coordination controlled the timing of the body parts and the release itself produced that speed *simply because he wanted to make the club go as fast as possible!* His wrists or hands or arms alone could not possibly have moved the clubhead as fast as the speed he produced using body rotation in this free, uninhibited, natural joyful exuberance. The velocity of the clubhead was a pure centrifugal result of the grip end of the club getting pulled by the hand being pulled by firm extended arms being moved by shoulder turn, and that beats muscling the club *shaft* every time.

"Bob, that was a 300 yard drive!" I told him. Obviously there was no golf ball there to strike— it was a "dry" swing. But if there had been, it would have been one tremendous drive!

My point is this. When he did not have any limiting and subconsciously driven need to steer the club to a ball, the swing was entirely physics-perfect— without muscular impulsiveness or inhibition (all of us have great practice swings!). Any steering (involuntary redirecting of the orbit to go to where the ball sits) or conscious muscular exertion in the arms or hands slows down the club, knocks it out of its own naturally pure orbit, and ruins the perfect motion that might have driven a golf ball 300 yards.

In order for *you* to achieve your maximum swing speed *you use to hit golf balls*, you must discover for yourself your own exuberant, free, uninhibited athletic readiness and *apply that* in your approach to the ball. First, ingrain perfect mechanics. Then measure well so that you *can* trust your setup for every shot and trust your eyes to find the ball during the swing. Eliminate unnecessary body motions during your swing that can move the swing orbit a hair or more out of its intended path. And rather than attempt to over-control/steer the club to the ball, trust the repetitive nature *of* your swing and the measurements of your setup in order to achieve perfect impact. Your attitude must be to swing with confidence, using the information obtained from the results of *previous* shots to make adjustments that may be indicated for your *next* shots.

Swing mechanics of particular significance

There are some things I wish to emphasize:
- maximizing your swing arc;
- taking up the slack at the top;
- using use of your right hand, arm, and shoulder;
- making the correct sequence of events during the swing;
- finding and using the driver best fitted to you;
- finding the club that gives you the best launch angle;
- positioning the ball properly;
- conditioning yourself physically.

Maximizing your swing arc The longer the amount of time a drag racing car has before the finish line, the more the speed he can reach by the time he gets to it, through constant acceleration. The longer your backswing, the more time you have to accelerate the clubhead.

Taking up the slack In a golf swing, the application of acceleration requires that there be no loose parts anywhere between the center of power of the swing and the clubhead at any time between the beginning of the forward motion and impact. The center of power is the hips, in rotation. And 'slack' exists when any body part does not get moved by hip turn. What you do, then, is simply hold firm with your arms and hands so that when the 'big motor'— the hips— acts (the water skier's tow boat), the hands are moved immediately (the tow rope is tight).

Maximizing the use of your right side The right hand gets *its* power from a firm right arm being pushed by a fast moving and firm right side. You often hear the phrase "fire the right side" to describe the driving force felt and needed for *that* hand to contribute its fair share. It will help if you picture that your right *arm* must not be allowed to drag, but *be pushed*, by the right shoulder. It does not lag behind but retains its relationship with your torso; it cooperates with the body turn. The right arm gets pushed into the ball. A camera above your head would record your right forearm moving around in unison with the shoulders turning— the angle between them remaining constant.

The correct sequence I need to emphasize here that the *correct* sequence of events permits the body to be in the most powerful position it can be for the application of its power— i.e., for its hip rotation. And it does this best not by twirling around the *spine, as happens when rotation occurs too early while your weight is still on your right side* (while you try to shove your hands from a planted right foot), but by getting *onto the left heel* before any rotation begins, and then using the mass of your body (for adults, between 100 to 250 pounds probably!) like the Olympic hammer-thrower who spins his entire body around his left leg and left hip. All powerful swings in golf do this.

Find the right driver While helping a pupil recently to buy suitable clubs at Wal-Mart, in his excitement he handed me a very beautiful looking driver from the rack and said, "Here, George, take this. It's inexpensive [under $40], and I want to give you something. If you don't want it, give it to someone else!"

His gesture turned out to be far more significant than I expected, because as soon as I hit the first ball with that club, I immediately knew it was the best driver I had ever had in my hands! It is as though the club found the ball automatically, and then launched it with more punch and authority than I had previously experienced with any club. Its launch angle was appropriate, my mis-hit shots deviated a lot less than with my other drivers, and it produced for me the most effortless and longest drives of my life.

I mention this for this reason: the correct fit of a driver is personal and I believe largely unpredictable. And obviously it is not related to price. And contrary to the 'book' on the appropriate shaft for my swing speed, the shaft on this 'best driver I have ever had in my hands' is quite soft.

When I told others of my experience with the club and allowed them to hit a few shots with it, nearly all of them went and bought the same one for themselves. And these people ranged from women with slow clubhead speed for whom 140 yards is a 'long drive' to men capable of 300 yard drives.

Launch angle We are told by physicists that a launch angle of about 13 to 15 degrees is the most efficient for total distance of most drives, taking into account both 'air time' and roll of the ball on the ground. There is a simple way to check the launch angle of your drives. It may not be as related to the club's nominal loft as you would expect. Get an old shaft from a golf club repair shop or by cutting off the head of a club you are discarding, and stick it in the ground at a distance of five times its height directly in front of where you tee up. Have someone watch your ball flight as you drive to see if your well struck shots pass above, below, or even with the top of the shaft. A ball launched too low hits the ground too soon; and one launched too high rises too much and drops too soon. Of course wind conditions and extremely fast swing speeds can have an effect on what is optimum for a given golfer, but using this procedure as a norm is quite reliable.

Recent studies have confirmed that most golfers are much better served to use more loft than they do. *Golf Digest* test results published in their November 2003 issue showed that slower swing speeds got *seriously* more distance with 16° loft clubs, and swing speeds between 85 mph and 115 mph benefited with 11° clubs over those with less loft. There are few golfers with 115 mph swing speeds 'whose egos will permit them to use an 11° driver' but their yardage could be considerably greater for it!

Ball position for the driver Because you want 1) to develop the most clubhead velocity for your shot (itself a function of the amplitude of swing arc before impact), 2) to hit the ball slightly on the upswing, and 3) to swing faster with a bit later release, it is a good idea to put the ball further left in your stance. Sometimes the best position is left of the left foot entirely, sometimes it is directly out from the toes, and sometimes it is out from the instep of the left foot. At the same time, if you have enough flexibility in your lower body to permit a full exuberant hip turn with your feet further apart than was suggested at the beginning of this book, it is a good idea to use the widest stance that allows you to make your full hip turn. Your added stability will permit you to swing with more force almost automatically, especially if your intention is to 'rip it!'

Physical conditioning and strength It is obvious that strength and conditioning are important to the serious golfer intent on taking his game to advanced levels. There are many excellent sources of this kind of information which is not appropriate for me to add here. A couple of things are worth mentioning however. They are the importance of warming up and stretching the muscles of your legs, your back, and your shoulders, before hitting any serious shots, and of course, the fact that stamina becomes an issue towards the end of a round of golf.

Range of motion— flexibility— does more for a golf swing than strength alone. A couple inches increase in backswing amplitude can easily make a difference of ten or fifteen yards on a drive. So you get a disproportionate benefit from a simple warmup routine before you practice or play.

Back injuries are common among golfers, so warming up and stretching have the additional benefit of helping you stay healthy.

Stamina permits you to concentrate and perform better both mentally and physically. And it is quite easy to establish and maintain stamina even as you get older. As I write this I am 71 ½ years of age, and I take an easy ride on my bike of about 5 miles (the total time is about ½ hour) 3 or 4 days a week. A recent physical exam showed my blood pressure to be 120 over 60, so I do believe that something simple like that kind of aerobic activity returns a *lot* of bang for the buck! And I selected that kind of exercise for a couple of reasons besides the direct aerobic benefits, namely that unlike running, there is no impact, and I prefer the outside and fresh air and variety to sitting on a stationary bike inside.

A few repetitions of standard arm and leg exercises also pays off with benefits much greater than the effort put into them.

A rule I use is never to do anything in kind or quantity that is unpleasant, and it is surprising how *it becomes easier and naturally makes me want to exert more* and do more simply by the good feelings I experience in the middle of the exercise. I *want* to pump my legs faster, I *want* to do a couple more reps, and I *want* the feelings of well being that are an almost immediate reward. My advice to anyone not familiar with the benefits from such simple things is, "Try it; you may like it!"

Notes

Chapter Nine

Direction and Distance Control

Direction Issues Related to Impact

Feedback from chalk or tape is used for diagnosis of impact, but feedback is necessary from *trajectory* to understand, correct for, and make precise, your control of direction.

Impact somewhere near the center of the clubface needs to be achieved before it makes sense to deal with the precise direction of your shots. Balls struck on any edge of the clubface are deflected wildly, and those struck on the clubface surface far from the center usually travel so short and erratic that interpreting their flight as a basis of adjusting the direction of your ball flight is not of much help.

If a ball is struck above its equator, it will obviously be driven down onto the ground and bounce forward. If a ball is struck on either the edge of the toe of any club, or on the hosel of an iron, it will shoot wildly to the right. Knowing which impact causes *your* wild right trajectory on such a shot is clearly very important, since correcting for toe impact requires a different procedure from that which corrects for hosel impact! A ball struck behind or under the heel of your club will dart sharply to the left, often bouncing off the turf (many drives from the first tee or over water are of this kind). And a ball struck on the top edge of a wood will pop up and travel high and short, depending on just how deeply the clubhead passes under the ball's equator. An iron shot struck high on the clubface sends a nasty shock to the golfer's hands *and* flies left, because it careens off the slanted top edge of the club.

All of the above mis-hits have to be understood and eliminated before you will be able to generate consistency in making good contact. When you *are* able to strike the ball fairly well, then you will want to read your ball flight and make adjustments to improve your accuracy and direction control.

You first need to understand how sidespin affects ball flight. It is always caused by a clubface that is not perfectly square to the line of flight at separation. Depending on how much the face deviates from square and on how much the ball lends itself to sidespin and reacts to it, any 'glancing blow' *will* cause some sidespin and curvature in flight after its initial launch. There are several trajectory possibilities. A ball can start right if the path of the club at impact is to the right, and then it can turn in either direction, or it can remain straight on that line. Or it can start straight at your target or left of it and then turn in either direction. Any shot can have no sidespin, in which case it will not curve in the air after it starts out straight or to the right or to the left. Or after it starts in any direction, it can curve left because of counterclockwise spin (hook spin), or it can curve right due to clockwise spin (slice spin).

There are only two issues involved in managing the direction of a ball struck near the center of the clubface, namely the *direction of the path of the clubhead*, and the angle of the club*face* at the instant the ball separates from it (after a very brief "impact interval" of about 5/10,000ths of a second). The initial direction and then the direction of any curve in its flight will both be immediately obvious. However it is not obvious how *much* of the initial direction is due to the angle of the clubface and how much is due to the path of the club in their collision. Dave Pelz's research has proven that in *putting*, the angle of the clubface is more responsible for the initial direction of the ball (where sidespin is virtually irrelevant) than the direction of the stroke. But experience shows that small deviations from square-to-the-line on *full* shots has little effect on initial direction, and the effect of those deviations only shows up in the curvature of the flight of the ball. So it requires judgment from experience to know how much the initial direction of your shots is due to clubface alignment either left of, or right of square-to-the-target line. After you learn how to adjust *for* straight ball flight by making small changes in the strength of your grip, you can then adjust *to deliberately shape your shots* by using a weaker or stronger grip to automatically produce the fade or draw you seek. When experimenting with weakening and strengthening your grip to find out how to 'work the ball,' realize that the initial direction of the flight of the ball *will* be affected even by a slightly open or closed clubface, so if you wish to fade your shot around a tree on the right side, for example, be sure to aim enough left *of* the tree so that the open clubface doesn't actually start the ball at the tree itself. The open clubface will *both* change the initial direction and cause a fade, so you need wiggle room in addition to what you are allowing for the curvature of the ball in flight!

Alignment and Direction Control

You have been shown how to control direction by monitoring your club's path through the ball, namely by tracing the target line with your left hand, and then adjusting the strength of your grip based on feedback from ball flight so that the ball flies dead straight on that line. In addition to using this procedure routinely and on a daily basis with ever more care and fussiness, there are a couple of other things you can and need to do if you wish to attain a high level of skill. They are that you choose your target line with care (using something on the ground in front of and close to the ball as an intermediate target), especially in driving, approaches, chipping and putting (did I leave anything out?), *and* **that you always use the same tempo and rhythm.**

The rate of closure of your clubhead into impact is related to rhythm. Any variation in your timing will either hasten or delay the rotation of the clubface (slightly or a lot, depending on how erratic the rhythm for a given swing), hence changing the alignment of the clubface at the instant of impact, and with that, the direction of the ball. So you need to spend a good deal of your practice time to focus on and develop the rhythm that best suits your own personal temperament and preferences. We often hear about tour golfers who practice on a daily basis for hours at a time just hitting wedges or bulleting 4-iron shots, all in the quest for the consistency that requires a repeatable and unchanging rhythm.

Ball position and direction

A ball played too far back in your stance will be struck before the direction of the clubhead gets parallel to the target line, while the clubhead is moving on a path out towards, instead of along, that line. So a ball placed too far back will be struck as the clubhead is still swinging to the right, and the ball will get 'pushed' right of the target line.

A ball played too far forward in your stance will be struck while the arc of the clubhead is moving to the left, and a ball struck from that position will be 'pulled' to the left.

Because of the nature of the curving path of the clubhead, then, you need to place the ball where its path is directly at the target. If you have made a proper weight shift onto the left heel for the forward swing, you have placed the hinge of rotation of your body onto the left side of your body, and that hinge position is the center of the arc of your clubhead. So it means that the arc of your swing will be on line as your clubhead passes your left heel, approximately even with the left side of your head. It is also the point where the clubhead reaches the lowest point of its arc ('low point') and where its path changes from downward to upward.

With an iron, there is sufficient tolerance, and good reason, for placing the ball approximately opposite your nose in front of you. It is because the downward arc of your clubhead early before low point makes it easier to catch the ball cleanly than would be the case if the ball were closer to low point where the path of the club is just about level with the ground.

However with longer clubs like your long irons and fairway woods, their flatter trajectory permits the ball to be played a bit more forward, closer to low point. And due to the slower rate at which the clubhead closes on swings with the longer woods, it is more likely the clubhead will arrive 'on time' than if the ball is placed earlier, namely, more to the right.

For a driver, a *more* forward ball position is necessary for you to achieve on-line and square contact. It is due to the slowness or lateness with which a driver head does close or arrive in line with the left arm. It is also because when driving the golf ball you normally stand with your feet further apart— with a wider stance— with your weight and your hinge at impact more left of the center of your stance than with your other clubs. It explains one of the most common problems off the tee for many golfers, namely, a push-slice trajectory— a ball flight starting right and then curving to the right even more. And almost always the remedy for both the push and the slice path of those shots is simply to tee the ball more to the left in your stance. So instead of having a swing problem, if you have this kind of trajectory, nine times out of ten you will discover it is a ball-position problem! Of course with the ball on a tee, you do not have to hit it before low point. The tee's height permits the clubhead to pass low point and to be rising prior to impact, and that adds other benefits to your drives, such as a higher launch angle, less backspin, and greater clubhead speed. SEE THE DIAGRAM ON PAGE 311.

Distance Control

Full shots: Calibration of the distance you hit your irons and woods for full shots is an ongoing and flexible process. When you have achieved some consistency and confidence, you of course record a range of distance you achieve with full shots for each club. I say range, because depending on how warmed up, energetic, strong, or exuberant you feel at various times on different days, the impact-to-impact distance of your 'full effort' 7-iron may actually vary by 20 yards or more— say from 125 to 150 yards (or 140 to 170 if you are a longer hitter), simply depending on 'how you feel,' the temperature, the moisture and heaviness of the air, the altitude, and other factors. Most of us also overestimate the distance we do hit our irons, and for that reason it can be stated categorically that missed greens in amateur play can be attributed to under-clubbing 90% of the time. So it should go without saying that honesty in the creation and use of your calibration chart is important.

Calibration requires that you find a place to practice where you have accurate distance markers, or some other way in which to determine the distance your balls travel. Many of us now own laser range finders which are extremely accurate, and if you are able to place something at the spot you hit *from* and then read back to it from the center of a cluster of well hit balls, or count paces (normal walking steps) to the center of that cluster, you can record *quite reliably* (by converting your steps to yards) the distances you are striking the ball with each club. As I said earlier, when you choose a club for a given situation, you need to be realistic with the expectations you place upon your game and to take into account the conditions of the day and how you feel. And you will soon discover quite a lot of variation day to day. Wind is, of course, a force to be dealt with, and you will experience situations where your club of choice can range from driver to 6-iron, for example, simply because of its intensity and direction.

Keep your chart or card with you and use it. Be prepared to make changes in it as your skill improves or if you lose some of your distance or if you use different clubs. Note the range of 'impact-to-impact' distance of each club in your bag, information which is sometimes critical for flying a bunker or water hazard, for example, or dropping an iron shot onto a particular part of a tiered green. You will also discover that different types and brands of balls produce different distances, and allowing for *them* is equally important, especially for distance control on approaches.

Let me promise you that you will have a thrill one day, after you have some accuracy in applying good information to your play, to discover that your 'guesses' as to which club to hit will be right on the money, and that indeed you are in one-putt range *on many holes per round* because you are hole high!

Less Than Full Shots One way to control distance for shots requiring a bit less distance than what you get with your normal full swing with a given club is to choke up on the club. Find out how many yards shorter the ball travels using the same full swing with each club but with your left hand an inch or two lower down from the grip cap. You may find a correlation that simplifies using this procedure, such as "choking up by one inch reduces distance by 8 yards" or something similar.

A preferred procedure for controlling distance for approach shots shorter than full wedge shots is to calibrate the distance you hit the ball with each of your wedges using partial swings, as follows. If with a full swing your left hand rises to the height of your right shoulder in the backswing, you will hit the ball somewhat shorter than full-swing distance when you use the same pace of swing but stop your backswing before reaching that height. For example, I did my own calibration by using parts of my body to mark the place to which my left hand travels on partial swings. I used breast height, stomach height, belt height, and pants pocket height. After hitting several shots with backswings measured to those 'markers' on my body and checking their distance (averaging the distance of the well hit ones), I wrote down the results and taped them on to each club.

So now when I have an approach shot that calls for less than full distance of any of my irons, I choose the wedge appropriate for the shot, check the yardage, and hit the ball with the backswing amplitude that produces the distance I want. It is far more reliable than guessing by using 'touch' or instinct.

Distance Control for Putting and Chipping

More and more instruction about how to control distance in the short game applies a simple concept of physics known as "the law of the pendulum." What it means is since the time for a complete period of a swinging pendulum is always the same, regardless of whether the stroke is very short or fairly long, the speed of a clubhead at impact will depend simply on how big the stroke, and not on muscular effort to control its speed, when the stroke uses gravity to govern its pace. This way you can control distance with an extremely simple process, namely, by first achieving a consistent pace in the same manner you did when doing the 'pendulum swing drill' taught in Chapter 6. Simply hang your putter or chipping iron between the thumb and forefinger of your right hand and swing the entire arm and club back and forth across your body several feet in each direction. It becomes clear immediately how the club responds to gravity, and in few moments you will be able to move your hand **exactly as fast as the club moves, and reverse direction at the same pace at which it turns around at the end of both the forward and backward strokes.** Like a mom with her child in a playground swing, you will be able, with attention, to time your own motion to match the timing of the motion of your club held in this manner, regardless of whether the stroke is wide or narrow. Note also that *the total amount of time for a stroke will be the same whether you swing it widely, say two or three feet back and forth, or with a short stroke of only a few inches in either direction.*

Putting When you *use* a 'pendulum tempo' stroke for your putting, do not try to swing faster for a long putt or slower for a short putt: instead, stroke *all putts with exactly the same pace, and in so doing allow amplitude alone to control the energy given to the ball. In that case, the ball will respond reliably by rolling the distance that tempo and that amplitude stroke make it roll because of the laws of physics and momentum. If you change the pace of the whole stroke and attempt to control it with effort instead of amplitude, your results will be less reliable as they will be based on instinct and impulse rather than physical laws.*

If you are an instinctively good putter in your control of distance, I will not suggest that you abandon your good touch for the sake of a mechanical and self-conscious stroke. But I do think it makes sense to use *both* your sense of touch *and* your chart as a way of keeping an eye on things so that you don't deviate into a procedure that may not stand up later as you get less chance to keep in tune, or after a break, such as over the winter.

Calibrate your putts by recording the average distance the ball travels with putts of 12", 18", 24", 30" and 36" backstrokes, for example. Count the number of actual normal walking steps from where you struck the putts to where they travel on a level surface. Allow for slower or faster greens as you make a chart (I have three different rows of numbers on mine, one for each kind of surface), and the chart is taped right on the top of the shaft of my putter. I consult it for every putt and adjust for slope, speed, and conditions. I always add one step to my distance to step to my distance to the cup so that I won't be short (most short putts don't go in), and I putt short putts with as much authority as possible to try to minimize any effect of slope, grain, and defects near the cup. If I miss a short one it should travel about 2 feet past the cup.

The most common technical error made by golfers is starting their forward stroke before allowing the time necessary for nature and gravity to reverse the direction of the backstroke. It was mentioned that a tree does not fall suddenly: it starts its fall gradually. A playground swing does not careen from the top of a stroke: it turns around gradually and *then* gathers speed. If you try to start the putter forward faster than nature wants it *to* fall forward, you cause a jolt in the connection of the putter to your hands, and the stroke is ruined, deflecting both the angle of the blade at impact *and* the pace of the stroke.

Another common problem is that of looking or even *thinking about looking* at where the ball will travel once struck. Even if you do not move your head, you may easily cause some slight muscular impulse in anticipation of looking up, and that again will cause a deflection of the stroke itself or of the alignment of the clubface. Often during a TV broadcast the camera will be focused on the eyes of the golfer during his putt, and the announcer will point out the virtue of those putts where the eyes do not follow the ball, and the problems that are caused when the golfer's eyes *do* move at or an instant after impact. In the latter case, the damage has already been done even though the impulses are tiny and invisible to the naked eye. But the golfer's *eyes* are the tip-off of the problem.

It should go without saying that making contact on the sweet spot is a critical detail, but I need to explain how you ought to hold the putter so that you minimize off-center hits. It is this:

you need to hang both your hands and the putter without trying to hold it in a fixed position, allowing it to find its own position by gravity acting on it. Then when it is stable, *walk yourself over to your ball, do not reach out for it.* By doing this you can allow the putter to remain hanging where it is automatically stable, instead of placing it into a driving lane that requires you to *hold it there with effort* to keep it from slipping into another lane.

Ideally, the ball should be directly under your eyes to minimize optical distortion. But this issue is about the tendency of the putter to 'change lanes on the way to the ball' if it does *not* hang. Effort to hold it other than as it hangs is jeopardy, and without perfect muscle control while attempting to hold it out there, it probably will fall back closer to your feet and create a toe impact, resulting in a "short right" putt.

Chipping By using the position of hands on a clock face as markers for backswing amplitude, it is easy to create a calibration chart for the clubs you wish to use for chipping. Record how far the ball travels for the same kind of strokes as is described above for putting, where gravity with a little help in the downswing creates a reliable and repeatable stroke, hence reliable distance control. Make a chart for how many steps the ball travels using 7, 8, and 9 o'clock backswings, and when actually using the information, allow again for slope and conditions using common sense. There is a jeopardy in hitting *to* a slope: an upslope can sometimes almost stop a chip and hitting to a downslope can cause a ball to leap forward. The common rule is to use a club that puts you past the fringe and onto the green as soon as possible, rather than one that flies to the pin. Shots higher in the air are harder to control, and their ball behavior is more erratic than when the ball rolls to the pin.

Chapter Ten

Chipping, Putting, Sand, and the Rough

CHIPPING

Since chipping involves short distances of ball travel and concerns about impact are not the same as for other shots, a different setup is needed. Common sense applied as to how we naturally go about wielding tools, understanding our instinctive reactions in sensitive motions, and the need to minimize potential problems give rise to the stance, setup, and the swing used for this part of the game. Chipping represents about 15% of the total number of shots you will execute in a normal round of golf— close to the percentage of shots with your driver!

So we establish a setup that will enable us to perform the function as easily as possible and that must deal with the following:

- the necessity to impact the ball before hitting the ground in different kinds of grass;
- the sensitivity of distance control, specifically that it is affected and controlled by solid, center impact;
- the clumsiness of the long golf sticks used for the purpose and the distance to the ball from our *shoulders* (to illustrate this concern I to ask my pupils if they would find it easy to do watch repair using three-foot long screwdrivers and tweezers);
- correct alignment;
- choosing the best tool for each particular chip shot;
- controlling distance using pendulum timing and technique, and amplitude of stroke.

Impact before low point Clearly the best way to minimize interference with the grass surrounding the ball is to approach it from above, as much as possible, rather than to try to sweep through it, where almost any grass off of the fringe is so deep that the ball would be partially buried (balls on the fringe often provide the easier option of putting them, but of course can, and often should, be chipped) and the club's momentum seriously jeopardized. So a ball position back just inside of the right instep, or even to the right of the right foot in some deep grass situations, is better. Your hands *need to hang under your chin* as already discussed so that there remain no tendencies for the clubhead to be disrupted by gravity or downswing forces, for the same reasons as for full shots and putts. Failure to let the arms hang for shots around the green can result in costly extra strokes many times in a round!

Since the ball will be on its way immediately after impact, *there is no need for the clubhead to continue with the kind of follow through normally associated with 'a good swing,' while there is plenty of reason to allow the club to hit, or even smash down into the ground after impact, instead!* There is a need to swing *through* the ball, but the club is often stopped in impact with the ground, and it helps to realize it will happen and fully accept it so you don't flinch. The instinct is to execute your chipping as a sweeping stroke, but that is not efficient in grass denser than what is on the fringe itself because it grabs the clubhead and disrupts the shot too easily.

This needs more comment because of a tendency of some golfers to scoop the ball instead of stroking it well. Many a club golfer will suffer several mis-hit chips *in an average round* where his club gets caught by deep grass on the way to the ball or by hitting the ball fat. This could cost him 5 or 6 extra strokes. And I am always struck by how golf analysts at professional tour events dwell on the difficulty of chip shots from deep grass, for that very reason. So you need to adopt and make habitual a procedure where difficulty is minimized.

My advice is, then, that you make a habit of *letting the club continue down after impact and get stopped by the ground* when the grass is deep, instead of trying *any* kind of through-stroke. The procedure for doing this is using body turn to move the arms and club, and in the forward stroke, after the wrists have received a minimal wristfold in the backswing, to retain that wristfold and let shoulder turn alone bring the arms and club back down through the ball. *The secret to delivering the club to the ball correctly is to hold the angle of the wristfold attained in the backswing with the right wrist bent back and then to use the base of the right wristbone against the left hand as the sensor that moves the club, while the arms and club act as an inflexible unit as the stroke is made.* Another way to key your stroke is to use

---

the left thumb to guide the club through the ball to control its line, and to hold your left wrist 'frozen' in its cocked position throughout the stroke to control impact.

These methods allow for a smooth body turn and a smooth stroke, and either one brings the clubhead to the ball with your hands ahead of the clubhead automatically for a clean impact. The club may or may not continue forward after low point depending on ball position and its resultant angle of attack (the angle between the clubshaft and the ground). In heavy rough, using a ball position further to the right, the lofted clubface descends onto the *'top of the ball' and* causes the ball to bounce up and forward. There simply is no need *to* scoop the ball, ever, for any conditions, because of the loft built into the clubhead. And to simplify your chipping, use the same technique for all your chip shots, whatever the lie, varying only the ball position according to the depth of the grass. (A sand wedge used in very deep grass is very effective in driving a ball out and onto the green....)

The following sequence of pictures shows the setup, backswing, impact, and follow-through of a chip shot you would make from the fringe or from fairway grasses. You would vary this by putting the ball 'back in your stance' even more when the grass is deeper and when you want the club to come down onto the top of the ball.

Centered clubface impact on the ball: It is critical that you eliminate any slack in the connections of your swinging mechanism (body, arms, hands, and club) because during a swing that slack will allow the clubhead to hit the ground first, before it hits the ball. Take up the slack by a) choking up some on the grip, b) allowing your left arm to be completely straight; b) raising your shoulders until the clubhead hangs a couple inches higher than the ground, for a moment; c) allowing the clubhead to fall so as to take up *wrist* slack, until *it* has no more 'range of motion' from which the clubhead can fall further; and d) standing with your upper body about 45 degrees open to the target, where body turn— torso rotation— will pull your arm and the club through the ball.

Correct alignment: When the ball is further back in your stance, as it is for chip shots, you need to use a *much stronger grip* than normal. It is because your hands are closing during the swing, and the earlier impact occurs in your stance, the more open the hands remain— they haven't closed as much as they would for a ball opposite your left eye, for example. Therefore, a square-to-the-target line alignment for the club*face* for a ball position far to the right requires that the back of your left hand be turned a lot more towards the top of the clubshaft than for your normal iron shots! (If the ball were forward of center body, the naturally rolling left arm would have rolled toward the left a considerable amount, so a naturally square-to-the target impact from *there* would require a much *weaker* grip.) The further forward, the weaker the grip needed: the further back, the stronger the grip needed *in order for the clubface to arrive square to the target line.*

    There is another variable in chipping that is often overlooked. It is this: when you choke up on the club and stand closer to the ball than for a full shot, as you must in order to use your arms and hands comfortably, the heel of the club gets lifted higher than the toe. **Such a position changes the direction of the striking surface of the club!** You have, in effect, created a "toe down" lie angle for these shots, *so you must align the striking surface itself, not the leading edge* or the club will hit the ball to the right! Learning how to aim that *surface*, in place of the normal procedure of aligning the *leading edge*, will take some getting used to. But there is no escaping the reality that your shots will all go right of target if you do not deal with it.

The magic of the left thumb: Using my left thumb as a guide, there is procedure I use for making my swing that controls everything— alignment of the path, alignment of the clubface, amplitude of stroke, and impact with the hands ahead of the clubhead, as you saw in the pictures. It is deceptively simple and easy, and it goes like this. Once you have set yourself ready to chip with the setup shown, hands ahead, ball inside the right foot, with a fairly strong grip in your left hand, *guide your club completely with your left thumb. Direct it away from the ball by tracing the target line with its* <u>*tip*</u>, *and then on the downswing, direct the shaft back to the ball without uncocking your left wrist at all* <u>*with the pad of your thumb pressing onto the shaft and squeezing your fingers to help hold your wrist firm.*</u> There is no simpler means of controlling the path, the clubface alignment, the impact, and the stroke itself than swinging your arm with your left wrist held firm, using the tip of your thumb going back and the thumb-pad to bring the club back to the ball. This procedure works best on the fringe and the stroke will normally brush the ground and continue in a small follow through. To use it in deeper grass requires the ball be back further and you may not have any follow through as the club comes down onto the ball and stays in the heavier grass.

Choosing the right club: Trial and error, personal preference, and common sense will inform you of the right club for each situation. The universal rule is to use as little air time and as much rolling-on-the-green time as possible, so choose a club that will get the ball to the green in the air. The lower the loft, the lower the height of the chip, and the more roll.

Chipping into an uphill or downhill slope, whether on or in front of the green, requires judgment of the effect of the slope on how much the ball will bounce forward on a level or downhill landing area, or be 'stopped' by an uphill slope, hence whether you might prefer to fly the ball *over* such a problematic landing point.

A single club works for many golfers; using several clubs of different lofts works for others. I suggest that you familiarize yourself with your 9-iron, pitching wedge, and gap wedge for chipping from the fringe, and perhaps use your sand iron for balls in heavier rough where its added weight is an advantage.

More about controlling distance: Once this chipping technique has been learned, as mentioned, I strongly urge you to calibrate distances for the various amplitudes of backswing for each club. Make a chart for each club for use as a guide when using that club, and tape it to the club. Referring to that information before your shot will provide confidence for it and indicate an exact stroke to practice a few times before actually striking the ball. I don't believe I have ever seen a professional golfer execute a chip shot without several rehearsal practice swings. When I watch, I can almost feel him searching for 'just the right swing before giving himself permission' to finally strike the ball.

Find your natural tempo. Look for and use a tempo that feels natural to you, that meets your comfort level. It is necessary to use it consistently in chipping and putting in view of the delicacy of distance control, especially on fast greens. Having a reliable 'up and down' game is, when you look at great golf, what ultimately makes for lowest scores. I have seen Tiger Woods for several years now perform astonishing miracles of scoring even when his driver was erratic, to say nothing of seeing so many other golfers with less skill achieve similar results. It is universally known that practicing 'the short game' will do more for low scores than perfecting any other golf skills. I adapt the quip quoted earlier, "old age and cunning (read, 'a short game') will overcome youth and skill (ball striking and booming drives).

PUTTING

There are many different styles used in putting, based, I suspect, on differences in how we are wired for coordination regarding minute motor skill. (In the world of piano performance, differences in 'wiring' are immediately obvious when we observe phenomenal dexterity, speed, and accuracy in some young people, capable of playing diabolically difficult passages. Compare this to fairly elementary levels of the same skills in so many other people who have studied and practiced for years.) We see many variations of grip used, in type of club used, and in putting styles used by tour golfers for this reason.

What is universal in good putting, however, is conformance to principles and common sense in how to aim the club, how to hold it to keep it from wobbling, how to move it, and most of all, how to manage *ourselves* in the process. Putting accounts for *almost half* of a final score (between 42% and 45% of the total strokes in a round), yet it receives precious little practice, and very little of the putting practice we witness is of any real value for creating skill.

Principles that govern our technique:

- The club must be held in a way that its face angle is not easily deflected during the stroke or its sweet spot is subject to getting moved closer to or further from your feet during the swing.
- A stroke must be used where the golfer can easily control the amount of energy given to the ball with the finest imaginable sensitivity, and for this reason I advise the use of pendulum timing and amplitude, on a natural arc [as opposed to one that is unnaturally manipulated to travel along a straight line] in cooperation with instinct.
- A procedure for aiming needs to be used where optical concerns such as distortion due to standing parallel to the target line are taken into account and problematic areas are handled *automatically* by the procedure.
- The golfer needs to deal with the most problematic issue of putting, a phenomenom called 'the yips,' which is ultimately an instinctive and impulsive adjustment, mid-stroke, that 'something is wrong with this picture' and a last minute, in-swing impulsive effort to adjust for what is perceived to need correction.
- The entire routine for putting needs to be installed so that no details or necessities are omitted at any time, so that just like in a pre-shot routine for full shots, the golfer

does not need to think mechanically, but uses a habitual and identical procedure for the entire preparation and stroke itself that accounts for and handles every important detail automatically.

Holding the club: I usually putt with two hands for short putts (up to about 12 feet), and with my right hand alone for longer putts as well as for many short ones. The principles I observe are to let my arms *hang* directly from their sockets so that their at-rest hang is not subject to a 'change of lanes' due to gravity acting on the club during the swing. I hold the club in a way that will not induce or even permit the face angle to change during the stroke; and with all the slack removed so that the putter won't drop to where it could bump the grass during mid-stroke and so disrupt the putt. I use a ball position directly in front of and below my two eyes (which is about mid-body in my stance), and stand with my shoulders parallel to my chosen line so that the natural movement of my arms and shoulders *is* directly along that chosen line at impact. (I allow a natural arc rather than try to trace a straight line if viewed from directly above the ball, since the natural arc really *does move* in a straight line if it is viewed looking down to the ball from the shoulders instead of from *directly above* the hands.) The plane *line* is straight, but the illusion created from looking at the path of the club from the eyes which are above your shoulders makes it appear that the path is curved from inside to on line to back inside again.

The first of the next two pictures is my setup for a right-hand only putt. This is my personal preference for all but short putts. The second picture is my setup with two hands.

In the photo on the opposite page, the ball is directly under my eyes, and my arm is simply hanging by gravity. It is not visible to an observer that I have firmed my fingers and wrist considerably, so that during my stroke, which will cooperate with gravity, there will be absolutely no wobble in my wrist. My backswing will be a true *swing* of the club, activated by weight shift and an imperceptible 'heave' of my shoulders, and the turnaround to the forward swing will be timed so that the arm, hand, and club move forward as a single piece in unison. Neither my hand nor the clubhead will 'lead;' both will move forward together in a smooth continuous 'fall through impact' stroke. In the second photo I show how I address the ball with a two-handed grip. Both elbows are pulled back to my sides, and this causes both palms to face outwards towards the camera. That palms-outward grip creates great stability for the putter in my hands, eliminating any wobble or potential opening or closing of the putter blade during the stroke: it 'locks' the putter in my hands effortlessly to create an extremely stable unit of shoulders, two arms, hands, and putter. It secures the club because of opposing tension created in over-rotated hands working against each other— the left hand is rotated so far left it wants to spring back. The right hand is rotated so far right it also wants to spring back. That built-in spring in both the hands because of their over-rotated positions 'balance' each other, resulting in a lock that secures the club. No energy or tension remains to turn the clubface from its set position in my palms. I hold the club gently but with firm fingers in my palms with my right forefinger down the shaft for the support it offers. When I make my stroke with this grip, I also use a 'heave' for the backswing and the same timing and respect for the natural speed that gravity creates in my turnaround and forward stroke. And as with all shots, *the base of the right wristbone is the 'touch point' that marries that hand to the instrument and which moves it* without the wrist flexing or the *palm* moving forward during the stroke. That **bone** moves the club, *not* the palm. This next photo is to draw your attention to the base of my right palm, and whether I am putting with one or two hands, *that* part of that hand is what I use to move the putter so as not to allow my hand to flex. The putter and my arms act as a rigid unit, not two parts.

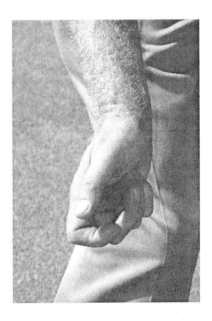

Another procedure I like is that used by my editor, Karen "1-Putt" Roberts. It is simply a left-hand-low putting grip, and it has the benefit of three controls: it holds the putter steady without wobble at the wrists, it holds the putter-face square to the line effortlessly, and by using the back of that hand to direct the *stroke*, a smooth, controlled pendulum tempo. That procedure is largely responsible for her extremely accurate putting, from which her nickname is well deserved.

Sensitivity in the stroke: As the years went along in my own golfing experience that began when I was 14 years old (and when

I felt I could sink any putt from anywhere, with no technique, principles, or thoughts to bother me), my instinctive putting skill gradually deteriorated. About 20 years later I discovered that I not only had not *developed* a sense of touch, I actually *lost an instinctive touch given to me as a youngster* that worked well for me for many years.

My frustration led me to develop a system for controlling distance by taking advantage of a very reliable natural phenomenon, namely gravity and how it makes hanging objects behave. The system permits a golfer to reproduce extremely sensitive degrees of impact energy by managing the consistency of his tempo and the amplitude of his stroke, within remarkably small tolerances, if he tunes into and uses the natural tempo that gravity moves his arms and club hanging from his shoulders. In other words, the "system" it offered me made it *much* easier to control the distance of my putts. And this is something people can install at the outset of their golfing experience, as opposed to requiring months or years of practice to learn.

How to do this has already been discussed, but I restate it because just like in infomercials and public speaking, important things need to be repeated frequently and some details need more clarification.

First find your own natural pendulum tempo. Realize that it takes the same amount of total time for a short stroke as for a long one. One of the traps is to decelerate a stroke for the short ones and force a stroke for the long ones! While using a gentle but positive, naturally slow motion, find out how far the ball travels for given backstroke amplitudes. Make a little chart that shows the number of steps the ball travels on level greens for various backswing amplitudes to the best of your ability, (mine estimates it for slow, medium, and fast greens), attach it to your clubshaft, and then for every putt, count steps to the cup, add one for good measure so as not to flirt with an inch too short, and on the green **use the amplitude it tells you for the putt at hand.** First adjust sensibly for slope, grain, green speed, and wind, and then just trust the stroke and watch how your distance control becomes astonishingly accurate in a very short time.

By using your right wristbone for your contact point and for moving your putter (the same as you do for chipping and full shots) it is easier to keep your palm and with it the clubshaft from folding forward. All movement applied to all golf shots, and particularly putting and chipping, require that you 'hold the angle of the right wrist' as you move the instrument forward, and in putting and chipping this is by consciously using the wristbone to direct the club.

Aiming: In the first chapter mention was made of the problem of refraction from eyeglasses. How our two eyes are used for aiming *putts* is more of an issue than refraction, however, since *everyone* has to putt and align his shot, and two eyes parallel to the target line while you stand over the ball do not offer the most accurate way to align your stroke and your putter face. Triangulation, the ability to see the target with both eyes the same distance away at the same instant, is not possible from a putting stance.

To handle this specifically for putting and as Jack Nicklaus and others advise for full shots, I select a spot on the grass on my intended target line *with precision and care*, a spot which becomes the target for aiming both my stroke line *and* my putter face. To do this I sight along the shaft of my putter by placing it in my line of sight through the middle of the ball to the target, and I find a spot that sits exactly somewhere on that edge of the shaft on the target line. I then substitute that spot entirely for the cup or distant target (even on short putts where eyes are still unreliable from above the ball), deliberately using the type of stroke and the amplitude necessary for the putt.

Putting is a matter of making decisions I have found that all putting concerns can be condensed into a series of decisions which, if routinely executed, are capable of making even novices into excellent putters of the golf ball in a very short time. These are the decisions:

- Decide on the line, *to the best of your ability*, with confidence that since it is the best you can do, there isn't any other resource to use *for* that information, so you simply accept it in that spirit. *Take whatever time you need, and get away from the ball and target, etc., long enough and far enough, to become settled in your mind in this regard.* When you complete your setup, you will also align your eyes, your shoulders and your feet parallel to the chosen target line.

- Decide on the stroke amplitude you are going to use, *to the best of your ability and judgment. It is because you are going to trust this judgment for the same reasons as above.* This attitude is extremely important because it eliminates the indecision that gives rise to the yips (changing your mind mid-stroke). The amplitude you choose will be based on the calibration of your putter already done, and on the adjustments you need for the sake of green speed, slope, and wind.

- Decide to advance the putter with the base of your right wristbone or the back of your left hand and to hold it to allow no wobble at the connection of the putter in your hand(s). Your swing back and the turnaround will be paced so that no looseness in the connection allows the putter to swing independently of or out of synch with the arms and hands.

- After taking up the slack in your arms in a manner that is comfortable for you, hang the center of your clubface precisely at the back of the ball, align the face to your target and eliminate any gravitational action on your arms or club by inching your feet to where the natural hang of your arms places the sweetspot of the club directly behind the ball. This allows the club to swing and return to the ball with nothing built into the setup that could act to move it 'to a wrong lane' on the way to the ball, resulting in an off-center impact.

- Decide to watch impact! This is much more important than you may realize. It is because any uncontrolled eagerness to see where the ball goes as it leaves your club is likely to cause you to flinch in some imperceptible degree and to deflect your putter prior to impact itself. And unknown to you perhaps for *years*, this anxiety and its invisible but real deflection of the stroke will remain a flaw that few teachers or observers would ever notice. (Even more effective, however, is watching a spot an inch or so to the left of the ball--impact will already have occurred before the club passes in front of your eye, eliminating the problem entirely!)

And finally **EXECUTE YOUR DECISIONS**: the *line* (for your feet, your shoulders, your eyes, and for the face of the putter), the *amplitude* of stroke, the *fluid and slightly accelerated stroke, the movement of the putter with your wristbone, and the need to watch impact* as you 'accelerate' (deliberately continue your motion) with your club *through the ball.*

Installing Your Putting Procedure; Correct Putting Practice

This is how I give a pupil his first putting lesson. I take the pupil to the green and put a ball down about 10 feet from the cup where the putt intended has no slope or grain to affect its path, and where it is expected to be perfectly straight. I will ask him to get ready to putt, allowing him all the time he wants. When he indicates he has aligned his putter to the best of his ability, I then freeze it in the position he has placed it. I then move the ball away and place my laser flashlight device against its blade. The laser indicates exactly what the putter is aimed at— I use a backstop behind the cup to show where the red laser beam is aimed.

Invariably when I do this— probably eight out of ten times at that distance— the laser will actually be aiming either right or left of the cup by some significant amount, sometimes more than a foot! I then ask the pupil these questions:

1) "If you were to practice your stroke for 2 hours a day for a year and then I gave you 10 balls to stroke *using that line for your putt,* how many of them would go in the hole?" Obviously the answer is, "None of them!"

2) "Will putting practice do you any good if you believe the target is where you are aimed?" Answer, "No, of course not."

My next step is to use the laser device to aim his putter precisely at the center of the cup, and after freezing his putter in *that* place, I replace the laser with a golf ball. I then ask the golfer to make sure he doesn't let the blade change its alignment, *and without any instruction whatsoever about technique, amplitude, or mechanics,* I ask him to stroke the putt, being sure only to hit it hard enough to get the ball into the cup. While the results are not always perfect, most of the pupils do sink the ball (at ten feet). My next question is, "What do you think is more important, good aim or perfect technical execution?" Answer, "Aim."

The lessons learned from this simple routine are priceless. They are:

- MOST PEOPLE DO NOT KNOW HOW TO PRACTICE PUTTING.
- MOST PEOPLE'S PUTTING PRACTICE TIME IS WASTED WORKING ON THE WRONG THINGS.
- MOST PEOPLE WOULD BE ABLE TO LEARN HOW TO TWO-PUTT IN A VERY SHORT TIME BY PRACTICING THE RIGHT THINGS.
- MOST PEOPLE WOULD, THEREFORE, BE ABLE TO REDUCE THEIR STROKE AVERAGE BY AT LEAST NINE STROKES IN A VERY SHORT TIME BY PRACTICING A COUPLE OF HOURS— BY CALIBRATING, AND BY GOING AT IT AS FOLLOWS as opposed to 'practicing putting' in their usual manner. I remind the reader that putts represents about 45% of the score on the card!

What to Practice...ooops, NO, What to LEARN:

- Learn how to aim.
- Learn how to produce a smooth repeatable stroke.

- Learn how to maintain the alignment of the blade of the putter from end of 'aim' to final impact on the ball.
- Learn how to watch the putter actually impact the ball.

Learning to aim starts with learning how to find intermediate target spots in front of the ball *with precision* that you substitute for the actual target that is much farther away. You may find a way to do it by standing behind the ball and sighting down the line and then picking out a spot. I like to do it as I said and wish to repeat, by picking out a spot but not from behind the ball: I do it while standing above the ball where I will be standing for the stroke itself (so I minimize movement of my head away from where I was when I found the spot resulting in loss of the spot!). Using my putter shaft as a straight edge that defines the line from the center of the ball to my target, I pick out a blade of grass, blemish or whatever for my intermediate target somewhere along that straight edge. To check the reliability of this method and whether I am accurate enough with it, when I practice I stick something like a tee or a pencil into the ground at the very spot I have chosen and then walk away behind the ball to see if the spot I picked *is* on my target line.

When using a laser device, it is best if you have help holding your putter or the device. I made one by obtaining a laser flashlight (I got mine at Radio Shack for about $15) and mounting it on a small board so that its beam is precisely perpendicular to the flat edge of the board. I can place it against the blade of the putter when getting ready to stroke the putt to check if I *did* aim it correctly. It also helps to draw perpendicular lines on white paper which you can set on the floor and use with a golf ball and your putter to train your eyes to recognize a correctly aligned putter face with a ball at the sweet spot. You need to know how a perfectly aligned putter looks from your normal address posture. Finally, any practice where you can aim at a target, set the putter so it won't move and walk away to check to see what you really *are* aimed at is good 'aiming' practice.

How to find your own tempo, hence a reliable repeating smooth rhythmic full swing stroke, was covered in Chapter Seven, and just a few words are all that are required to apply the advice to putting. A natural pendulum tempo stroke is slower than most people actually do move their putter, so in getting familiar with your own, please expect to discover how much slower it seems than what you may be used to.

The turnaround: The critical detail that sets 'perfect stroking of the ball' apart from muscling or manipulating it is the manner in which the change of direction is handled, i.e., by patiently waiting *for* the turnaround (like Mom waits for the playground swing to start back *of its own accord)* before she assists it— sometimes fairly exuberantly— for the forward stroke. Calibrate the distances your ball travels with various amplitudes of stroke using a stroke that honors the rate of gravity in this manner. And when using it for play, respect the time it takes for turnaround, and then choose and use the same pace, the same tempo, the same "effort" stroke after stroke, day after day, and month after month. This is possible if you seek and install the tempo that feels most natural and enables consistency for you. One of the check-points that your stroke is neither decelerating nor being accelerated too much is the follow through. If its amplitude is equal to, or a bit more than, the backstroke amplitude, it is likely an excellent stroke. If the clubhead covers less distance after impact than its backswing distance back away from the ball, it clearly is a poor, decelerating stroke.

Maintaining the alignment of the putter blade once its direction is determined is done by the use of a two-handed grip like the one described earlier in this chapter, or with the right hand alone, with your palm square to the target line, and where you do not allow your wrist(s) to flex. Your arms and hands and club should constitute a single firm and inflexible pendulum (right arm, right hand, and putter being the unit for one-handed putting, or both arms, hands and putter the unit for two-handed putting), and by holding the hands, fingers and wrists firmly, wobble is minimized. But as mentioned, *turnaround* at the end of the backswing is the instant when problems get introduced by starting forward too early or rushing its motion, because any change in the behavior of the club introduced by muscles in the wrists, however slight, *will* cause the putter blade to open up slightly. Moving the *hands* forward while the putter *head* lags waiting for gravity to move *it* is a sure way to cause wobble. Execution must respect this critical detail by moving the hands and putter shaft and head in unison, 'as one.'

Another area that you need to watch out for (one that is not uncommon even in professional events among the world's best players) is the tendency to pull putts, and the main reason for this is having a body/shoulder position somewhat open to the target line. *Any* mis-alignment of the shoulders to the left can cause the golfer to pull his putts because the hands do tend to swing parallel to the shoulders. In order to eliminate the tendency to begin with, simply stand parallel to the target line, not with an open stance.

Exactly How to Practice Putting

In actual play of the game it is not possible to 'remember' a lot of detail, nor is it wise to try to 'think your way around the course.' But because there really are so many details that turn out to be critical for success, good practice absolutely requires *memorizing and installing* **an entire routine** *in which all necessary technical details get programmed into habit to the point where they operate automatically without thought.* So I suggest the following practice routine (after the individual elements that make up the whole have been developed somewhat) using a single golf ball. Always start from the beginning, and run through the entire routine, hitting only one putt at a time as though it were for score on the golf course. The entire routine is as mentioned before:

- Choose your line (make up your mind, and stick to it) using an intermediate target point.
- Choose the amplitude you need after you make up your mind to the best of your ability, and then stick to your decision.
- Finish making your stance by adjusting your body to your aligned putter, take your grip, take up the slack, and adjust to *hang* the putter and arms correctly.
- Mentally rehearse the exact stroke tempo and amplitude.
- **Execute all your decisions, where you are not finished until you have watched your putter impact the ball.**

In a word, you are not teaching *the putter* how to putt automatically. You are teaching *you* how to think, act, and to perform the entire routine which you will use for every putt on the golf course. In a short putting session (this is very hard work and it is not easy to continue the practice for long periods of time), you may hit about 10 putts over a period of 10 minutes. You may prefer to break up your practice a bit with other concerns. But when you are about to "see if I can putt perfectly," and when you go to execute a putt on the golf course, go through the entire routine in the same order that you have determined works the best for you. You need to learn and embed it in its entirety.

A final word: if you do choose the line to the best of your ability, if you do choose the amplitude appropriate to the best of your ability, if you do align your putter face to the best of your ability; if you do execute the physical stroke to the best of your ability, *you will have made a perfect putt regardless of whether it drops into the cup.* Many subtleties on the green surface and human error are realities that we deal with. So we need to keep these things in perspective, since beating yourself up for something beyond your control is inappropriate, even if it is a mental error— no, all the *more* so if it is a mental error. After a putt *is* executed, feedback gives you information about whether you read the line or speed well and what adjustments you need to make *on the next putt, but for the stroke at hand, accepting the results constitutes an extremely important part of the psychological frame of mind that allows you to putt with confidence, hence to execute with the best mechanics themselves.* Mechanics *do* operate with better efficiency when your mind is at peace over the task at hand. And be assured: confidence that you have made your best judgment as to line and amplitude gives you a relaxed attitude, hence it reinforces your chances of success.

Sports psychologists tell us to 'trust' our swing. Well, if you know that you have done everything you can before your shot, you don't have to *pretend* to trust, while below the surface you are unsure. You truly *can* trust, because you have covered all the bases, and when you make your stroke, you can be free of subconscious anxiety.

The greatest rewards of a day of golf are the freedom and exuberance we experience in an athletic activity in the open air, the joy of challenge in the game, and the thrill of executing some good shots. And on top of those, preparation for this specific skill that is responsible for such a large percentage of your final score has to be very high on the list of priorities for golf. I hope this section helps in that search, and that what is written here enables you to make significant progress quickly.

SAND

The secret to successful sand shots is to understand the bounce feature of the club you will usually use for that purpose so that you can cooperate with it.

A sand wedge is designed to slide through the sand so that it will neither bounce out of the sand before impact to strike the ball directly, nor dig in and get stuck. The trick is to find out just how much "bounce" the club has for the different ball positions available to you. If you put the ball too far forward relative to where the butt end of the club is at impact, the built-in slope of the bottom of the sole of the club will cause the clubhead to slide quickly to the top of the sand, where you will cuff the ball directly with the club's leading edge. Such a shot is called "blading," and the biggest fear the golfer suffers is that he will blade his shot way over the green if he "hits it too hard." What he often will do as a result of such fear (the IRS factor) is to quit his stroke before getting through the ball place producing insufficient clubhead momentum to carry the sand and the ball to the green. It helps to imagine that you are going to cut a divot 2" wide by 8" long with the ball in the middle, and that the ball is part of the sand. Your job, Mr. Phelps, is to toss all that sand onto the green!

The result of overriding your fear and swinging without quitting, if your club's bounce was too much, is to do exactly what you feared— i.e., to cuff the ball *way* over the green! What has to be determined is the best *place* to put the ball for that club. If the ball position is too far to the rear of your stance, the leading edge of the club digs into the sand too much and it fails to slide through in your intended "divot," leaving the ball in the sand. So the task is to locate the point between these two extremes that will work correctly for you.

Sand wedges are designed, normally, to slide through the sand correctly when the clubshaft is directly vertical at impact, or stated another way, when the ball position is at mid-body for a swing that puts hands mid-body at impact. A ball sitting mid-body position with impact occurring with the shaft vertical uses the club's bounce correctly, and the path taken by the clubhead through the sand will be horizontal. Such a stroke will slide appropriately if there is a good strong delivery through the sand, and it will throw the sand and the ball onto the green.

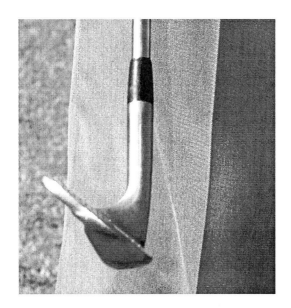

This photo shows my sand wedge, and you can see clearly how the shape of the sole will allow or cause the clubhead to slide up or skid through sand without digging in. Depending on how sharply the clubhead enters the sand, the club will either slide along or dig in.

When you have found exactly where to place the ball (forward, dead center, or back from mid-body) for that correct sliding action to occur, you will conquer your fear and the jeopardy of sand shots. The position will vary depending on the consistency of the sand. Experience alone can teach you the differences, and practicing in different kinds of sand conditions is really the only way to learn how hard, how big, and how deep, your greenside sand shots need to be. The simple way that I tell people how to use the club is this: *THROW SAND!* Consider that the ball is part of the sand, so throw sand by slashing through it with the leading edge low enough below the bottom of the ball that it doesn't strike the ball before it strikes sand. And use a ball position that permits the club to slide along under the ball without skidding back to the top where that edge strikes the ball and sends it either into the banking or over the green. With experience you will come to find out how hard to swing, and how far or back the ball position needs to be for the results you want.

Longer iron shots from sand, hardpan, or other questionable surfaces need to be struck by the clubhead before the sole of the club gets to the ground, and there isn't a lot of tolerance for quality impact when the surface is sand, mud, or anything hard. It is no small feat for you to acquire precise depth or low-point control of your irons using the methods for controlling and measuring that have been explained earlier in this book. That skill pays off more especially when the surface is less tolerant of error than fairway grass, in addition to its value for normal fairway shots rewarded by greater consistency.

PLAYING FROM ROUGH Problems with rough are grass lying between the clubface and the ball that reduces the effect of friction between the clubhead and the ball, and the grab of the grass holding and possibly twisting the clubhead during impact. Good judgment and experience are necessary to make the most of bad situations, but being aware of the geometry (the loft and bounce of your club) of impact is especially necessary in high grass.

As in sand, the cutting edge feature of a club and its bounce help to get into then get out of grass, provided that its entry is sufficiently DOWN to get to the ball. The loft of the clubface will get the ball up or out, so the golfer needs to be sure he uses *enough* loft for the circumstances. The temptation will be to force a long iron (that has insufficient loft to cut down to the ball), or to use a wood that could be poorly suited to the task, to get to a distant green rather than to accept your punishment with a realistic shot back out of trouble to a good spot for the next shot. Sometimes the shape and size of a small headed wood club is better suited to getting through heavy grass, if its loft is sufficient to get the ball up.

The geometry of the clubface's loft gets the ball out *after it is struck* but the geometry of the angle of attack gets the club to hit the ball to begin with. The "angle of attack" is the angle of the clubshaft relative to the ground at impact— i.e., either erect (90º), or maybe with the hands a bit ahead, say 60º. The other "angle" often referred to is the "angle of approach", which is the angle of the clubshaft relative to the target line at impact as read from above the ground looking down, so with your hands leading the clubhead, that angle is also less than 90º, and ideally the clubface is open to the target line until separation after impact.

You need to adjust your club's path to the ball so that it comes down onto the ball from above it enough to minimize grab, rather than sweeping into the ball from behind where grass will ruin the shot. One possible solution is to put the ball back in your stance, more before low point than usual, as required by the density and height of the grass you have to deal with.

As with sand, only practice will teach you the tolerances, but I'll mention again that it makes sense to override the temptation to force a club by taking the safe way out, because the more common situation is overestimating your strength, leaving the ball in trouble.

I have always known that I can get par on a hole if my shot to the green is close enough, and truth be told, you can have two bad shots before you get to a green and still salvage a par with an accurate fairway to green approach shot. So I give myself a much better chance to save par from a mid length fairway shot to the pin than a *closer* shot from deep *rough*.

Using 'Loose Hands'

One of the skills you would do well to develop is the use of what is called 'soft' or 'loose' hands. As implied it simply means that you grip the club softly and with wrists quite loose. Swinging with such a procedure produces a soft landing of chip shots and of easy pitches and lobs, even with 7, 8 and 9 irons of 70 or 80 yards. When you have worked with this technique with very easy but very accurately produced motion all the way up to the 80 yard range with any of these approach clubs, you will discover that you can drop a ball onto a green nearly lifeless, where it then runs less than it usually does with a firm grip. That kind of a shot is one of Lee Trevino's trademarks, so different from the 'muscle and spin back' approach. Its energy is totally in torso turn pulling soft arms and hands. I think this technique produces more reliable results in the way it just plain "drops" the ball dead on the green than a procedure that creates a roll backwards after impact due to backspin.

Final Comment about the Short Game

The short game, golf shots of less than full amplitude and effort, accounts for about two thirds of your golf score. While it is tedious to practice it as opposed to the fun of practicing with your driver and irons in full swings, it really doesn't take a lot of time to install the procedures taught in this chapter. We all tend to procrastinate about things that are less pleasant to do, but the payoff for your scoring by practicing things in this chapter is considerable. And be prepared to be flexible and ready to change your expectations, hence your calibration charts, as you make small changes in your tempo, procedure, or preferences.

This Concludes Instruction in the Skills You Will Need for Playing a Satisfactory Game of Golf

In the first chapter of this book it was pointed out how there are several different individual things that go into making golf pleasurable and rewarding, and that trying to compress learning them all would be to put yourself on overload. This chapter ends the instruction on all of them with the one exception, that being the actual application of your skills on a golf course for pleasure and probably in a desire to compete. Most of us wish to compete and compare our scores with ourselves from day to day. Many of us like to compete in tournament play of various kinds. The very last part of your learning and preparation for this is in the next, the last section of this book, where I give some advice about how to bring your skills to the golf course. Common sense, realistic expectations based on actual results, and exuberance are the best ingredients for your success.

The most demanding part of exceptional golf may well be this element, namely, realistic expectations as to what you can expect to be able to bring off in actual play. This was addressed on page 251.

Notes

Conclusion

How to Practice For a Round of Golf

Playing golf bears little similarity to practicing on a range. During a round of golf the considerations for each shot will occupy your mind, and there just is no opportunity to "work on your swing" at that time. This means that your warm-up on the range the day or hour before your round needs to be conducted with an entirely different procedure and purpose than what you use when you are working on your swing. You need to accept the fact that on the golf course you will not be able to change your swing or procedure from "what it is" despite your most recent practice thoughts and swing changes. If changes have been "installed" they will be there. If they have not, you cannot put them into your game at that time. And that is ok, because you don't need them for that round.

So do not practice your 'swing' when you are preparing for a round of golf. Practice for the purpose of finding out exactly how you are going to set up, how you are going to measure to your ball for perfect impact on the center of the clubface, and how you are going to align yourself for straight shots.

Before you start your practice, install the following pre-shot routine *for every single golf shot you make during practice and for every shot you will later make on the golf course.* Some teachers suggest you visualize the trajectory of the ball you are about to hit, a process which for some people seems to pull everything together in a way that 'causes the swing' to create the trajectory envisioned. It means that you picture the direction, the flight of the ball, and an intention to make the ball go to your target. I do not find that this visualization is possible or workable for everyone, but a *'motion rehearsal'* visualization is quite easy to learn to do, and in my opinion, more effective in producing good shots.

It goes as follows: every golf shot requires a line of direction along which you move your left hand for guiding your hands and the club away from the ball, by tracing it with your left thumb. You also direct the grip cap with your left hand in the downswing back through the ball. In addition, the forward swing will normally use a lot of energy to produce appropriate clubhead speed with an accelerating swing, as opposed to a mechanically contrived act in which you steer or 'put' the club to the ball. So the rehearsal procedure you will use is a mental run-down of these three things just before takeaway, after you have set yourself to the ball with grip, posture, stance, alignment, and balance in place as you have been trained.

Just before you take the club back, 1) picture moving your hands to the right tracing the line you chose for your backswing motion; 2) picture where your hands and the clubhead will arrive at the top of your swing; and 3) picture yourself making the full-effort downswing motion pulling the gripcap with your left hand down toward and then along the target line and through the ball at the target (not in any old direction!) *And then as soon as you have envisioned these things in the order they occur, make your swing in conformance with that mental rehearsal. Do what you just imagined.* It is a different than taking a swing first, even a practice swing, because in either of those cases you find out *after* the swing or the shot that you did something wrong or badly. In this motion rehearsal *you actually program the right and good motion before making any swing at all!* You can, of course, swing badly even after a good mental rehearsal of the motions, but you are much less likely to do so! And such a procedure does not mean that you can't or won't make a practice swing on the golf course later, but it does focus your attention on *those exact things that are responsible for results, namely what you are going to do.* I do not believe that 'feelings' alone control a golf swing. I know that cognitively directing your hands to exact places is doable, and *such an action produces* the feelings that occur during good shots. *The mental rehearsal of what you are about to do* is the secret of playing your next shot the best it can possibly be!

Start your practice with some stretching and dry swings to get warmed up and comfortable with the athletic motion, the exuberance, the freedom, and the sheer joy of a free-swinging golf club. Then take your PW and hit some short pitches, say 60 or 80 yards, one at a time, each time *deliberately rehearsing your takeaway line, your top of swing position, your downswing motion, the down and through direction, and the effort you will use in that forward swing.* Then, since you will need to make adjustments to fine-tune impact, do not hit two shots in a row. Limit yourself to one shot at a time. *Practice swing* as often as you wish, but don't *strike* more than one ball in a row without using the entire routine. It's hard work but you learn rapidly when you practice like this.

When ready, rehearse the actual swing as I just showed you. Then hit one ball. Look at the results of the shot. Did you hit it fat? Pull it? Hit it thin? Exactly what were the results as compared to perfect? Did you fail to address anything in your setup or in the 'mental image of your swing,' or is the mis-hit cured by a small adjustment. Understand that in real play it's too late to do anything *about that shot* if it was mis-hit, so both in practice, and on the course, proceed to hit your next shot. Fix any problems or make adjustments that show up in your last shot before the next one. During your practice session, stay with the process of creating perfect impact before going on to longer swings or longer clubs. In actual play, trust the measurements you think are right for the shot, rehearse the three steps of the swing, then swing away. In practice, before proceeding to longer clubs, continue hitting short shots to perfect your impact. When you are ready to advance because you *are* hitting your easy shots perfectly, work gradually to longer clubs.

When you have consistent impact, it is a good idea to 'practice playing' the full shots you will need in an actual round. Imagine the first hole of the course you are going to play, and first 'locate its fairway and its green,' where "Your mission, Mr. Phelps, is to get that ball on that green." Make a drive. Miss the fairway? Notice the penalty: on the course you may need to play a safe shot back onto the fairway out of the rough. Now make your approach. 'Miss the green?' — too bad, next shot would have to be a chip. That's also likely to cost you one shot in normal play (it is unrealistic to hope for miraculous chips or long putts to cure bad approach shots). Or did you land your shot on the green? — great!

Now go to "the next hole" with your driver. Again you have one chance. You *must* be careful to try to make this a perfect drive, ending in the fairway! Do whatever it takes not even to *flirt* with potential problems like the rough or bunkers. If your tendency is sometimes to fade the ball too much, *take precautions or aim so as not to be punished* for it. You have an obligation to keep that ball in the fairway! In real golf, there are no second chances.

In the process of practicing in this way, an amazing thing happens. You start to be a much more accurate golfer. And that is because of the power of what we call "focus," a characteristic exemplified by a miracle that goes by the name of Tiger Woods. Focus taps into a capacity of the human mind that I like to say "knows more than you do" for its unbelievable ability to "get the job done" *when we really are thinking of the right thing during the action to bring it about. Focus is the absence of distraction from the essential!*

And then as you apply the corrections and adjustments to correct any mis-hits, you gradually make very serious progress and get the taste of single digit handicap golf!

Use a similar approach when you practice your putting. When you go to the green, take only one ball with you, and after you have practiced to achieve a good smooth stroke and have determined the green speed and conditions (by calibrating the distance of travel for a given length backstroke), then practice *single putts* with the intention of holing or just passing the cup with every one. Make all the decisions you need before you stroke the ball. Visualize your backstroke and forward stroke before making the putt. Follow your rehearsal with a deliberate stroke exactly the same as your rehearsal. If you were impatient and stroked before thinking of your stroke ahead of time, realize it was your impatience to make the stroke that caused the problem by doing it before you were ready, not your ability! Again, give yourself 'no second chances.' Map out a four- or five-hole putting course, and hole out at each cup. *Realize that you cannot train the putter to putt automatically for you. You are not teaching the putter to putt. You must train yourself to use your complete putting routine for every single putt!* This is what you will need to do when you are on the golf course. You are training yourself how to *think*, how to *prepare yourself* to putt, and how to stroke each putt, because it is in the preparation and the rehearsal and its execution for every putt that you fail or succeed, not in some automatic response of your putter to motions you went through on a putting green!

Exercise Caution in Your Pursuit of Instruction

I will draw an analogy with the medical profession. We are becoming more and more health conscious at this time in history, and I now have many senior friends for whom the best available medical care is a serious issue. It is common for heart patients to choose to go to a famous clinic in Texas or to one of the Mayo Clinics for surgery instead of to one of the local doctors in the same specialty. When I ask someone why he would go so far and pay so much more than the local doctor, the answer is "because I want a specialist who really knows what he is doing." The reasons are obvious, of course; the issue is often life or death.

While learning how to swing a golf club doesn't have that much at risk, I consider it pretty important to choose a golf teacher carefully. **Good golf instruction is far from generic!**

Recently I was watching one of the three most famous teachers in the world talk with an authoritative tone to a national audience on *The Golf Channel*. This man's credentials are absolutely without parallel, and to express a difference of opinion with the man in public would be unthinkable because of the acclaim he is given by the media and by virtue of the fact that he works with the best golfers in the world. But much of what he said was contrary to the principles explained here, and obviously contrary to what pictures of great swings actually show. I listened to him use the language of the present culture of teaching, a style and manner which continues to be the most prevalent, and which could be characterized as, "Do it this way because people like me know it works and I've proven through the successful pupils I've taught that it is right." I call this "the authority syndrome," and I believe the problems with such an approach are considerable, namely:

- Virtually all teachers have fundamental theories in their instruction about which they disagree with others, and the pupil has to make a choice between "styles," teachers, or actual techniques. A good example is the highly visible "Natural Golf" program, claiming to be an easier way to swing than a "conventional swing." My answer to that is it is *not* easier, but that *unclear instruction* has made the conventional swing seem hard, and therefore they are able to capitalize on their claim of an easier way! IT IS NOT HARD. This misperception is unacceptable to me, in light of the fact that the simple dynamics and geometrical realities that are specific, operative, and demonstrable in great swings are teachable in the same way that basic math concepts and bridge mechanics are teachable, i.e., by principle. In many ways learning to play good golf is no harder than learning how to do math or build a bridge. It is because when you know how things work, you can learn how to produce good results.

- No reasons are advanced to the pupil for *why* specific things need to be done, hence no solid understanding from which a pupil can apply good golf swing information to his own body type correctly. And it takes only a hair of a misalignment or measurement to trigger horrendous compensations. By virtue of perhaps a single "imperative" put forth by any given teacher, to create a subconscious belief in that pupil's head that the compensations to which his instruction gives rise are a necessary part of the technique of golf. The broad-brush approach just doesn't take into account the differences in golfers.

- What is taught is incomplete because it does not address the correct *exertions* to use, which are invisible, and as you've now discovered for yourself, *which* muscular exertions you use and when you activate them determine the success or failure of your shot and your swing.

- The entire subject matter of dynamic motion and the operation of physical laws is ignored (for starters, how centrifugal release is produced and used to achieve distance, or how the behavior of the pendulum must be dealt with or it will do you in).

- Much of what is put forth is *irrelevant* to the exertions that the golfer needs to make, hence are distractions from what he ought to be thinking. The implication of stressing some things as opposed to others is that the things that *are* mentioned are somehow central and the important things (by implication, where the "secrets" of success are hidden), and things that are *not* mentioned are *not* important. We now know that to be completely false and damaging. I have witnessed far too many 'lessons' in which while the point being made may be valid, it is as irrelevant to the pupil's needs as it would be to use fine sandpaper on boards intended for a table that haven't even been planed yet.

There are universal physical principles operative in golf, and I didn't either invent them or discover them. History points to geniuses who surfaced centuries ago that proved to us that a pendulum obeys its own laws, that momentum going into a collision equals momentum coming out from it, and that gravity pulls at its own rate or force. Besides the club and ball themselves, a pencil and paper, a compass, and a straight edge are simple instruments that can make most of the principles involved perfectly understandable. And it is not hard to show pupils how feedback from the trajectory of his shot and the point of impact on his clubhead can be used to indicate exactly what adjustments are needed to correct bad shots.

So this book has been written to provide the complete story. It is a hands-on textbook, a comprehensive resource on the golf swing, usable by any golfer. It is not based on a computer analysis of the swings of the best 150 golfers in the world. It is not based on 500 years of "this is what we did and it works." And it does not require three scientists to analyze one's body type in order to know what anyone must himself do to be able to swing well.

It is based on principles of physics, geometry, and simple common sense in terms and images that are immediately recognizable and familiar to anyone. It is written to convey the essence, not the appearance, of what happens in the golf swing. (On *The Golf Channel* just one day prior to my writing this a teacher was analyzing a swing and made mention of a feature of the swing that was an irrelevant effect. The impression given was somehow one should 'try to achieve' the position he was pointing out. The appearance was, in my opinion, totally unrelated to anything a pupil should actually *do*, and whether that feature would appear in a given swing had nothing to do with good or bad mechanics or technique: it was simply how *that* golfer's body looked at that instant, not how *every* golfer's body should look!)

This is written with great care to include all of the detail that I consider essential, and I hope without being unduly tiresome in its repetition. And it is my hope that you, the intelligent reader, will take the effort truly to grasp it and thereby be enabled by it.

I do wish you success and I hope that as a result of applying this information that you will take lots of strokes off your handicap. I thank you for your faith in considering these things, in your patience and time spent working with it all, and I promise you that it will pay off for you— quite possibly, big time! I truly hope it will and I invite you to phone/email/write to me at any time for clarification or just to chat, because I am incurably addicted to the joy I experience when someone "gets it" as a result of something I told him.

With best wishes, I am sincerely yours,

George Hibbard

Critical Details,
and
Why They Are Critical

The lie of your clubs must fit you. It is because an incorrect lie angle will induce you to take a setup that will compromise good mechanics, as well as lead to harmful compensations for misdirected shots.

The shaft of your clubs must be soft enough to permit feedback from the clubhead. It is because your natural instinctive responses to the clubhead are extremely important in the development of your technique; a too-stiff shaft will induce you to force your swing and ruin good mechanics.

A forward press (a small weight shift to the left just before takeaway) is necessary to trigger athletic responses that govern subconscious reactions during your swing. Those natural gifts are more likely to work well than a swing that is controlled and contrived without those specific instinctive triggers.

Your stance needs to be narrow enough to allow and induce ample lower body turn. It is because the swing needs to be powered not just to, but also *through* impact, with hip turn. Feet placed too far apart prevent lower body turn. Your feet also need to be angled sufficiently

302

for ample turn in either direction without allowing the collapse of leg support in the backswing.

The axis of body rotation for the forward swing needs to be on the left leg before, or immediately at the beginning of the downswing. It is because such a procedure uses physics-perfect responses in the body to produce the power and efficiency of body rotation, relieving muscles in the legs or upper body of tasks for which they are not as well suited.

Your body must be balanced between heels and toes before your takeaway. It is because any motion caused by a need to rebalance during the swing causes your upper body, and with it the clubhead, to move closer to or further from the ball during the downswing, with a resultant mis-hit of the golf ball.

At setup, your arms need either to hang by gravity under your armpits, or to lay upon your chest (for longer clubs) which acts as a support. It is because any reaching out of your upper arms at setup will be nullified in the downswing by gravity and downswing effort by bringing your upper arms back to your chest, causing toed impacts and fat, weak golf shots.

Your left hand must hold the club so as to be able to fully fold the clubshaft to a 90° angle with the left forearm at the top of the backswing. A grip taken too diagonally across the left palm prevents such an angle and greatly limits the potential energy of the flail action of the releasing clubhead in your effort to create clubhead speed.

Your right hand grip must not limit that same backswing wristfold, nor apply pressure on the clubshaft at the top of the swing. It is because any limitation to achieve the 90° wristfold, or pressure to dissipate it at the top of the swing, will again destroy the mechanical advantage of the flail for producing appropriate clubhead speed.

Your hands must move parallel to the target line on the backswing as the torso turns. It is because if they 'follow the torso' as it turns, they move the swing mechanism of arms and club off plane and destroy the alignment of arms, clubshaft and clubhead necessary for on-plane delivery of the club to the ball on the downswing.

As the hands reach waist high in the backswing, the clubshaft must be directed along a line running up to and past the tip of the right shoulder. It is because that is the plane on which the shaft must lie in order to be correctly aligned for the downswing.

The sequence or transition of the downswing must allow for both your body weight to fall back onto the left heel, and then for a downward motion of the hands, before any rotation occurs either in the hips or in the torso. It is because rotation that starts before either of those two actions will send the hands and club outward, off plane immediately in a direction from which it is not possible to recover for an on-line delivery of the clubhead. An outward motion of the hands commits them to a wrong path back to the ball, causing an over-the-top swing.

Body parts must be 'connected' with all slack taken up at the top of the backswing. It is because the entire swinging mechanism of body, arms, and club must move as a single unit, not as disconnected parts, as the downswing proceeds. Disconnected or slack parts will behave in the same way as a car being towed with a slack rope, getting jolted and disrupted as the downswing proceeds.

The left hand must retain the same 'dish angle' throughout the swing that existed at address, except when it gets pulled flat through impact by the force of the pulling club. It is because any change in that angle in an effort to flatten or bow it will change the alignment of the clubface and/or dissipate power, or both, during the downswing.

Your back must turn away fully from the target in your backswing. It is because that position is necessary to make available the downswing power in your arms as your hands move down from above your right shirt pocket to pants pocket level.

Your right hand needs to be positioned with its lifeline *atop* the left thumb in your setup and on the way down to the ball in the downswing. It is because your right wristbone needs to apply its force to the top of the clubshaft at the fulcrum during the downswing, directly on the line of delivery of the clubshaft down towards, and then along, the target line.

In the backswing your weight needs to move toward, but not *onto*, your right leg. It is because standing *on* that leg prevents gravity from moving you by itself over to the left leg prior to the downswing. Leaning *towards* that leg instead of standing on it allows gravity to move you back onto the left leg for the downswing with a correct natural and uncontrived weight shift.

Your spine must be tilted to the right a bit in your setup in order to place your body and swing on line and on plane correctly. And then you must maintain your spine angles throughout the swing to prevent any change of upper body position during the swing, where any change at all would impair your ability to hit the ball on the sweet-spot of the clubface.

You must use an intermediate target as a marker through which you draw a line for aiming your motion through the ball. It is because all golf requires extreme precision of aim during a shot, and unless that line is deliberately traced with your hands in your backswing and downswing, there is no reliable direction control to your shot.

Your forearms roll open in the backswing and closed during the downswing, in response to body turn, or even deliberately, in order to work smoothly to correctly position the club for its top-of-backswing position, and to return the clubface square for impact. After doing this rolling motion deliberately at first, it needs to become natural and uncontrived in your learned golf swing procedure.

The law of the conservation of momentum requires that, during release, as the clubhead *speeds* up, the handle *backs* up. What is not realized is how *much* this backup or slowing down of the hands during the impact interval affects clubhead speed. The reality is that if you can maintain great force to continue the speed of the hands as you approach the ball, the clubhead gains *unbelievable* speed for impact due to the momentum transferred from hands to clubhead (when you snap a wet towel, the speed of the tip exceeds 700 miles per hour!). So a slow, powerfuly supported swing (or, of course, a fast, powerful swing such as is exemplified by Ernie Els) actually produces more clubhead *impact* speed than a swing where the hands may be moving faster than Ernie's on the way down, but get slowed down more than his do as the clubhead catches up. So you will produce more clubhead velocity for impact with pressure and firmness *through impact* than with a fast-to-impact INTERVAL without support as the clubhead catches up!

There will be several other critical details in your own setup and procedure which you will have to discover and fit to yourself through trial and error. They include how you measure for perfect depth control, how much tilt of the spine you need, how weak or strong your grip needs to be for string-straight ball striking (so that you don't need to manipulate the clubface during your swing), and you even may have to accommodate the refraction of your eyeglasses by aiming 'north' or 'south' of the ball in order to make center-of-clubface impact. But having an understanding of *all* of the realities and often extremely tiny details or adjustments that a golf swing and good impact require, you will be able yourself to find and install all of them if you are attentive.

Finally, I repeat the premise of how you need to produce and control your golf game. It is that you will swing your arms and hands freely and independently, directing everything in a way that most truly corresponds to everyday human activity, which is to say, through your hands, your reactions, your built in sense of balance, and your natural instincts that 'know more than you do.' Do not turn your swing over to body exertions as the prime focus of what moves the club, even though they play such a major part. Do the drills, train yourself to coordinate body response and reactivity for the demands put upon them for moving your hands and arms, and remember what I have called the very first mandate of good golf mechanics, namely, an attitude of exuberance and the mindless freedom and joy of a child of five, playing in the leaves with his friends, oblivious to the consequences of his trust that everything is going to be just fine, thank you.

Index